*Stolen Words*

Burnt Pearls

*It is not just because my words quiver*
*Like broken hands grasping for aid,*
*Or that they sharpen themselves*
*Like teeth on the prowl in darkness,*
*That you, my written word, substitute for my world,*
*Flare up the coals of my anger.*

*It is because your sounds*
*glint like burnt pearls*
*discovered in an extinguished pyre*
*and no one—not even I—shredded by time*
*can recognize the woman drenched in flame*
*for all that remains of her now*
*are those grey pearls*
*smoldering in the ash.*

*—Abraham Sutzkever, Vilna Ghetto, July 28, 1943*

UNIVERSITY OF NEBRASKA PRESS
*Lincoln*

# Stolen Words

## THE NAZI PLUNDER OF
## JEWISH BOOKS

Mark Glickman

THE JEWISH PUBLICATION SOCIETY
*Philadelphia*

Thanks to Dr. Ben Outhwaite for assistance with photo 8.
Many thanks to Anne Graham, senior computer specialist
of the University of Washington Libraries Digital Initiatives
Program, for scanning images for figure 10.
Thanks to Gisele Levy and Carlo di Cave of the Unione delle
Comunità Ebraiche Italiane for their cooperation in getting photo 17.

Library of Congress Cataloging-in-Publication Data
Glickman, Mark, 1963-author.
Stolen words: the Nazi plunder
of Jewish books / Mark Glickman.
pages   cm
"Published by the University of Nebraska Press as a
Jewish Publication Society book"-Title page verso.
Includes bibliographical references and index.
ISBN 978-0-8276-1208-2 (cloth: alk. paper)
ISBN 978-0-8276-1276-1 (epub)
ISBN 978-0-8276-1277-8 (mobi)
ISBN 978-0-8276-1278-5 (pdf)
1. Jewish libraries—Europe—History—20th century.
2. Libraries—Destruction and pillage—Europe—History—
20th century. 3. Libraries and national socialism. I. Title.
Z675.J4G55 2016
027.04—dc23
2015031831

Set in Minion Pro by L. Auten.
Designed by Rachel Gould.

*For my parents*

*Ron and Sharon Glickman,*

*Harriet and Joel Katz,*
*and Vicki Nelson,*

*who have taught me to bask in the*
*paradise of books.*

# Contents

# Acknowledgments

During the months I've spent working on this book, I have been blessed with support from many wonderful individuals, and I'm grateful to them all.

I thank Phil Hanrahan, an editor with the uncanny ability to look into the mire of my early drafts and find within them the stories I want to tell and the ways I want to tell them. The faults of this book are, of course, my own, but its merits bear the indelible imprint of Phil's incredible handiwork.

I am also grateful to Rabbi Barry Schwartz, director of The Jewish Publication Society, whose early enthusiasm and ongoing support for this project were indispensable in bringing this book to publication. Thanks also to JPS managing editor Carol Hupping for her invaluable guidance and unending forbearance; to Ann Baker, managing editor of the University of Nebraska Press and project editor of this book; and the amazing copy editor Debra Corman, without whose keen eye and skilled craftsmanship this book would never have become ready for print.

There were also many individuals who willingly shared their time and insights with me and without whose contribution this book would not have been possible. Heartfelt thanks to Michael Strong, my good friend and invaluable guide to all things books; Robert Ericksen, of Pacific Lutheran University; Devin Naar, of the University of Washington; Aaron Lansky, director of the Yiddish Book Center in Amherst MA; Chaya and

Jay Pomrenz; Eli Genauer, Jewish book maven extraordinaire; Walter Lachman; Ursula Behr; Marie Luise de Vries; Jacob Glickman; Shoshana Glickman; David Gilner, of the Hebrew Union College–Jewish Institute of Religion; Lydumila Sholokhova, of YIVO; Shoshana Baron Tancer; Corina Remes; Dario Tedeschi; Gisèle Lévy and Carlo di Cave of the Unione delle Comunità Ebraiche Italiane; and Ann Brener, of the Library of Congress. I owe special thanks to Patricia Kennedy Grimsted, of Harvard University, and to Dana Herman, of the American Jewish Archives, both of whom regularly and enthusiastically made themselves available to me and the constant barrage of questions I threw their way.

I am deeply grateful to Charles Knapp and the Knapp Family Foundation for their generous support of this project, as well as to the many private donors who helped make its publication possible.

Words cannot adequately express how grateful I am to my parents— Ron and Sharon Glickman, Harriet and Joel Katz, and Vicki Nelson—for their ongoing love and support.

I am especially grateful to my children—Shoshana, Jacob, Kyleigh, and Taylor—for making it all worthwhile.

And above all, thanks to my wife, Caron—my life-partner, my best friend, my rock when things get tough. Her world—especially her husband—smiles far more brightly thanks to her many invaluable gifts.

*Stolen Words*

# *Introduction*

In the fall of 2004 a deliveryman came to my home and handed me what would prove to be one of the most fascinating packages I've ever received. It was a heavy cardboard box—about the size of a large briefcase—and clearly it had traveled far on its way to my doorstep in suburban Seattle. It bore a patchwork of frayed brown packing tape, my name in large handwritten letters, and a generous spray of American and Israeli customs stamps. The return address indicated that it had come from an antiquarian bookseller in Jerusalem.

"Glad you're here!" I said to the man in brown. "I've been expecting you."

"Lemme guess," he said. "eBay?"

"Yep," I responded. "eBay. They haven't failed me yet."

I carried the box to the kitchen table, opened a pair of scissors, and using only the tip of one side, carefully cut along the seams. Slowly, I pulled back the cardboard flaps, and there, nestled in a protective frame of crumpled packing paper, was what I had been waiting for. My *Alfasi* had arrived.

*Hilkhot Alfasi*, to be precise—a work whose title literally means "Jewish Laws of the Guy from Fez." Its author was Rabbi Isaac ben Jacob Alfasi, a prominent eleventh-century Moroccan sage who is still renowned as one of the greatest Jewish legal scholars in history. Born in a small

1. A seventeenth-century volume of *Hilkhot Rav Alfasi* (*Alfasi*). Photo by Shoshana Glickman.

Algerian village in 1013, Alfasi studied for the rabbinate in the Tunisian city of Kairouan (whose incoming and outgoing parades of cargo-bearing camels gave us the modern English word "caravan") and then spent most of his adult life in Fez, namesake city of the tasseled Shriners' cap.

For Alfasi and other Jews throughout North Africa, the eleventh century was a time of immense political, cultural, and intellectual change. The power of Islam rose rapidly during those years, bringing with it magnificent art and architecture, advanced science and math, and a series of relatively pluralistic Muslim dynasties. Partly as a result of this progress, Muslim leaders were becoming increasingly tolerant of Jews, and Jews in the region tended to live more peaceful lives than did their counterparts in Europe. In Muslim countries there were successful Jewish merchants, high-ranking Jewish government officials, and Jews with Arab names who spoke Arabic as their first language.

Jewish and Muslim communities both became far less insular, and the friendly atmosphere allowed Jewish religion—Juda*ism*—to encounter

Islam as it never had before. Jews saw how Muslims studied ancient texts; Jews heard discussions of Islamic mysticism; Jews saw the Muslim legal system at work. All of these new ideas and perspectives gained toeholds in Jewish thought, and as a result Jewish life would never be the same. Still today Judaism bears hints of its encounter with Islam—the exactitude with which Jews parse the words of sacred texts, the methodology of rabbinic courts, the meditative practices of Kabbalah.

The foundational text of Jewish study was then—as it is now—the Torah. But coming in as a close second was the Talmud, a record of the Rabbis' debates in the ancient academies of Babylonia and the Land of Israel. The Talmud, codified by stages in 200 CE and 500 CE, is an enormous, meandering, fascinating, frustrating, baffling, bewildering, and brilliant text. Divided into six major "orders" and subdivided into sixty-three individual tractates, it addresses all areas of life—everything from blessings to bathing, marriage to menstruation, and Sabbath to sacrifices.

It is also notoriously difficult to study. Some of it is written in Hebrew, but even more is in Aramaic, the Jewish vernacular of the ancient Near East. Its arguments are often governed by logical principles utterly foreign to modern readers, leaving vast swaths of the text incomprehensible even to those who can decipher its language. Its passages often seem to wander from law to lore and back again, with no apparent reason for the journey. Perhaps most frustrating is that the Talmud is notoriously impractical as a guide for daily practice and behavior. Many of its passages are about Jewish sacrifices—rituals last practiced almost two millennia ago in Jerusalem's ancient Temple. Other sections are purely theoretical: "When a wedding procession and a funeral procession meet at an intersection, which has right-of-way?" "What happens if a mouse carrying a piece of bread enters a Jewish home during Passover?" "When we build a sukkah [the booth in which Jews reside during the festival of Sukkot] is it OK to use a dead elephant as one of its walls?"[1]

Despite these difficulties, however, the Talmud was the primary text of Jewish study during the eleventh century. Many rabbis had released legal opinions by then, and others had written Torah commentaries. But none of this material had ever been assembled into collections of any significant size. Therefore, after the Bible, the baffling and bewildering Talmud was about the only Jewish text left for the serious student of Judaism.

With such an intensifying rumble of political and ideological change afoot, the rabbis of the Arab world grew concerned. Islam was thriving; now it tolerated Jews; some Jews even considered converting. To make matters worse, the oppression and intolerance that did occur in Muslim society *also* induced some Jews to consider jumping ship and adopting the majority religion as their own. Many Jews, the sages noticed, felt drawn to the growing light of Islam. Somehow they needed to resist the allure of that light, but how?

A big part of the problem was that in their resistance campaign the rabbis had only one arrow in their quiver—the Talmud, replete with all its difficulties and complexities. The Talmud may have been good for scholars, but now teachers needed sound bites and slogans, not complexity and hermeneutics. For the rabbis' efforts to succeed they would need to capture Jews' minds and hearts, and the Talmud was rapidly losing its ability to do so. Clearly, they needed something else—a text that, compared to the Talmud, was snappier, clearer, and far more applicable to everyday life.

Enter Alfasi. As an acclaimed scholar and rabbi of one of North Africa's largest and fastest-growing communities, he was well-positioned to devise this new tool. Obviously the tool would need to be a text; the written word was the best way of communicating with large audiences of Jews across the Arab world. And just as obviously the text would need to be based on the Talmud. But it would need to repackage and reframe the Talmud's contents in a way that eleventh-century students could understand.

So Alfasi got to work. He couldn't—and certainly wouldn't—simply dispose of the Talmud. Instead, he pored through twenty-four tractates of the ancient text, copying only those sections that he felt had practical import for Jews of his day. Out went the material about sacrifices and other no-longer-practiced rituals; out went talmudic passages recording the arcane back-and-forth of ancient Rabbinic debate; out went the sages' nonbinding minority positions and much of the Talmud's entertaining but legally extraneous folklore.

What remained was a Talmud digest, a shortened and far more usable version of the massive ancient text. Now Jews wanting to know what they could eat, how they should celebrate Jewish festivals, or what constituted appropriate conduct in business had a source to which they could turn for help. The Talmud, as a result, was no longer under the sole purview of scholars and sages. Now, suddenly, it was far more available to the Jewish rank and file. Just as *Reader's Digest* would render modern classics widely accessible to twentieth-century Americans, so too did *Hilkhot Alfasi* open the Talmud to the Jews of North Africa nine hundred years earlier.

The book was enormously successful, drawing praise on all fronts. Maimonides, the renowned rabbinic sage of Cairo who lived a century after Alfasi, wrote, "The Laws of our great teacher, Rabbenu Isaac, of blessed memory, have superseded all their predecessors, because they include everything useful for the understanding of the decisions and laws that are now in force." Maimonides's contemporary, Isaac ben Samuel Hazaken, joined in praising the compendium. "A man will toil in vain to produce such a work," he wrote of *Hilkhot Alfasi*, "unless the spirit of God rests upon him."[2]

Isaac Alfasi died in 1103, but scribes copied his Talmud digest, and it spread quickly throughout the Jewish world. Soon it became a common "first stop" for students on their way to the study of Jewish law—almost, but not quite, as central as the Talmud itself. Over the years, other sages would compose clearer and more concise codes of law, often citing Alfasi as their inspiration. Unlike Alfasi, however, these newer law codes tended to be so concise as to make it difficult to trace their teachings back to the Talmud. The newer works may have been more user-friendly than Alfasi's, but it was Alfasi who remained the primary bridge between the Talmud and contemporary Jewish practice.

A few centuries later the Catholic Church inadvertently helped sell Alfasi's books. In 1553 the Pope banned the Talmud in Italy—existing copies were to be burned, and printing new copies was absolutely forbidden. At the time Italy was the world center of Jewish printing, so the ban had a huge effect on Jewish communities everywhere.[3] For a while, most Jews realized, the Talmud would need to go underground. *Hilkhot Alfasi*, however, wasn't technically Talmud, so it escaped the papal ban. Unlike the Talmud, Jews could still get copies of *Alfasi*; and unlike the Talmud, studying it was perfectly legal. As a result the influence of *Hilkhot Alfasi* grew even further.

An edition of *Alfasi* is said to have been printed in Spain as early as the late 1400s—one of the first printed Jewish books ever—and a printer in Constantinople is known to have come out with another edition in 1509. In due course Jewish presses elsewhere published their own *Alfasis*. There were Venice additions in 1521 and 1552. Another was printed in Alfasi's hometown of Fez and released in 1523. Then came Riva de Trento in 1558, Krakow in 1597, and Amsterdam in 1720. And in the 1760s yet another edition—the tenth, if you're counting—was published in the Bavarian town of Sulzbach.[4]

Sulzbach, a small hamlet in the rolling hills of southeast Germany, is just a few miles from the borders of France and Luxembourg. In the eighteenth century its Jewish community numbered only a few dozen people, two of whom were printers, Meshulam Zalman Fraenkel and his son Aaron. Their press released each of *Hilkhot Alfasi*'s three volumes individually, in 1762, 1764, and 1767, probably in print runs of about one thousand copies. They are large, folio-sized books, each about ten-by-fifteen inches, and three inches thick. They have black leather spines and matching heavy-cardboard covers.

Although the Fraenkels of Sulzbach sold their books all over the Jewish world, their largest market was certainly in eastern Europe. Hundreds of thousands of Jews lived in Russia, Poland, and other eastern lands—some in large communities such as Kiev, Vilna, or Odessa, others in small *Fiddler-on-the-Roof*-type shtetls, with names like Bedzin, Yazlovets, and Plock. Most Jews in these areas eked out meager livings in small shops and other businesses, often under the looming specter of oppression from non-Jewish neighbors and governments. Despite their hardships, however, the shtetl Jews needed books—lots of them. Children of all ages needed reading primers and Bibles for school; older students and adult learners needed volumes of Talmud, rabbinic commentaries, and prayer books; and sometimes women needed prayer books with Yiddish translations, because they hadn't received the education they needed to learn the original Hebrew and Aramaic. To be sure, there were printers throughout eastern Europe who could supply many of these needs, and they printed countless schoolbooks, novels, and other literature. Books such as the Talmud and *Alfasi*, however, were far more difficult to produce. Each page used several typefaces of different sizes, marginal notes demanded columns of varying width, and the books were huge. The demands of such printing often exceeded the resources of the printers in these small, impoverished Jewish communities, so eastern European Jews had to import their Talmuds and *Alfasi*s from areas whose printers were better equipped to tackle such difficult jobs. As a result, prominent Jewish publishers arose in places such as Warsaw, Amsterdam, and Prague. And, yes, in Sulzbach too.

We can imagine, then, the large, freshly printed editions of *Hilkhot Alfasi* coming off the Fraenkels' press in 1764. There, behind the small shop, two or three brawny workers load boxes of the heavy books onto horse-drawn carts. Aaron Fraenkel, forty-four, shouts orders, and his seventy-one-year-old father Meshulam Zalman watches calmly from inside.[5] When loaded, the carts, creaking under the weight of their cargo, roll out of Sulzbach and into the Bavarian countryside, parting company with one another as they head to their different destinations.

Most of the carts head east, toward Russia, Poland, and other nearby lands. One cart in particular goes to Vilna, the largest Jewish community in Lithuania, where its driver sells several books to a local itinerant book dealer. The dealer thanks the driver politely and heads to his home in a small nearby shtetl. The next day he makes his normal rounds to the surrounding towns, and one of his first stops is to see the rabbi of a *beis midrash*, a house of study. "The rabbi is a regular customer," the dealer reminds himself. "Surely he'll be interested in this new stock from Bavaria." Carrying a perilously tall stack of books, the bookseller walks toward the wooden building, and the rabbi greets him warmly at the door. "Yankel! *Sholem aleykhem*—it's good to see you. Please come in."

In just a few minutes, the deal is done. Yankel leaves with a shorter stack of books, and the rabbi places his heavy, newly purchased volume of *Hilkhot Alfasi* alongside other similar books on one of the shelves lining the walls of the *beis midrash*.

The following morning the students file in, and soon they are engaged in *khevruse*—tandem Torah study with a partner. A pair of young men walk to the shelf, take down the new *Alfasi*, and carry it to their study table. Opening its black covers, they quickly find the page they are looking for, and across the centuries Alfasi begins to speak.

For almost two hundred years the book remained in that *beis midrash*, allowing generation after generation of students to plumb its depths and discover its riches. Some of the students surely found the experience frustrating; others found it deeply satisfying. Still they came back, year after year, parting the book's covers to read the words inside.

And then one day in late 1941, the door of the *beis midrash* opened. This time what came into the study house was not a hopeful salesman or a group of eager young students. This time what came through the doorway was darkness.

Carefully, I removed the large book from its package and laid it on the table. There were some rub marks on the cover, but otherwise it was in remarkably good condition. The pages were soft and un-torn, the text was completely readable, and the age-old binding was still doing an excellent job of holding everything together. I turned to the title page. For me, seeing the frontispiece of an old Jewish book is just as exciting as feeling an airplane's final acceleration before takeoff or first stepping into the summer sunshine at Wrigley Field. Despite my middle-aged jadedness and cynical remove, it never fails to give me a thrill.

This book was no exception. Bold, banner-sized letters across the top of the page read, "Part Two of the Laws of Rabbi Alfas." (The letters spelling the author's name were the largest ones on the page—an author's dream!) Then, in slightly smaller letters, came the words "Containing all that is found in the versions of *Alfasi* printed until today—new, and old as well." Moving down the page, the font size grew smaller. Tiny letters listed all of the commentaries included in the book and the previous versions of *Alfasi* that the editor consulted as he assembled his own. Then came the ornate printer's mark; inside the intricate logo was a Hebrew banner reading "Zalman the Printer." Just underneath, once again in a larger typeface, "In Sulzbach."

The page also bore a couple of haphazard stamps indicating that the book had once been at Heichal Shlomo, the office of the chief rabbi in Jerusalem. That's probably where the dealer who sold it to me first got it. Near the left side of the page, somebody had written "Z 302/2" in large penciled letters. The Z was crossed, European-style; it looked like it had been put there in the twentieth century. What could that strange marking mean?

A horizontal black line crossed the page near the bottom, beneath which was a phrase in Latin: "*Cum Licentia Serenissimi Domini Electoris Palatini qua Ducis Solisabacensis*"—"Licensed by His Most Revered Lordship, the Elector Palatine and Duke of Sulzbach." Evidently, printers needed copyright protection back in the 1700s, too. Next came the printer's credits—"In the publishing house of the honorable Meshulam Zalman (may his Rock guard him and give him long life), son of the

2. Title page of *Hilkhot Raf Alfas* (or *Alfasi*) written in the eleventh century and published in Sulzbach, Germany, in 1764. Photo by Jeff Hersh.

renowned and honorable Rabbi Aaron (may the memory of the righteous be a blessing)."[6]

Finally, at the very bottom of the title page, came the date: "In the year, 'And I became great and surpassed all who came before me.'" That phrase, of course, isn't a year. It's a *phrase*! The passage is from the Bible—Ecclesiastes 2:9, actually—a lament of how vain our life's labors can be. But in a certain sense, the phrase *is* a year, albeit an encrypted one. Classical Hebrew, you see, has no numerals and instead uses Hebrew letters to represent numbers—*alef* is one, *bet* is two, *gimel* is three, etc. To provide a book's publication date, Jewish printers customarily quote a passage from the Bible, printing a few of its letters larger than the others. To figure out the book's publication date on the Hebrew calendar, all you have to do is total the numerical value of those large letters and add 5,000. Then, to convert that Hebrew date into its corresponding year on our Gregorian calendar, you simply subtract 3760, and—*bingo!*—you have the year the book was published. Simple!

This particular verse had four enlarged Hebrew letters, *dalet, peh, tav*, and *mem*, representing the numbers 4, 80, 400, and 40 respectively. With pencil and paper, I totaled the value of the letters—524—and added 5,000. The book was printed in the Jewish year 5524. Subtracting 3760, I got its date on the Western calendar—1764! The fact that I'd known this date ever since I first saw the book on eBay diminished the thrill only slightly.

After figuring out the year of publication—refiguring it, actually—I noticed there was a blank page covering the book's frontispiece. Turning it back, I found a decal pasted to the inside-front cover. It was printed in pale blue, and its logo featured two concentric stars of David. The caption read "Jewish Cultural Reconstruction."

"Jewish Cultural Reconstruction"? I'd never heard of it. Puzzled, I did what rabbis have always done when faced with such mysteries. I booted up my computer and went to Google.

לתחיה לחקר ישראל רוח הנצח

Jewish Cultural Reconstruction

3. Bookplate inside the front cover of *Hilkhot Alfasi*. Photo by Shoshana Glickman.

What I discovered while researching the bookplate was an epic story of looting and recovery. Jewish Cultural Reconstruction, I learned, was the organization that processed unidentified Jewish books and other cultural treasures discovered in the American Zone of Germany at the end of World War II. The Nazis had stolen millions of books during their reign. Some they burned in spectacular bonfires, but most they saved, stashing the literary loot in castles, abandoned mine shafts, and warehouses for future use. It was the largest and most extensive book-looting campaign in history. And if their collection of stolen literature could appropriately be called a library, then at the time it was the largest library of Jewish literature ever amassed.

I try to imagine the last person to study this book before the Nazis took it. In all probability, he died during the Holocaust. Was he single or married? Old or young? What color was his hair? Was this man the victim of a massacre in the woods near his home? Was he herded along with hundreds of others into a gas chamber? Or did he avoid the gas chambers only to die later of disease and starvation? And as he endured his final travails, I wonder whether he carried with him any of the wisdom he learned from this book. Did Alfasi's teachings strengthen him as he faced the horrors? Was he able—even furtively—to perform any of the rituals it prescribed? Might his memories of studying this book together with teachers and friends have brought him at least a fleeting moment of warmth during his final days?

Although we'll never know the answers to these questions, what we do know is that there were millions of books just like this one—books stolen and later redeemed. Some bear traces of the people who once read them—a thumbprint, a doodle, maybe even a handwritten name inside the cover—but most of the books lost their stories in the catastrophic upheavals to which history subjected them.

How is it that the book on my shelf survived those upheavals? How is it that the long trajectory of its path through history led it to my home in Washington State? And what, if anything, is there to be learned from its story?

This, then, is a book about books—millions of books. It is the story of the journey these volumes took from the places they were printed, to the homes and libraries of those who read them, to Nazi castles and warehouses, and back into the hands of Jewish students and institutions around the world. It is a story of great cultural and human loss and also of how a regime bent on destruction preserved its enemy's literary treasures. It is the story of how a free civilization decides what to do with the remains of a largely destroyed world and of how those remains connect individuals who survived the destruction with their past. It is the story of Jews everywhere struggling to understand the new realities of their post-Holocaust world and of Western society's gradual realization of the magnitude of devastation wrought by World War II. Most of all, it is the story of people—of Nazi leaders, ideologues, and Judaica experts; of Allied soldiers and scholars and scoundrels; of Jewish communities, librarians, and readers around the world. The story of European Jewry's books during World War II is one that runs eerily parallel to the far more tragic story of European Jews themselves. Like the Holocaust's human victims, many books were hidden in attics and cellars; once discovered, few of them survived; sometimes their survival was by design; often it was due to sheer luck.

Most of the people who directly experienced the darkness of the Holocaust are gone now. Among the only remaining physical relics of them and their world are the books that survived the war. One of those volumes was written in Morocco, published in Germany, studied in eastern Europe, and now sits on a bookshelf just a few feet from me as I type these words. This is the story of that book and of millions of others that also survived the calamitous destruction of European Jewry.

Still today, despite the darkness, the light hiding inside these volumes can shine. And maybe—just maybe—knowing the books' stories can help that light shine even brighter.

# 1

## Loading the Jewish Bookshelf

> My son! Make your books your companions; let your book-cases
> and shelves be your pleasure grounds and gardens. Bask in their
> paradise, gather their fruit, pluck their roses, take their spices and
> their myrrh.
>
> —*Ethical will of Judah ibn Tibbon, Provence, twelfth century*

The Nazi pillage of Jewish books was an assault on the very core of
Jewish life. To understand the effect of the attack, we begin with an
imaginary journey to a real place. The place is the Strashun Library in
Vilna, Lithuania. It is early 1939.[1]

Vilna is a bustling, lively city. Long the capital of Lithuania, sover-
eignty over the city bounced between Germany, Poland, Lithuania,
and the Soviet Union during and after World War I. The Polish army
seized Vilna in October 1920, and it has been under Polish leadership ever since.

As we approached the city a few minutes earlier, we came to the
Vilna River and looked across to a sea of red-tile roofs covering buildings with white walls. We drove down wide boulevards lined with
majestic palaces—some are grand neoclassical structures, others
imposing medieval fortifications. We saw the pillared white façade
and the sturdy bell tower of the Vilna Cathedral; the ornate, russet,

Gothic-style steeples of the sixteenth-century St. Anne's Catholic Church; and the green onion-domes of the St. Michael and St. Konstantin Orthodox Church, erected only twenty-seven years ago.

The metropolis is home to more than two hundred thousand residents, and from the number of steeples, we would never guess that 30 percent of the city's population is Jewish.[2] There are theaters, banks, and museums on the wide boulevards, and looking down the narrow side streets, we glimpse twisty lanes packed with small shops, peddlers, and cramped multistory apartment buildings.

Our guide explains that Vilna's Jewish community thrums as actively as the city itself. It is home to prominent Jewish scholars, artisans, poets, and educators. There are dozens of "mutual aid societies" in Vilna—among them organizations supporting Jewish orphans, Jewish brides, Jewish war veterans, and Jewish beggars. For the hungry, there is the famous "Inexpensive Restaurant," with a seven-hundred-seat dining room that serves hearty meals at minimal cost. There are Jewish theaters in Vilna, which stage a veritable Broadway's worth of plays in Yiddish, Hebrew, and Polish. There are two daily newspapers published in the city, *Tag* (Day) and *Jüdische Zeitung* (Jewish Times). There are Jewish writers' groups, art academies, and orchestras. There is even a Jewish opera company that has presented classics such as *Aida* and *La Traviata* in Yiddish. Vilna is home to more than one hundred synagogues, dozens of trade organizations run *kloyzes* (study houses), and there is a rabbinic court whose rulings the local government accepts as law.

It should be of no surprise, our guide continues, that Vilna has long been called Yerushalayim d'Lita—the Jerusalem of Lithuania.

Soon, we turn down a narrow street and arrive at the *shulhoyf*—synagogue courtyard. There are actually several small synagogues in this complex of buildings, but the largest by far is Vilna's Great Synagogue, a large, slant-roofed building built in the Baroque-Renaissance style that was popular back in the 1600s. Adjacent to the synagogue,

4. The Strashun Library, Vilna, Lithuania. Courtesy Yad Vashem Photo Archives.

we see a long two-story brick structure, its arched second-floor windows evoking images of the tablets from Mount Sinai. The building's front door swings open every few seconds; men, women, and children—lots of children—come and go, often holding one or more books under their arms. When the door shuts, we notice the sign: "The Library of Rabbi Mattityahu son of Rabbi Samuel Strashun."

Our guide tells us that the library's namesake, Mattityahu Stras-hun (1817–85), was a man with a life perfectly situated to create a literary study center of this size. His father, Samuel, one of the most renowned rabbis of mid-nineteenth-century Vilna, had left Mattityahu a huge collection of books, and as Mattityahu himself became a successful businessman, his growing fortune allowed him to enlarge the collection with purchases of his own. Mattityahu, who died childless, bequeathed his library to the Jewish community of Vilna. A catalogue compiled shortly after his death listed 5,700 items in the library, but it clearly contained far more—manuscripts, collections of rabbinic legal rulings, secular books, and thousands of volumes of Judaica in a variety different of languages.[3]

It took years to organize the collection, and as the catalogue grew, Strashun's heirs feared that its secular literature would lure readers away from Judaism and were reluctant to open the library to the public. Finally, however, in 1892, in a building that was once the home of Mattityahu Strashun, the doors of the Strashun Library opened.

Almost immediately the collection grew even larger. The library received monetary donations and was able to purchase more books; educated Jews from Vilna and elsewhere commonly bequeathed their own books to the library. It was becoming a major institution.

By the late 1890s it had become clear that the collection had outgrown the home of its donor. Funds were raised, the site on the *shulhoyf* was selected, and in 1901 the Strashun Library moved to the building before us.

As soon as we arrive, a man in his late fifties comes out of the building to greet us. He is a short man, with a graying beard and a large friendly smile. He is neatly dressed, though his black gabardine suit is slightly faded and fraying at the edges. "*Sholem aleykhem,*" he says. "Welcome."

5. Khaykl Lunski. Courtesy YIVO Institute.

Our guide introduces our host as Khaykl Lunski, the scholar who has served as the Strashun's librarian for the past forty-four years; he began working there in 1895, when he was fourteen years old.[4] Lunski speaks quickly, exuberantly, and with a slight lisp. We have to listen closely to understand him.

"Welcome," Lunski says again. "I'm glad you're here. Please. Please, come this way. Let me show you around."

Lunski, it seems, is friends with everyone he sees. "Professor Gradstein," he says to a man entering the library, "I hope you're well today. I put the material about the Vilna Gaon on a table inside, and I added a few more books and articles I thought might be helpful . . . Moshe, how is your research on early Yiddish novels progressing? Come later and I'll show you some material nobody's studied before . . . Rabbi Kopnick, I heard that you'd like to be able to speak more loudly at shul. I have some material on elocution that you might want to see."

We walk through the Strashun Library's reading room. It is long and well lit, full of people sitting at tables looking at open books. There are men and women, old people and teenagers, bearded rabbis wearing black hats and young, fiery-eyed revolutionaries.

"I thought we would do our tour chronologically today," says Khaykl Lunski, "starting at the very beginning. Let's go over here to our collection of Bibles." He points to a set of bookshelves lining a short wall from floor to ceiling. There are hundreds of volumes of Jewish Scripture on those shelves. Some are very old; many are in Hebrew; others have been translated into a variety of different languages. It is a Babel of Bibles.

"As you know," Lunski explains, "the earliest Jewish texts weren't books. Nor were they even scrolls. Nor, for that matter, were they even written on paper. No, our first texts were inscribed in stone. And the very first of those stone texts began with the second letter of the Hebrew alphabet . . ."

Lunski is called away mid-sentence, having been approached by a young, scholarly looking man with a question he seems anxious to have answered before our tour goes any further. We are on our own for a moment, left considering the start of Jewish literature.

6. The reading room of the Strashun Library, Vilna. Courtesy YIVO Institute.

### *The Tablet*

What many believe to be the world's first Hebrew text, as Khaykl Lunski was about to tell us, opened with a *bet*, a letter whose name and shape once invoked the image of a house—*bayit* in Hebrew. A horizontal line to the right, another narrow one down to the baseline, and then a final rightward stroke along the bottom.

Moses is said to have inscribed that *bet*, chiseling it into the stone tablets that God had told him to bring to the mountaintop. More letters followed that *bet*, and soon the *bet* became part of a word—*b'reishit*, "in the beginning." Still more letters emerged from Moses's chisel, and the word became part of a verse, the verse part of a chapter, and the chapter part of a biblical book telling the story of Creation and of the formation of the Jewish people: Genesis. Moses chiseled still more words—79,847 of them in all—and what resulted was the Torah, the complex, bewildering, and often baffling mix of narrative and law that has served as the basis for countless works of Jewish thought and literature ever since.

One letter. Three strokes. Across, down, across. In its wake came millions of other letters—billions, perhaps—composing vast store-houses of Jewish literature. It is doubtful whether Moses could have even imagined it.

There were, of course, two sets of tablets. The first was a set that God carved, which Moses smashed when he discovered the Israelites worshiping the Golden Calf. The second was the handiwork of Moses himself; it survived much longer.[5] Those two sets of tablets were the first Jewish texts ever and are the stuff of Jewish legend. Legend has it that God conceived of the first set long before the creation of the world but actually formed it on the eve of the first Sabbath. Having made the tablets, God kept them safe for many centuries until it was time to give them to Moses. Originally, others taught, the tablets were not made of stone, but of fire—black fire written on white fire. They were heavenly, spiritual tablets, and it was only when God handed them to Moses that they assumed physical form.

When Moses brought the second set down to the Israelites, they remained intact. Soon the Israelites placed the second tablets, along with the shards of the first, in an ornate box called the Ark of the Covenant. They placed that sacred coffer in the innermost sanctuary of the Tabernacle, the portable Temple where God's presence manifested itself during the Israelite's desert wanderings. Yes, both sets of tablets were in the Ark—even the shattered ones. In Judaism sacred words remain sacred. Even when they seem broken; even when they no longer seem useful. Jews cherish words—the broken ones as well as those that are intact—and abandon them only when forced to do so.

That's why, when things settled down after the Israelites' desert wanderings, they placed the tablets holding their foundational text in the most sacred spot in the universe. To Jews, the center of the world is the city of Jerusalem, capital of the Land of Israel since King David first established it as such around 1000 BCE. In the center of that holy city stood the Temple, built by David's son, Solomon. In the center of the Temple was the Holy of Holies, a small chamber accessible only to the High Priest on the Jewish Day of Atonement; and inside the Holy of Holies was the Ark of the Covenant, holding the tablets from Sinai inside it. At the center of the universe sat a book—or at least the closest thing to a book that existed back in ancient times.

In 586 BCE Babylonian forces invaded the Land of Israel and destroyed Jerusalem's magnificent Temple. Soldiers carried away the Ark of the Covenant, plundering it and the holy text it held as war booty. It was a theft of sacred Jewish words, an eerie foreshadowing of what would happen to the descendants of these Jews in Europe two and a half millennia later. In the centuries to come, some would argue that the Babylonians hid the Ark somewhere in the Temple complex, where it still waits to be found. Others believe that today it is in a church in Ethiopia. And millions of movie fans think that the "Lost Ark" was discovered on the eve of World War II by Indiana Jones and now sits in a large warehouse somewhere in the United States.

Most historians, however, believe that the bejeweled Ark of the Covenant ended up in a Babylonian chop shop and that its captors simply threw away its old engraved tablets and focused instead on the precious materials adorning the box itself. The loss of such a sacred national treasure might have destroyed other nations or cultures, but by this time the Torah had been copied and recopied. Like many books of today, the Torah was able to survive even though its original copies had long since disappeared.

Within fifty years Babylonian dominance had waned, and the Persians who succeeded them allowed Jews to return to Israel and rebuild the Temple. Only a small number of Jews took the Persians up on the offer. Those who did decide to return immediately set about rebuilding the Temple. As soon as its foundations were laid, there was a grand ceremony of dedication, replete with trumpets, cymbals, and joyous songs of praise. "All the people raised a great shout . . . because the foundation of the House of the Eternal had been laid" (Ezra 3:11). After fifty years of exile, finally the house of God could stand again. Finally Jewish life could be glorious just as it had been in the past.

But as the songs and sounds of celebration erupted, a group of old men stood off to the side—priests, Levites, and tribal leaders. They remembered the First Temple from their youth: the gigantic stones of its base, its rich cedar planks, its gleaming bronze pillars and altar. Here, however, lay a simple foundation roughly hewn into the ground. No sanctuary, no ornate carvings, and perhaps worst of all, no tablets from the mountaintop. When they saw this pitiful sight, the book of Ezra tells us, they wept.[6]

Almost immediately, the sounds of their cries were drowned out by the far louder celebrations of the younger men around them. Evidently Jewish life *could* continue, even without the sacred stone tablets at its center. Evidently memories of the text would do just fine.

### *The Scroll*

Having attended to the young man's query, Khaykl Lunski returns and continues our library tour. "Now step over here," he says. "I have something very special to show you." He walks through canyons of crowded bookshelves and enters a door near the back of the library. Holding it open, he lowers his volume to a stage whisper. "This room is not open to the public. You'll understand why in a moment."

It is a small room, lit by a single light bulb hanging from the ceiling and a reading lamp on a table against the wall to our right. To our left is a wall lined not with bookshelves, but with wooden cubbyholes of various sizes. A few of the cubbyholes are empty, but inside most of them, we see, are scrolls in various states of preservation. Some of the scrolls have one roller, others have two, and still others are simply coiled-up parchments that evidently lost their wooden centerpieces long ago.

"This is where we keep some of our greatest treasures," Lunski tells us. "This here, for example, is a Scroll of Esther. I believe it is from the eighteenth century. Persian, perhaps." From one of the cubbyholes he pulls out a small scroll wrapped around an ornately carved wooden roller extending into a handle beneath the scroll. He sets it on the table, gently unrolls it, and before us unfurls a parchment illuminated with bright, intricate pictures and designs in the margins of every page.

We're fascinated, but Lunski doesn't leave us much time to ooh and aah. He rerolls the scroll and keeps talking as he returns it to its place on the wall. "Some of the scrolls here are far older, of course, but they're usually incomplete." He pulls a tattered roll of parchment from another cubbyhole and carefully lays it flat on the table. It is about eighteen inches high and three feet wide. "Once—back in the seventeenth century, I think—this was part of a Torah scroll. Now all we have is this small section. If only I knew what happened to the rest of it."

"Most of the scrolls in this room," Lunski continues, "are complete Torah scrolls." Many of the older ones, we see, are simply unadorned parchments with no rollers or covers. Some have only a single roller, others have two. Many scrolls have lush velvet covers, silver breastplates hanging in front, and crowns or finials on top.

Someone asks Lunski why the scrolls are dressed in such regal garb. "Why?" he responds, as if it should be obvious. "For Jews, the Torah is the most regal prince of all."

The history of the written word in Judaism is one of ongoing and explosive proliferation. Ever since the first *bet* appeared on the first tablet at Sinai, Jews have copied the words of their ancestors, recorded the words of their teachers, and written words of their own. Even Moses himself was a copyist. Yes, God wrote the first set of tablets that Moses smashed during the Golden Calf fiasco, but it was only the second set—the one that Moses copied from God's original teaching—that made it down from the mountaintop and into the hands of the people.

What did change in the generations after Moses was the size of the "print runs." That's because Jews *need*—and have always needed—written texts in order to lead Jewish lives. Other religions emphasize the times when God speaks to individuals, but Judaism focuses on shared revelation—the shared revelation that happened at Mount Sinai. Personal moments of transcendence might be moving, but what really counts is what God said to the Jewish *people*, collectively. And what God said to the Jewish people collectively is called Torah. To study Torah, therefore, is to study a thunderous moment of divine revelation. To study Torah is to hear the voice of God.

That's why Jews have always been such passionate learners. Over the years millions of Jews have devoted as much time as they could to exploring sacred Jewish texts. There was a lot to learn and not a moment to waste. Frivolity, from such a perspective, wasn't just a waste of time, it was a *bittul Torah*, a waste of Torah time, study time. And it was downright sinful. And with so many Jews hungering so passionately for text, the texts needed copying. On stone. At least that's how they did it in antiquity. But it didn't take long to realize that rock-made tablets rendered the task of writing excessively slow and that a newer, more efficient surface would be desirable, to say the least.

Long before Jews began producing Torah scrolls, Egyptians had been experimenting with other writing surfaces. In the twenty-eighth century BCE the Egyptians began weaving reeds into papyrus.[7] Papyrus was cheaper and easier to write on than stone, but it was fragile and very sensitive to the ravages of heat, moisture, and time. It was a good writing surface, but it wasn't great. Sometime later, Egyptians discovered that they could also write on animal hides. Scribes could stretch and treat it to turn it into parchment, which, though somewhat costlier than papyrus, was also more durable.

In the coming centuries, the two surfaces, papyrus and parchment, would battle it out for dominance. Eventually, especially as writing spread to the comparatively reed-less lands of Europe, the durability of parchment won out over the affordability of papyrus. By the early centuries of the Common Era, scribes throughout Europe, the Middle East, and North Africa could be found washing, liming, de-hairing, scraping, stretching, powdering, and pumicing animal skins of all sizes into parchment writing surfaces. They used hides of goats, calves, sheep, and other animals, and the process yielded a smooth, pale, absorbent surface that could grab the letters inked upon it and hold on to them for centuries. Jews could be found writing on papyrus in Egypt as early as the seventh century BCE.[8] During the following century, however, the growing Jewish community in Babylonia learned to write on parchment, and for the next several hundred years parchment increasingly became the primary surface used to record Jewish texts.

The earliest Torah scrolls contained not the entire text of the Five Books of Moses, but only parts of it—sometimes just a single book such as Genesis or Exodus, and sometimes even shorter passages. According to ancient Rabbinic literature, the priests read from Torah scrolls at the Temple on Yom Kippur, the Day of Atonement, as part of a spectacular public ceremony.[9] There were a few other Torah scrolls back in First Temple times, but only one—the Temple scroll—was actively a part of Jewish life. And after the Temple fell, its Torah scroll disappeared, and Jews dispersed so widely that even if they did still have it, they couldn't all gather together to hear its words as they had previously.

As a result, soon after their arrival in Babylonia, small groups of Jewish exiles began meeting in homes and other gathering places (probably on Saturdays) to spend time together, have a little nosh, and most significantly to read Torah. The gatherings were important to the exiles, for those exiles were a tiny, threatened minority still coping with enormous loss. They needed to do everything they could to maintain their connections, and Torah study was the glue that held them together. Life in exile is rarely any good, but gathering to read their ancient Scripture gave these Jews a ray of hope for the survival of their sacred tradition. The synagogue had been born.

The synagogue wouldn't firmly establish itself as the central institution of Jewish life until after the destruction of the Second Temple in 70 CE. But as its bare outlines first emerged in Babylonia, Jewish Scripture had been copied and recopied enough to make it available to the growing audience of Torah-hungry Jews. Even in these early "proto-synagogues," it was clear that the presence of the written word would play a critical role in Jewish life. Scrolls, of course, are a cumbersome and highly impractical way of recording and storing sacred text. Round scrolls don't allow for easy storage, and sewing the pages together is difficult; one slightly off-kilter seam can render the entire document crooked and unrollable. Despite its drawbacks, in its day the scroll was a revolutionary development, allowing texts of all kinds to be more widely accessible than ever before. Nowadays we have the Internet, in the late Middle Ages they had the printing press, and in antiquity they had the scroll.

Still today, in our age of high-speed, high-tech, and high-volume printing, Torah scrolls are created just as they have been for centuries. A scribe painstakingly prepares the parchment. He etches faint guidelines into its surface to keep the text straight and neat. He mixes the ink—a unique batch for each page to maximize its ability to grab the particular parchment before him. Then he begins to write. Letter by letter, word by word, column by massive column. To prevent mistakes and to fully immerse himself in his work, the scribe will often chant the name of each letter as he writes it. Minor errors can be repaired, but if the scribe makes a mistake writing one of the Bible's names for God, he must dispose of the entire page and start again.

Slowly, from the nib of his quill, the Torah text flows out toward completion: 5 books, 245 columns, 5,845 verses, 79,847 words, 304,805 letters. A good day's work, I'm told, is one column of text. With a few days off and proofreading time, it typically takes about a year to create an entire scroll. Every synagogue is supposed to have at least one Torah scroll, and because some holiday readings are from different parts of the text, two is even better.

As Jewish religious objects go, the Torah scroll remains the holiest and most precious of all. Usually it is dressed in a plush mantle, adorned with a breastplate and crown—kind of like an ancient priest. When the ark holding the Torah scroll is open, the congregation rises. One of the greatest honors in a synagogue is to be given an *aliyah*, an invitation to recite blessings before and after a Torah reading. And if, God forbid, someone should drop a Torah, Jewish tradition prescribes fasts and other penance not only for the person who dropped it, but also for those who saw it dropped, and sometimes even for *everyone* in the community, whether or not they were present when the Torah fell to the ground.

Over the centuries, Jews have danced with Torah scrolls, run with them from burning towns and villages, and plumbed the depths of their content for every spark of meaning they could find. In one sense a Torah scroll is just inked parchment coiled around wooden rollers. But for Jews it is far more. For Jews it is nothing less than a sacred portal; to open it up is to reveal the splendor of heaven.

## The Manuscript

Unfortunately those heavenly scrolls didn't protect the Jewish community from earthly troubles. In 66 CE Jews in the Land of Israel rebelled against their Roman rulers, and Rome responded by vanquishing the Jewish rebels and destroying the Temple. Looking at the devastation, the Jewish survivors couldn't help but fear that Judaism itself lay in ruins.

And indeed Judaism might have come to an end right there and then were it not for one courageous, forward-thinking, and highly resourceful sage named Yohanan ben Zakkai. As the Roman army stood poised to conquer Jerusalem, Yohanan realized that everything was about to change and that Judaism would need an utterly new paradigm if it was to survive the new challenges it faced. He snuck out of Jerusalem, approached the Roman authorities, and received permission to build a new institution in the city of Yavneh. It was a *beit midrash* (house of study), a place where Jewish sages could gather to discuss and explore the words of Torah. Maybe with such an institution in place, Yohanan hoped, Judaism could thrive even though the Temple was now gone.

The plan worked. The Temple lay in ruins, and the priests had therefore fallen from power. Now, however, Rabbinic Judaism had been born—a new type of Judaism that allowed the study of text to fill at least part of the gaping hole that the destruction of the Temple had left in Jewish life. To Yavneh the scholars came—men with names like Gamaliel, Yosi Hakohen, and Joshua ben Chanina. Later generations of sages came too, and some of them moved to other cities and opened academies of their own. Their teachings addressed every element of Jewish life: holidays, marriage, tort law, and even the sacrifices they hoped would soon take place in the rebuilt Temple. The growing body of material was recorded not in writing, but in memory, passed down orally from teacher to student. An oral library, of course, can be impermanent. The limitations and inaccuracies of human memory often rendered it scattered, disorganized, and sometimes faded beyond recognition. With such limits it tended to do better with the pithy, the rhythmic, and the simple, rather than with the nuanced detail of elaborate law and lore. Even in the early days of Rabbinic life, the need for a written text was becoming increasingly evident.[10]

The first century led to the second. More sages came and went. The canon of Rabbinic teaching grew. By the end of the second century, the amount of material had grown so large that students inevitably quoted its teachings incorrectly. Some, whether accidentally or on purpose, let their own interpretations creep in to muddle the lessons.

By the end of the second century, a leading rabbi named Yehudah Hanasi had come to fear that the original text was getting lost in the transmission. Resolved to stanch this knowledge drain, Yehudah standardized Rabbinic teaching, establishing a single version of the material for everyone to accept and through which to preserve the inherited teaching.

What emerged was a work called the Mishnah, a compendium of a century and a half's worth of Rabbinic wisdom codified in the early third century. It is divided into six major "orders"—agriculture, festivals, family law, damages, sacrifices, and laws of purity; and subdivided into sixty-three tractates—one on each of several holidays, another on blessings, one each on marriage, divorce, menstruation, and so forth.

And yet, despite all of the Mishnah's advantages, the Rabbis still found it unsatisfying. For one thing, scholars suggest that Yehudah Hanasi didn't actually write down its text; he only standardized it but still kept it oral. Some help *that* was. For another, it may have clarified the Rabbis' positions on many issues, but it too demanded interpretation. The Mishnah, it turns out, was hardly the definitive text it claimed to be. Perhaps most important, the Rabbis had *liked* the fact that the Torah was an oral text. To them "Torah" was what happened when teachers taught students. "Torah" was a vibrant, lively encounter between one generation of its adherents and the next. "Torah" was relationship; "Torah" was the stuff of noisy classrooms, animated argument, and passionate discussion. Writing the sacred teachings down therefore didn't enrich them or preserve them. Writing them down only ossified them into frozen relics of the past.

Rabbis from Mishnaic times onward therefore resisted writing down the texts. "Those who write down legal traditions are like those who burnt the Torah," said one. In fact, said another, when God told Moses to "write down these words [of Torah] for yourself" (Exodus 34:27), God was actually giving permission only to write down the written Torah; transcribing the words of oral Torah was forbidden.[11]

With each generation of sages, the rabbinic "family tree" widened even further. More students jumped in. More academies opened throughout the Land of Israel and, beginning in the early third century, also in Babylonia. And they did it all by word of mouth, adding a new set of textual inaccuracies and variations of their own.

The size of the textual record—the original manuscripts available still to modern scholars—waxes and wanes during these centuries. Today the oldest known Jewish manuscripts are the Elephantine Papyri, a collection of several hundred legal documents and letters, mostly in Aramaic, written in the fifth century BCE, and now housed in Berlin and New York. A group of four Egyptian biblical fragments from the second century BCE called the Nash Papyrus is now housed at Cambridge University. The Israel Museum in Jerusalem houses the Dead Sea Scrolls, a group of 972 manuscripts of biblical texts, sectarian literature, and other ancient material, first discovered in cliffside caves during the 1940s. They are variously dated anywhere from the fifth century BCE to the second century CE. The Israel Museum also holds a handful of scraps representing correspondence from the Bar Kokhba revolt, a rebellion of the Jews of Palestine against their Roman rulers during the second century CE.

And then the record goes dark for nearly eight hundred years. From the early second until the late ninth century CE, there are hardly any Jewish or Hebrew manuscripts of any kind. Maybe this is because the rabbis of these centuries remained reluctant to commit their teachings to paper. Or maybe Jews did write during these centuries, and for whatever the reason their manuscripts were lost to the passage of time.

As antiquity yielded to the Middle Ages, the Jewish people became more geographically dispersed. Fewer Jews now lived in the Land of Israel; other population centers grew. Babylonia housed a vibrant Jewish community, as did Cairo, Kairouan, and other cities in North Africa; the Jewish community of Spain grew and prospered. As the Jewish map widened, Babylonia and Israel had plenty of rabbis to teach the old texts, but the outlying communities found themselves with far fewer. Repeatedly Jews in Spain, Yemen, the Maghreb, and elsewhere had to write to rabbis in the major population centers for advice. These teachers responded as well as they could, but the strain of distance was rapidly making the situation untenable.

In the eighth century, a new tool for the dissemination of written text reached Babylonia: pressed sheets of wood pulp pressed into folios for writing. Paper was far easier to work with than animal-skin parchment, and the Muslim world produced ream after ream of the stuff to help them record their sweeping scholarly achievements. Paper, in turn, made being a scholar much easier than it had been back in the vellum days, and its arrival in the Muslim world allowed even more scholarship to unfold. Such literacy couldn't help but rub off on the region's Jews, and Jewish literature in the lands of Islam flourished as a result. In places such as Cairo and Baghdad, Jews had been producing manuscripts as early as the sixth century, but with the arrival of paper came a huge writing boom. Jews transcribed biblical passages, sayings of their rabbis, and even letters to their friends and family. And as writing became stylish, the major Rabbinic academies in Babylonia and the Land of Israel were able to respond more easily to queries from Jews in faraway lands.

For all of the reluctance of early rabbis to write down their teachings, the laws that they composed came to consider those writings to be sacred. The words of Torah, these rabbis said, are never to be destroyed. Instead, when no longer usable, the texts are to be buried or placed in a *genizah*, a closet or an attic in the synagogue designated as a repository for damaged or destroyed sacred literature. Originally Jewish law required only the words of Scripture to be stashed in *genizah*s, but over time the understanding of which texts were sacred often became far broader. Soon Jews were depositing rabbinic writings as well as scriptural ones into their *genizah*s. Later, they included any document even mentioning God and sometimes documents bearing any Hebrew at all. In fact, by the tenth century—particularly in the highly literate lands of the Middle East and North Africa—many Jews seem to have considered any document of *any kind* worthy of preservation in their *genizah* repositories.

"We Jews treasure our old words," says Khaykl Lunski during our library tour. "That's why we hold on to our old papers. Even the scraps. Over here, we have several collections representing different kinds of papers." He points to three shelves of matching albums near the ceiling. "Those on top are Vilna community archives—property deeds for synagogues, birth and death records, and minutes of our community council meetings. Some of the papers are almost 150 years old. These volumes in front of us? They are collections of correspondence from Jewish travelers between 1750 and 1850.

"And here," he continues, "are some of our most precious treasures." Lunski walks to a padlocked cabinet in the back of the room, reaches into his pocket, and takes out a jangling ring of keys. In the open cabinet we see more volumes like the others. "These albums might at first seem similar to the others, but look . . ." Inside the albums are brown, tattered papers—handwritten, faded, and crumbling. "These are some of the oldest manuscripts in our library; I'm not even sure where they're all from. Here we have three pages from Leviticus—they may have been written five hundred years ago. And these letters are in Judeo-Arabic—Arabic words written in Hebrew letters—obviously from the Middle East. And here we have some handwritten scraps of Talmud that are at least three hundred years old. Word has it that they came from a *genizah* somewhere . . ."

Lunski's voice trails off as he explores the albums. We know he's studied them before, but he looks at each manuscript as if it is a new discovery.

"*Ach*! If only we had more time."

## *The Book*

"Let's go back out to the main collections now," says Lunski. He waves us out of the room, locks the door behind us, and leads us through the stacks to another locked room.

"And here are the books that we guard most carefully." Like the manuscript room, this chamber is also lined with books on three walls. Unlike the identical binders on the shelves of the manuscript room, however, here there are books of all sizes, shapes, colors, and conditions. A faintly musty smell greets us when we enter.

"On these shelves," says Lunski, "are our rare volumes of Talmud. And over here are signed copies of the greats of modern Yiddish literature: Sholom Aleichem, Mendele Mocher Seforim, and others.

And look here . . ." Again, out come the keys; again, a padlocked cabinet opens before us; again, we eagerly peer inside. We see several dozen volumes, particularly worn and tattered. "These books are called incunabula," Lunski says. "They were all printed during the first twenty-five years of Jewish printing—between 1475 and 1500." Slowly and gingerly, he takes one out and lays it onto a nearby desk. "This, for example, is an edition of the books of Isaiah and Jeremiah, published in Lisbon, Portugal, in 1491." Lunski pauses. "The entire community of Portugal was expelled from the country six years later."

During the Middle Ages, many Jewish texts splintered into variance. Jews were moving to places where there had never been Jews before, and to get there, the texts had to travel great distances, usually carried by hand or on the back of a camel, horse, or donkey. The journeys took a long time—sometimes many months—and the words had a way of morphing over the course of long trips. A rabbi could issue a clear-cut ruling in Cairo, but by the time it reached its destination in Casablanca, the paper on which he wrote it was likely to have gotten folded, copied, torn, dropped, or mistakenly "corrected" by an overenthusiastic scribe, thus changing it into a text that was fundamentally different from the original. As a result the distances made it difficult for the rabbis and academies to exert the influence they wanted. To keep everyone in line, they needed to get everyone on the same page. Literally.

One area of Jewish practice that particularly needed standardization was prayer. As early as the second century CE, the Rabbis of the Talmud had begun scripting Jewish worship, but as prayer customs developed, the wording of the liturgy often varied from place to place. So too did the order of the prayers. And so did the very selection of prayers that Jews recited during their daily services. A traveling Jew visiting a synagogue therefore had a very real chance of becoming lost in a strange ritual that was supposed to be identical to his own.

The first Jewish *book* ever written didn't come out until sometime around 850 CE—a prayer book written by a sage named Rav Amram, from the Babylonian city of Surah (near modern-day Najaf). Noting the prayer pandemonium that had erupted in the Jewish world, Rav Amram set out to standardize Jewish worship once and for all. In response to a question from Barcelona about Jewish prayer, he compiled *Seder Rav Amram* as a comprehensive collection of Jewish prayers for the Sabbath, weekdays, and holidays; it also included laws and customs about how, where, and when the prayers were to be recited. Never before had anyone assembled such an omnibus, and *Seder Rav Amram* was soon copied and circulated widely throughout the Jewish world.

Others before Amram had written page-length documents or small pamphlets, but as the first Jewish book per se, *Seder Rav Amram* was of far more lasting significance.[12]

Or at least it was the first to be compiled. Amram, after all, *collected* the prayers; for the most part, the words in his book were not his own, but those of others that he deemed fit for inclusion in his standardizing text. The first person ever to *author* a Jewish book was a rabbi named Saadia Gaon, who lived a century later. Born in Egypt, schooled in Israel, and employed for most of his adult life in Babylonia, Saadia wrote dozens of books during his rabbi-philosopher career, addressing topics as wide-ranging as linguistics, hermeneutics, prayer, the Jewish calendar, and much more. It's not clear which of his books came first, but what is clear is that Saadia was first to pen books under his own name.[13]

His method—indeed his very view of what a book is—would have made later writers and publishers cringe. In a foreword to one of his books, we learn that Saadia didn't want a copyright for his work, but instead gave his readers free rein to correct his errors.

> I . . . adjure by God, Creator of the Universe, any scholar who, upon studying this book, sees in it a mistake, that he correct it. Or should he note an abstruse phrase, that he substitute for it a more felicitous one. Let him not feel constrained therefrom by the fact that the book is not his work, or that I had anticipated him in explaining what had not been clear to him. For the wise have a tender solicitude for wisdom . . . [whereas fools] are devoted to their folly and are loathe to forsake it.[14]

Even as early as the ninth or tenth century, Saadia Gaon had learned to crowd-source his work.

The works of Saadia and others morphed into new forms with each new copy. The constant change was a threat to the sacred texts. With such frequent editing, earlier versions of the text could easily disappear forever. "Medieval writing does not produce variance," one modern scholar noted. "It is variance."[15] Only the written Torah, the Five Books of Moses, remained sacrosanct. The Torah, after all, came from Sinai; its every letter was a sacred revelation from God. It may have been all right to change words that *people* wrote, but God's word was best left as is.

Rabbis soon realized that the only way to preserve their other texts was to get people to see those texts in different categories than before. As human texts, the writings of the Rabbis were subject to wanton editing, but if the sages could show that *God* had written the Talmud and other Rabbinic texts, then maybe fewer contemporary readers and scribes would mess around with their content. The Rabbis realized, in other words, that they needed to persuade Jewish readers to view Rabbinic writings just like they viewed the Torah itself.

And this is exactly what they did. In the eleventh century Rabbi

Hananel ben Hushiel wrote, "In *Talmud* is found the meaning of Torah and of Mishnah and of the commandments that are in the tradition, law given to Moses at Sinai" (emphasis added).[16] In praising the work of a previous scholar, twelfth-century scholar Rabbi Abraham ibn Daud wrote, "He acquired many books of sacred writings [i.e., Torah]—and of Mishnah and Torah, which are also sacred writings."[17] By the Middle Ages, Rabbinic writings had risen to the level of Torah itself.

With this newfound prestige, the content of Rabbinic literature could finally become permanent, just like that of the Torah. In the twelfth century a group of French and German scholars known as Tosafists standardized the pagination of the Talmud and began reproducing all of its tractates together rather than individually. The Talmud, once an amorphous, orally transmitted, shifting agglomeration of Rabbinic wisdom, had become a book.[18]

The Torah and the early Rabbis, as we have seen, established many laws regarding the creation and handling of Torah scrolls—and with a scroll or two in each synagogue's ark, those laws provided important guidance. But now, with Jewish bookshelves filling up as well, Jews began applying many of the laws concerning Torah scrolls to bound volumes. Those books were, after all, Torah. They were sacred, from God, and in some fundamental way a heritage that the Jewish people had received at Mount Sinai.

Perhaps the most noteworthy codifier of this principle was Rabbi Yehudah He-chasid (Judah the Pious), leader of a thirteenth-century movement of die-hard Jewish pietists called Chasidei Ashkenaz (the Righteous of Germany). In his book *Sefer Hasidim*, Yehudah He-chasid devoted an entire section to the proper care and handling of Jewish sacred books: It is forbidden to touch a book after wiping one's nose. One is not to kiss a book after kissing a dirty child. A teacher may not hit a student with a book, nor may the student use a book to shield himself from those blows unless he has good reason to believe that they are life-threatening. Using a book to hide your face from smoke or sunshine is off-limits as well.[19]

As the Middle Ages progressed, Jews continued to write books of all kinds—Jewish law, biblical commentary, interpretations of the Talmud, collections of Jewish lore, mystical works, and much more. They were all handwritten manuscripts, of course, painstakingly copied by students and scribes to become part of a literary legacy for future generations. As more books appeared, Jewish communities began collecting them for their citizens to read; wealthy individuals amassed large numbers for their private libraries; rabbis opened academies and found funding to provide books for their students to study. Bookshelves could be found in adult-education facilities, schools, private homes, and independent libraries. And the shelves filled quickly.

## The Printed Word

Lunski is on a roll. He is speaking even faster now, one word sibilating into another as he hurriedly points out various parts of the library's collection. "Not all of our books are rare or of particularly great monetary value," he reminds us. "Altogether, I think we have about forty thousand volumes in our collection. As you can see, a lot of the material is fiction—Hebrew, Yiddish, Polish, some Russian too." We round a corner, and Lunski points to a brightly decorated room with low tables. "We also have children's literature here, and as you can see, our kids love to read.

"You may have noticed," he continues, "that there is no card catalogue in our library. In fact, there has never been a complete catalogue of any kind listing the books you see here. We're working on it, and we have partial catalogues from when we were smaller, but with forty thousand volumes on these shelves, it's a big job. If you're looking for a particular book, I'm afraid that for now you'll have to come to me.

"Some of the books I showed you earlier are handwritten manuscripts," he reminds us, "but the vast majority are printed. Jews, as you know, got into the printing business very early—not long after

Guttenberg—and since then, the Jewish presses have never stopped rolling. Many of our books were published here in the Vilna area, but others come from very far away. We have books from Amsterdam, Venice, Constantinople, Warsaw . . . I could spend all day listing these places. It's an amazing and powerful tool, printing is, and its effect on the history of our people has been quite profound."

By the time Johannes Gutenberg printed his famous Bible in the mid-1450s, at least one Jew, David de Caderousse of Avignon, was known to have been involved in the printing industry for about a decade. By 1465 two German Jews, Conrad Sweynheyn and Arnold Pannartz, had migrated to Italy and begun printing Latin books in Subiaco, about thirty miles from Rome. They took on apprentices, and by 1470 there was an active cadre of Jewish printers producing books in and around Rome.[20] The Jewish presses had begun to roll.

In 1475 a publisher in Calabria, Italy, printed an edition of Torah commentary written by the renowned eleventh-century sage Rabbi Shlomo Yitzchaki (Rashi); it is believed to have been the first Hebrew book ever printed.[21] Almost immediately the technology caught on. By the end of the fifteenth century twenty-two Jewish print shops had come into operation—twelve in Italy, nine in Spain and Portugal, and one in Constantinople. Together, during the first three decades of Jewish publishing, they produced fully one hundred to two hundred separate editions of Jewish books, many in print runs of two hundred copies or fewer.[22]

If writing itself had standardized Jewish texts since antiquity, printing all but sealed the deal. Yes, printers had to decide between conflicting earlier editions of the texts they printed, and yes, the decisions they made were often controversial. But now, with one copy rolling off the press exactly like all the others, such disagreements became the exception rather than the rule. Now every Talmud was pretty much like every other Talmud. Now every *Alfasi* was identical to every other *Alfasi*. Now, finally, there were standard versions of Jewish texts accepted by readers all over the world.

Printing also made the very act of studying sacred Jewish texts far more efficient. Remember, Jews rarely study any text in isolation. Foundational texts such as the Bible and the Talmud are almost always read through the lenses of later students and sages. Before printing, this meant that a student of Talmud needed to lay open a lot of books in order to study the text—the Talmud or the Torah itself, of course, along with a veritable library of later commentaries. Before, printing, in other words, studying Talmud and Torah necessitated very large tables.

In the age of printing, however, passages from the Torah or the Talmud could appear not only in the same *book* as their associated commentaries, but even on the same *page.* It utterly transformed the study of these texts and is evident in the very first printed edition of the Talmud, which appeared in Soncino, Italy, near Milan, in 1483. Here, Talmud itself appears in the center and around it the various commentaries, extending outward like rectangular ripples in a pond. Rashi appears toward the book's spine to keep him safe from wear and tear, across from him is a group of commentaries called the Tosafot, and further out are later commentaries, cross-references to other related texts, biblical citations, and so on.

This new page layout allowed students to study a page of the Talmud and consult its commentaries all in one book. Suddenly the page had become a conversation. Rabbis in the Mishnah debated, their successors held forth in the Gemara, Rashi chimed in, and so did the Tosafot. It was a discussion—a drama—and on every page, it unfolded over the course of centuries.

And now students of Talmud could get by with far smaller tables.

With each step on our tour through his library, Lunski grows more excited. "Yes," he says, "printing did unify the Jewish people. In standardizing our sacred texts, it set a single framework for religious practice, dialogue, and debate; in bringing different texts together

## מאימתי

**מאימתי** קורין את שמע בערבין. משעה שהכהנים
נכנסים לאכול בתרומתן עד סוף האשמורה
הראשונה דברי ר' אליעזר. וחכמים אומרים עד חצות. רבן גמליאל אומר עד שיעלה
עמוד השחר. מעשה ובאו בניו מבית
המשתה אמרו לו לא קרינו את שמע אמר
להם אם לא עלה עמוד השחר חייבין אתם
לקרות ולא זו בלבד אמרו אלא כל מה
שאמרו חכמים עד חצות מצותן עד שיעלה
עמוד השחר...

7. A page from the Babylonian Talmud.

on the same page, it allowed Jews to study centuries' worth of commentaries all in a single glance. But printing also did something far more profound—it brought together Jews of different cultures and lands."

Lunski paused for an instant, looked to a shelf on his right, reached up high, and removed one volume from a four-volume set. "Here . . . here's the best example of all," he said. It was as if he had been magically transported to just the right spot at just the right time.

"This is the Shulchan Arukh," he said, beckoning us to gather in close. It's a law code—an encyclopedia of Jewish laws. As you know, it's often difficult to apply biblical principles to modern life, and you remember, of course, that the Talmud is almost impossible to understand in many places—the ancient Rabbis tended to be far more interested in discussion for the sake of discussion than for the sake of everyday practice. In terms of everyday practice, these texts aren't very practical at all.

"The Shulchan Arukh, however, is different. What prayers are you supposed to say when you get up in the morning? What kinds of meat are kosher? Does a pregnant woman have to fast on the Day of Atonement if she has a fever? These are the types of questions that the Shulchan Arukh addresses.

"The book was written in the 1500s by a rabbi named Joseph Karo . . . and Karo, we should note, was a Sephardic Jew—he and his parents had fled from Spain during the expulsion of 1492, and Karo eventually made his way to the Land of Israel. Because he was Sephardic, his Shulchan Arukh reflects Sephardic practices and customs. That made it fine for Sephardic Jews—Jews who lived in Greece, Turkey, and other Mediterranean lands—but not so useful for the Ashkenazic Jews in places like Poland, Austria, or Germany.

"But then another rabbi came along—an Ashkenazic one this time—and 'fixed the text.' This rabbi's name was Moshe Isserles, and what he did was to go through Karo's Shulchan Arukh and insert various additions that allowed it to be useful for Ashkenazic Jews as well as Sephardic ones. Here, look at a page of the book—you can see what's going on even if you don't know Hebrew."

Lunski motioned us in even closer. "The larger block letters are from Karo's original Shulchan Arukh; the smaller letters in the other typeface are Isserles's additions."

Lunski paused, staring at the book. His excitement seemed to grow even in his silence. "This is such a *Jewish* book!" he cried. "It deals with countless issues of religious law, and it does so in ways that reflect the views of Jewish communities living thousands of miles away from one another and in totally different cultural settings.

"And you know what?" he said more quietly while pointing at the book. "Without printing, this wouldn't have happened. Without printing, the text would have mutated into a thousand different forms, with Sephardic Jews practicing one way, Ashkenazic Jews practicing another, and the two cultures drifting ever further apart. It is printing that brought us all together."[23]

Jewish presses rolled slowly at first, but over time, they sped up. Whereas there were 100–200 printed editions of Hebrew books by 1500, a century later the number had grown to about 2,600. There were 3,600 such volumes at the end of the seventeenth century and 9,000 at the end of the eighteenth century. The list of the original twenty-two (mostly Italian) Jewish printers grew dramatically as well, particularly during the beginning of the sixteenth century. More presses opened in Italy; others began operating in Constantinople, Salonika, and Fez; and there were also Jewish printers in northern Europe—Prague, Krakow, and Lublin, and elsewhere.[24]

For a variety of reasons, printing caught on slowly under Islam. Although the Ottoman Empire's first printer of books in Arabic didn't open until 1728, the very first book of any kind published under Ottoman rule rolled off the presses in Constantinople in the late fifteenth or early sixteenth century. It was, perhaps not surprisingly, a Jewish legal treatise published by recent Jewish exiles from Spain and Portugal.[25]

One reason that the new technology eventually caught on was that hand-copied manuscripts had been enormously expensive, whereas printed books were comparatively cheap. Thus Jewish literature that had previously been the rarefied dominion of scholars now was available at low cost to Jews everywhere. Now, even relatively poor Jews had access to the Talmud, not to mention *Alfasi*, the Shulchan Arukh, and other volumes in the growing corpus of printed Jewish books.

As more Jewish books found their way into print, more manpower was needed to run the presses. The Jewish publishing industry—and by the sixteenth to eighteenth centuries it really *was* an industry—soon developed a veritable assembly line of workers. There were wood millers and papermakers, type casters and typesetters, pressmen and proofreaders, illustrators and illuminators, financiers, distributors, salesmen, and librarians, all of whom played crucial roles in the production and dissemination of the growing library of printed Jewish literature.

But the very idea of printing still gnawed at rabbis. Many welcomed the widespread dissemination of Jewish texts, but others felt threatened. This was sacred literature after all, and it was nothing to be toyed with. Like fire, knives, and the tablets from Sinai, you didn't want this material accessible to just *anyone*. In the wrong hands it could be deadly. Did Jews really want such powerful material to be available to every Tevye, Dovid, and Hayim who could scrape together a few rubles to buy a book?

Printing spread anyway. In the seventeenth and eighteenth centuries, thousands of new Jewish titles hit the market. Small pamphlets and monographs appeared, and these were even more affordable and easier to read than the hardcovers. Jews, it seemed, couldn't get enough books. Some Jews owned many books of their own; others read extensively from the collections of local Jewish libraries, schools, and synagogues.

As our tour continues, we round a corner, and Lunski points down a dark canyon of books. "Most of this aisle is our Kabbalah section—our books of Jewish mystical thought." Some members of our group wander down the aisle, looking at the enticing names of the books on the shelves before us—*Book of the Brightness*, *Gates of Light*, *The Nut Garden*.

"You'll note that we didn't see any kabbalistic texts when we looked at the manuscripts and the early printed books. That's because at first the Jewish mystics were leery of disseminating their books too widely. These weren't very humble men. They felt that the books that they wrote would allow readers to enter into God's palace—to behold God's very presence in the universe. In fact, one of the texts they focused on described what happened to four ancient sages who 'entered paradise.' To the kabbalists, 'entering paradise' was a euphemism for studying kabbalistic texts. Of the four sages, only one of them, Rabbi Akiva, returned unscathed. None of the others made it—one died, one went mad, and the other became an apostate.

"In other words, the kabbalists were frightened of their own books. Reading them, they felt, could expose someone to truth—overwhelming and destructive truth. Such was the power, they believed, of their mystical writings. Again, they were not very humble men.

"Eventually, however," says Lunski, "the kabbalists came around. In the 1600s, you see, life for Jews in Europe and elsewhere became especially difficult. There were horrible pogroms and attacks of other kinds—antisemitism was growing out of control. Jews everywhere sought salvation from these traumas, and Kabbalah—what with its promises of salvation and transcendence—seemed to be just what they were looking for. The mystical rabbis couldn't keep their books off the printing press; by the 1700s Kabbalah was wildly popular, and sure enough, so was its literature. Suddenly, kabbalistic works by the hundreds deluged the market. That's what you see on the shelves in front of you now."

The Kabbalah section of the Strashun Library seems particularly busy. In front of us an old bearded man in a black frock coat scans the shelves in search of a particular volume for his studies. In the next aisle a younger man in his early twenties peruses the collection, eagerly opening a book here and there as if on a quest for hidden secrets buried deep within the collection. Unlike those in other parts of the library, the Kabbalah aisles seem well traveled and widely used. These books get checked out often. On these books there is very little dust.

"As you can see," Lunski says, "our Kabbalah collection is quite extensive. People come from near and far to use it. It keeps me very busy."

"And then we have . . . ." Lunski pauses. "Some . . . other books related to Kabbalah." His voice has fallen almost to a whisper again, and he beckons us to follow him and brings us to a small alcove hidden behind a heavy door. "This," he says, opening the alcove to our view, "is our collection of Sabbatean literature."

"Your what collection?" whisper some of our group.

"Our Sabbatean collection. These are the books written by the followers of Shabbetai Tzvi." Lunski let out a puff of air (was that a spit)?

"Shabbetai . . . who?"

"Shabbetai Tzvi, a crazy man in the seventeenth century who persuaded about 70 percent of the world's Jews that he was the Messiah. In the end, this great 'messiah' converted to Islam, but some people continued to believe that he was their savior even after his apostasy. Once everything settled down, believers and nonbelievers alike read books of all kinds as they tried to make sense of what had just happened. Shabbetai Tzvi was a horribly destructive man, but I must admit that he did do a lot for Jewish books."

Lunski closes the door quickly and seems to breathe a sigh of relief. "It was shortly after these painful events," he says, "that a man came along who inspired millions of Jews throughout eastern

Europe to let their souls soar toward heaven. And to help them along"—Lunski smiles—"they read a lot of books."[26]

Into the disarray following Shabbetai's apostasy came Hasidic Judaism, a populist, often ecstatic movement that arose in eastern Europe during the early eighteenth century. Its founder was Israel ben Eliezer, popularly known as the Baal Shem Tov (Master of the Good Name). Originally an itinerant teacher and wonder-worker, the Baal Shem Tov taught that every Jew could attain great spiritual heights regardless of class and educational achievement. Study was important, of course, but the Baal Shem Tov also taught that a song sung from the heart or a dance danced with true fervor could bring a Jew to great religious heights.

His ideas caught on quickly—not as quickly as Shabbetai's but quick enough to give birth to a new religious force in Jewish life. Hasidic Judaism took the zeal and excitement of Shabbetai's time and channeled it into a religious movement that affirmed rather than denied the fundamentals of Jewish law.[27]

Hasidic Judaism was also mystical, and it too emphasized the centrality of the teacher-student experience. But Hasidic teachers, unlike those in the past, had a tendency to achieve rock-star status, and when they taught, fans everywhere wanted to get their hands on the latest releases of their wisdom. Yes, Hasidism affirmed, the teacher-student relationship is essential to Jewish learning. But why limit those relationships to classroom-size groups? Now, with printing, Jews' ability to connect with great teachers no longer need be limited by distance. Now, with printing, teachers and students can connect anywhere.

So Hasidic Jews bought books—lots and lots of books. Their books contained stories of Hasidic masters, as well as prayers, supplications, and advice regarding daily practice. There were prayer books, commentaries, and rabbinic anthologies. On the other hand, the books contained few of the lessons that the Baal Shem Tov and his students taught about deep meditation and hidden spiritual practice. Hasidic leaders decided that this material was so powerful that it really *should* be saved for teachers to teach directly to their students. Printing most Hasidic teachings, in other words, was perfectly fine; printing the really sacred and powerful material, however, was not.

Nevertheless it was books, in large part, that allowed Hasidic Judaism to grow. Books allowed the movement's popular teachings to spread, and by the early nineteenth century, a majority of the Jews in many areas of eastern Europe would proudly declare themselves to be Hasidic Jews.

From the sixteenth through the nineteenth centuries, the Yiddish-speaking Jewish communities of eastern Europe saw enormous growth; by the end of the nineteenth century there were almost four million Jews in the soon-to-be Soviet Union alone. Many Jews in these communities were religious, but with the rise of modernity, many others rejected religion in favor of secular ideas and attitudes. Soon novels appeared in print, as well as political tracts and secular philosophy.

Even religious Jews were known to crack open a secular book now and then, albeit in secret. One of them was Rabbi Jacob Emden, a towering and stern rabbinic sage who lived in Germany from 1697 to 1776. Late in his life Emden recalled that as a younger scholar, he developed a hankering to learn not only Torah but also secular material. He wanted to know it all—medicine and geology, biology and political science, arts and engineering, even European languages. Many devout Jews frowned on such study, of course, so in his autobiography, Emden made sure to mention that he studied this material in a manner that was perfectly kosher. "I remembered," he wrote, "not to read [secular books] or look at them except in a place where it is forbidden to think about words of Torah." Many of Emden's readers understood exactly what he meant. Emden could have "thought about words of Torah" almost anywhere. The only place where he wasn't allowed to think of them was in his dedicated secular-reading shrine—the toilet.[28]

Perhaps the most significant change in the Jewish landscape during early modernity was the addition of a new audience of Jewish readers—women. Traditionally only boys and men studied beyond elementary school. Girls usually studied for a few years at most, and few of them knew the Hebrew or Aramaic they'd need to read classical Jewish texts. Many women, however, did read Yiddish or other Jewish vernaculars such as Ladino (Judeo-Spanish). For Jewish women in eastern Europe, the growing presence of the Yiddish book was a boon like no other. Women by the millions, for example, read *Tsena-Rene*, a Yiddish compendium of biblical commentaries that was accessible even to women with the most basic of Jewish educations. The first known printed edition appeared in Hanau in 1622, and it has been reprinted at least 210 times since.[29] As early as the sixteenth century, Sephardic women were praying from their own Ladino prayer books, which also included laws relating to women's religious practice.[30] The mid-nineteenth century saw the rise of another form of Jewish literature, the novel, and by the nineteenth century there were countless book-length works of Yiddish fiction—some of very high quality, some quite trashy. Women were among the primary audiences of this literature, but the novels had many male readers, as well.

It was also the time of Haskalah—the Jewish Enlightenment. As Jews of western Europe left the ghettos and embraced the local culture and perspectives, they couldn't help but be influenced by modern European thought. Many Jews studied in European universities, and by the late eighteenth century fields such as science, history, philology, and archaeology had made an indelible impact on Jewish life. Many Jews who studied these topics did so with a secular focus, but others had a more pointedly Jewish approach. Until this time Jewish history, for example, hardly existed as an independent field. Now there were Jewish historians devoting their careers to the field. Similarly the nineteenth century saw the rise of the critical and analytical study of Jewish texts. It was called *Wissenschaft des Judentums*, the scientific study of Judaism.

Soon these modern scientific perspectives moved eastward, affecting

Jews in Russia, Poland, the Baltic States, and elsewhere. Jews in the east discovered these modern modes of thought with trepidation at first. As before, many rabbinic authorities opposed the study of such "forbidden" literature, but soon it seemed that everyone was reading the secular literature of western Europe.

The new accessibility of such literature helped allow for the growth of Jewish political movements and ideologies during the nineteenth and early twentieth centuries—Zionism, Communism, Socialism, and others. Each had their own literature, and each opened libraries of their own. The books of each filled community libraries throughout European Jewish communities large and small.

In the nineteenth century, particularly in eastern Europe, the lion's share of each community's Jewish books were stored in the local *beis midrash* (study house). With the rise of secular literature, however, many of the most prominent and widely studied collections of literature became those in public libraries. Libraries opened in communities throughout the east, and many readers from all sectors of Jewish society went to the libraries to use their resources every day.

Wealthy Jews collected books; Jewish scholars studied them; Jewish women read novels; young revolutionaries read political literature; children studied schoolbooks; libraries flourished; pious Jews prayed from prayer books and studied countless works of religious literature. Every day more books were added to Jewish bookshelves. Every day the shelves strained just a bit more under the weight of the literature they held. Every day more books lined the walls of Jewish homes and institutions. Every day the words in the books brought new light and new thoughts and new insights to the Jews who read them. The Jewish world overflowed with the literary riches of the books it cherished.

"So there you have it," Lunski says as we reach the front door. He is still speaking quickly, but he smiles warmly. "I haven't shown you everything, but I hope you've gotten a sense of what treasures we have in the Strashun Library. Please know that you're always welcome here, and if I can help you find a book to read, I'd be delighted to do so."

Within two years of our imaginary visit to this very real place, Nazi soldiers had destroyed or stolen all of the books in the Strashun Library. The library building was mostly destroyed along with the rest of the Vilna Ghetto in September 1943. There are conflicting reports as to the fate of Khaykl Lunski. Some say that a Nazi soldier beat him to death in 1942; others report that he was murdered at the Treblinka extermination camp several months later.

# 2

# Antisemites and the Jewish Written Word

Where men burn books, they will also burn people in the end.
—*Heinrich Heine, from "Almansor" in* The Complete Poems

What is a book? At one level, the question is absurd—a book is simply a bound stack of printed pages. But in many ways, we have always considered books to be more than just paper, ink, and bindings. This was especially the case before printing, when most books were precious works of art, wrought into existence through countless hours of devoted scribal labor. In many families, books are heirlooms; their musty pages bearing the faint aroma of a grandfather's cigar, a flowery inscription from a long-deceased aunt, or faded smudges of ancestral thumbs. Even when they're not family treasures, old tomes can carry inscriptions and bookplates and marginalia, all of which tell the story of the book's journey through time. In many homes, personal libraries fill shelves lining the walls of basements, bedrooms, and dens. The contents of the collections testify to the intellectual and literary scope of their owners, and many display the volumes with great pride.

Books represent their authors too, and to own a book is to possess for yourself something of its author's essence. William Shakespeare, Alice Walker, Stephen King . . . they're all sitting within a few feet of me as I write these words. They are mine.

Books, of course, hold words, and each word bears meaning both evident and hidden. Rainbow, heart, lamb, doorway . . . they and millions of others are not only tangible objects but also expansive metaphors. And just as words have multiple layers of meaning, so too do the phrases and pages and chapters that they compose. *Romeo and Juliet* tells readers of both a particular romance and a universal tale of love and fate. *The Color Purple* is the story of a young woman and also a celebration of the human capacity for triumph. Stephen King tears open the thin veneer of our calm to reveal the monstrous terror lurking just beneath it.

In short, books can be limitless. Reading them, we can find ourselves swept away by their words; *re*reading them can reveal more of their treasures, and rereading the good ones yet again can enrich us even further. The fullness of their truths may always remain just beyond our grasp. This is their greatness, for it means that they will forever hold the promise of new discovery—of glittering gems hidden in their pages, awaiting our seeking eyes.

As we have seen, there has long been a special place for books in the Jewish heart. From the very dawn of Jewish existence, Jews have relied on books as essential sinews, binding Jews to God, to friends and neighbors, and to other Jews in faraway lands and times other than our own. Even after the advent of printing, Jews continued to cherish books as some of our most precious possessions.

Through the centuries there have been plenty of attacks on people's furniture, homes, and foodstuffs; we respond to many such assaults with scorn and to others with sheer horror. Attacks on books, however, while not necessarily more evil than those targeting other forms of property, carry with them a different and often more profound symbolic value. To take or destroy a book is to sever the bonds it creates—bonds with family, bonds with authors, and for some, even bonds with the Divine. To take or destroy a book is to bring the stories that it tells—either as written literature or as a physical object—to an abrupt and irreversible halt. To take or destroy a book is to extinguish the hope of discovery that its boundless riches can offer.

To attack a book, in other words, is to attack an embodiment of things that make us truly human. Those in a position to do so hold the power of unspeakable destruction.

The Nazis were not the first oppressors to attack Jewish books—far from it. Rather the annals of history are replete with stories of assaults not only on Jewish people, but also on Jewish literature. In fact Jewish books have long been a favorite target of antisemitic attacks, and not surprisingly attacks on Jewish books have tended to go hand in hand with attacks on Jewish people. Whether they were imprisoning Jews, confiscating Jewish property, coercing Jews to convert to Christianity, or even burning Jews at the stake, oppressors of Jewish bodies and souls often trained their sights on Jewish literature as well. Sadly what Heinrich Heine wrote in 1882 was by then an age-old truth: "Where men burn books, they will also burn people in the end."

### Talmud Pyres in Medieval Europe

Later generations would view the confiscation and destruction of Jewish books with disgust, but the twelfth-century chronicler Thomas of Cantimpré saw such attacks as acts of great piety. In fact if he had any doubts about the practice, they were quickly dispelled by what he saw in the French city of Vincennes one day in 1241.

Two years earlier, in 1239, Pope Gregory IX ordered the rulers of Christendom to confiscate all copies of the Talmud on the first Saturday of Lent. Local officials were to subject the books to thorough investigations in search of anti-Christian content, and if any such blasphemies were found, the books were to be burned on a certain day in May or June of the same year. Some rulers disregarded the order, but in France— long a center of Jewish learning and scholarship—twenty-five-year-old King Louis IX obeyed it with gusto. He decreed that Jews throughout the land were to bring every copy of Talmud they owned to Paris by the specified date; anyone caught disobeying the order would be executed. To Cantimpré, the edict was perfectly justified. After all, he later wrote, "in [the Talmud], in many places, were written unheard of heresies and blasphemies against Christ and his mother."[1]

The Jews of France were overwrought. The Talmud sat at the center of Jewish life, religion, and culture. Its laws, its stories, and its wisdom served as the beating heart of Jewish religion and culture. How could they ever turn these books over to the authorities? How could they live without Talmud?

In the end, they had no choice—they had to surrender the books. From towns and cities throughout the land, Jews brought their Talmud volumes to Vincennes, a suburb of Paris. There a commission of high-ranking church officials took possession of the books and rooted through them, hoping to identify whatever anti-Christian heresies and whatever blasphemies they could find.

The job would have been easier for these officials if any of them knew Hebrew or Aramaic. They didn't, and the resulting delay bought the Jews some time. French Jewish leaders approached a high-ranking Christian official—probably Gauthier of Cornut, archbishop of Sens—and weeping, they implored him to intercede with church authorities to save the volumes from destruction. We don't know exactly how the Jewish leaders made their case; maybe they appealed to the authorities' moral sense, or maybe they made a financial argument. Whatever their tactic was, it worked. The archbishop went to the king and prevailed on him to spare the Jewish books. Relieved beyond words, the Jews reclaimed their Talmuds, went home, and declared that the anniversary of that date would forever be a solemn day of fasting, commemoration, and gratitude for their community.

Alas, their books would not remain safe for long. Exactly one year later, to the very day, Archbishop Gauthier traveled to Vincennes to visit the king. As soon as he walked into the royal chamber, Gauthier groaned in pain, keeled over, and died.

Gauthier's death, King Louis immediately concluded, was an act of God—divine retribution for the archbishop's role in rescuing Jewish books. Terrified that he himself would be the next victim of God's wrath, Louis ordered that the Talmuds of France be rounded up once again. Again the commission was convened, and again the Jews were distraught. But this time there was no Gauthier to intercede on their behalf. The commission staged a public debate as to the acceptability of the Talmud, but everyone knew ahead of time exactly what the results would be.

In the spring of 1242 the Talmuds of France were heaped together in Vincennes. Twenty-four cartloads of them. More than twenty thousand volumes.[2] Each one was the handwritten creation of a scribe who spent many hours—and often many months—carefully copying its words onto clean sheets of paper. A flame was lit, the pages burned, and the words ascended back toward heaven.[3]

The coming decades would see other book burnings in France, with prayer books and other sacred volumes joining the Talmud in the pyres. For a country that was once a vibrant center of Jewish learning and home to sages as great as Rashi and the Tosafists, it was an especially sad state of affairs. Some Jews succeeded in hiding their books, and many studied in secret. But for the most part, the conflagrations of the thirteenth century brought to a devastating and fiery close the study of Rabbinic literature in France.[4]

### The Long-Burning Bonfires of Banned Jewish Books

The first recorded incident of Jewish book destruction dates back to the second century BCE, during the Maccabean revolt. Seleucid emperor Antiochus IV ordered pagan altars erected in Jerusalem and other Judean cities. In the process, the first book of Maccabees tells us, "The books of the law which they found they tore to pieces and burned with fire. Where the book of the covenant was found in the possession of any one, or if anyone adhered to the law, the decree of the king condemned him to death."[5] The destruction of the Jewish book was part of a massive, violent campaign of physical and religious conquest. Evidently, even as early as the second century BCE, those bent on destroying the Jewish people used book destruction as one of their primary tools.

For the next 650 years or so, Jewish books escaped such attacks, mainly because at the time there were so few Jewish books in existence. Most of those that did exist were copies of the Jewish Bible—the "Old Testament," to Christians. Since the Jewish Bible is also part of Christian Scripture, it was spared the fiery fate of other Jewish books that came later. By late antiquity, however, Jews had begun studying the Talmud; the Mishnah had been around since 200 CE, and the Gemara, codified in 500 CE, was getting its "legs" in the Jewish textual landscape as well. The Talmud's longevity—not to mention its growing prominence in Jewish life—was great for Jews and Judaism, but by the middle of the sixth century, Christian authorities had begun to see it as a threat.

When the Byzantine emperor Justinian rose to power in 527, he found himself ruling a kingdom in decline. Byzantium, once the eastern half of the Roman Empire, had split away from the west almost two hundred years earlier, leaving it a mere shadow of its glorious past. The church was riven with conflict, a war raged with Persia, and in 540 the bubonic plague swept across the land, killing 40 percent of the population. In Justinian's view, one of the primary reasons for Byzantium's decline was its lack of religious unity. In order to restore its brilliance, he felt, he would need to bring the entire empire into the embrace of Christianity. Obviously Judaism—annoyingly persistent in its refusal to melt away into the religion that superseded it—didn't fit into his vision. Hoping to right this wrong, Justinian forbade many Jewish religious practices, denuded Jewish religious courts of their authority, and forbade Jews to read their books. They could still study their Bible, of course, preferably in Greek or Latin, but Rabbinic literature was a different story. Yes, the Talmud and other Jewish writings were *based* on the Old Testament, but they were distortions—they rejected the true meaning of Jewish Scripture as the forerunner of the New Testament.[6] In 553 Justinian issued his infamous "Novella 146," reading in part:

The Mishnah, or as they call it the second tradition, we prohibit entirely. For it is not part of the sacred books, nor is it handed down by divine inspiration through the prophets, but the handiwork of man, speaking only of earthly things, and having nothing of the divine in it. But let them read the holy words themselves, rejecting the commentaries, and not concealing what is said in the sacred writings, and disregarding the vain writings which do not form a part of them, which have been devised by them themselves for the destruction of the simple.[7]

Whether or to what extent Justinian's order was carried out is unclear. What is clear, however, is that his hostility to Jewish books established a precedent and that many Christian leaders in later centuries would honor that precedent, often with devastating results.

In 681 a church synod known as the Twelfth Council of Toledo also ordered the burning of the Talmud; in 712 the Visigoths in Spain declared that Jewish converts to Christianity were forbidden to read Jewish books of any kind. In 1199 Pope Innocent III, evidently wary of books in general, declared that Scripture is so profound a text that all interpretations of it should come only from the clergy—Christian clergy, of course. Henceforth Jews and their books were to be considered subversive. Later, in 1233, Innocent III's successors committed many Jewish books to flames, especially those of Maimonides, whose neo-Aristotelian philosophy many saw as dangerously pagan and potentially heretical.

In 1553 Pope Julius III also issued a decree ordering the burning of the Talmud. Jewish homes and synagogues were to be searched; the Talmud and other related literature were to be confiscated and destroyed. The age of printing had arrived by then, and during the century since Guttenberg, Italy had become the unrivaled center of Jewish publishing worldwide. With the pope's decree, however, the great history of Italian Jewish printing came to an all but complete halt, from which it would take more than a century and a half to recover. On Rosh Hashanah of

1553 thousands of Hebrew books were heaped into a huge pyre in Rome's Camp de' Fiori and set aflame. The city is said to have been inundated with shouts of glee and cries of anguish.[8]

In 1559, partly to quell the rising tide of Protestant sedition, Pope Paul IV issued the *Index Librorum Prohibitorum* (Index of Prohibited Books), a long list of banned titles, which included the Talmud as well as many other Jewish books. Ostensibly the *Index* was designed to protect Christian faith and morals, and it resulted in a new spate of book burnings in Cremona and elsewhere. In its wake Italian Jewish presses ceased production altogether. Although they were allowed to resume operations a few years later, the forced downtime forever removed Italy from its place at the epicenter of the world of Jewish printing

Subsequent popes issued their own variations of the 1559 *Index*, though the later lists were far less strict than the original. Nevertheless many Jewish works remained under official church ban for more than four hundred years. The final version of the *Index* was issued under Pope Pius XII in 1948 and contained many Jewish titles, including large sections of the Talmud, prominent rabbinic works, and the writings of Maimonides, Baruch Spinoza, and other Jewish authors. Soon after the release of that version of the *Index*, however, as the full impact of World War II came to worldwide attention, the *Index* and its fascist tone quickly made it an embarrassment for the church. In 1965 Pope Paul VI instituted a reorganization of the church, thankfully omitting the task of *Index* enforcement from its new organizational chart. The following June the Vatican announced that the *Index* had been officially abolished.

In 1985 the cardinal in charge of the church office that formerly enforced the *Index* wrote a letter to a colleague clarifying its 1966 repeal. Yes, he said, the *Index* was no longer in force, but even after its repeal, the books it forbade could be read "only after profound changes that neutralize the harm which such a publication could bring forth among the ordinary faithful." The *Index*, he said, "retains its moral force despite its dissolution."[9] The author of that letter was Cardinal John Ratzinger, later known as Pope Benedict XVI.

## From Incineration to Censorship

As we might expect, after the *Index* was instituted in 1559, attacks on Jewish books continued apace, now with official church sanction. In France, Italy, Germany, Poland, and elsewhere—during the early Middle Ages, the Crusades, and even into modern times—flames consumed the pages of Jewish books with tragic frequency. Not all Christian leaders shared in the obsession with the Jewish written word, but with almost cyclical regularity, many turned to the destruction of Jewish literature as a weapon in the imposition of antisemitic policies.

Often Christian leaders condemning Jewish books were able to draw active support from Jewish apostates—Jews who had converted to Christianity in hopes of avoiding the brutal antisemitism of medieval Europe. These converts were often of great use to Christian leaders who wanted to refute Judaism. Many knew Hebrew and other Jewish languages, were well read in Jewish texts, and were intimately acquainted with Jewish practice. And when one of these former Jews identified an anti-Christian Jewish text or a subversive Jewish ritual, the revelation was disinformation gold for antisemitic leaders, even when the "revelation" was totally fabricated.

By the thirteenth century France had emerged as the center of such attacks, and a standard pattern played itself out almost every time: an apostate would bring charges; the church would issue an order of confiscation; church officials would carry out the order; rabbis and Christian leaders would engage in a public debate—a disputation—as to the true nature of the condemned literature; the church would affirm its condemnation of the books; the books would be burned.[10]

Incineration was not the only tool that Christian leaders used to deal with Jewish books. Sometimes they only *threatened* to destroy the books when all they really wanted to do was to insert their own edits, usually deletions, into the text. The first to use this tactic was King James I of Aragon. In 1263 he presided over a four-day debate in Barcelona between a Jewish apostate turned Dominican priest named Pablo Christiani and Rabbi Moshe ben Nachman (also known as Nachmanides). In the end both sides claimed victory. As always the Christian perspective had the might of the church behind it, but this time it was a little more complicated. Nachmanides had earned the great respect of many Spanish leaders, evidently including King James himself. So when Pope Clement IV ordered an investigation into the Talmud and other Jewish writings, the king seems to have shown sympathy toward his Jewish subjects. Eventually Nachmanides had to flee, but King James did succeed in preventing the books from being burned. As an alternative tactic, he appointed another Dominican priest named Raymond Martini to peruse the books and simply cross out their offending passages. Raymond Martini thus became history's first official censor of Jewish books.[11]

In this way, censorship became yet another tool in the church's anti-Jewish-literature arsenal. Until the mid-eighteenth century, each generation of church leaders appointed official censors to scan and expurgate Jewish books. Typically the censor would certify his work by affixing his signature to the final page, often adding the name of his boss or of the agency under whose authority he operated. During some periods Jewish texts underwent intense scrutiny, such as in 1578 during the papacy of Gregory XIII, when a version of the Talmud appearing in Basel was so heavily redacted that it was all but unreadable. During other periods, when Jewish-Christian tensions eased a bit or when officials realized the utter futility of their efforts to permanently "edit" Jewish books, the censors were more lenient.

Ironically, even as church censors were crossing out sections of Jewish books, their work also played an invaluable role in preserving Jewish texts as well. Censorship, after all, provided a far less destructive alternative to burning Jewish books, and without the option to edit them, the church would undoubtedly have destroyed many of the volumes it

8. A censored prayer book from the fourteenth to fifteenth century.
Courtesy Syndics of the Cambridge University Library, CUL Add. 662.

deemed heretical. The censor's pen only marred the books. Most books not "fortunate" enough to be sent over to the censor were sent to the fireplace.

As a result Jews often found themselves pushing to have their books censored. Obviously no Jews *wanted* to see the content of their books deleted, but censorship was a far better option than burning, and many Jewish leaders pleaded with non-Jewish authorities to save their books from the fire and only have them censored instead. These efforts rarely achieved long-term success, but sometimes Jews were able to secure a "stay of execution" for the books, allowing them to be hidden away or at least to be studied for a little while longer than might have otherwise been possible. Sometimes intense negotiations did the trick. Sometimes Jews succeeded in getting a Christian clergyman or scholar to find favorable material in the books and to intercede on behalf of "editing" rather than complete destruction.

Censorship was thus the product of a very different dynamic than book burnings. The burnings were aimed at the utter destruction of Jewish literature, and they were carried out in a way that completely dismissed Jewish claims and the very validity of Judaism itself. Censorship, however, though humiliating, damaging, and degrading to Jews and their literature, reflected an underlying connection binding Christians together with Jews and Jewish books. For Jewish negotiations to have any chance of success, ruling Christians needed to have at least a little bit of respect for their Jewish interlocutors or at least for Jewish religion. For the church and its officials to bother with the time-intensive and laborious task of censoring Jewish literature, they had to acknowledge at least the possibility that there was something in the Jewish books that made them worth the hassle.

The church was not the only institution to censor Jewish books. Beginning in the late 1700s, eastern European governments did so as well. In 1783 Russia's Catherine II (Catherine the Great) instituted a set of policies that was relatively permissive with respect to books in general. Seven years later, however, in 1790, she didn't complain when the governor-general of Belarus, Pétr Bogdanovich Passek, ordered a shipment of Hebrew books from Poland detained in a local customhouse. He argued that the current rules didn't specify any particular protections for Jewish books and that Russian policy should therefore revert to older, stricter laws prohibiting the import of such literature. Catherine authorized Passek's decision and officially forbade the importation of Jewish books. She suggested that Jews get their literature from domestic publishers instead.

Russian Jews resorted to smuggling their literature across the borders and to finagling the purchase of what few books they could from the woefully inadequate number of local Jewish printers. Finally in 1797 under Catherine's successor, Emperor Paul I, the policy eased, permitting Jews to import their literature once again. The only catch was that the government insisted on inspecting all Jewish books—both imported and domestic—to ensure that they contained no subversive or objectionable content. Many of the volumes were in Hebrew and other Jewish languages, of course, so to expedite the process, the government hired two educated Jews to open a Jewish literature censor shop in Riga, Latvia.

Still, new Jewish titles were coming out all the time, and the size of the print runs were growing. To increase the capacity of their operations, the Russian government opened other censorship facilities in places such as Vilna, Warsaw, Saint Petersburg, and other major cities. At first they focused mainly on expurgating religious texts, singling out Hasidic literature for especially close scrutiny. But as more Jews wrote political tracts, academic texts, and secular fiction, the focus of Russian authorities broadened. Now any book written by a Jewish author or touching on Jewish subjects was considered fair game for the Russian censors.[12]

One example of their work is strikingly evident in *The Jewish Encyclopedia*, whose ten heavy leather-bound volumes were released individually between 1901 and 1906. Volume 1, *Aach–Apocalyptic Lit*, came out in 1901, and pages 347–48 of the densely printed tome feature a three-column article titled "Alexander III, Alexandrovich, Emperor of Russia." The article begins innocuously, with the first half-paragraph detailing the dates of Alexander's birth and death (March 10, 1845–November 1, 1894), the date of his ascension to the throne (March 14, 1881), and the circumstances under which he became emperor (the assassination of his father, Alexander II). Then, however, the second half of that paragraph describes the despotic tyranny that Alexander demonstrated during his reign. "[He] ruled with rigorous absolutism. . . . He permitted, and even encouraged, the oppression of the various foreign residents in Russia, and was particularly harsh in his persecution of the Jews. . . . [His] hostility against the Jews was fostered in order to divert the attention of the discontented elements."

At the time, Alexander's son, Nicholas II, sat on the Russian throne. Evidently when a copy of *The Jewish Encyclopedia*, volume 1, *Aach-Apocalyptic Lit* first reached the Russian censors shortly after it was published, they surmised that their boss wouldn't respond very kindly to its negative "spin" on his father's life. Surely the official who first read it took comfort in the fact that not very many copies of the expensive English-language encyclopedia were likely to make their way to Russia, so offensive passages would be easy to remove. All it took were a willing censor, a small brush, and good slathering of black ink. Within moments, the criticisms of Alexander III in Russia's copy of volume 1 of *The Jewish Encyclopedia* disappeared under a patch of black ink, and the book could safely be sent along to the library or individual who had purchased it.

Volumes 2 and 3 of *The Jewish Encyclopedia*, *Apocyrpha–Benash* and *Bencemero–Chananuth*, were released the following year. The latter contained a ten-page article by William Popper titled "Censorship of Hebrew Books." As he was writing the article, Popper evidently saw the censored Russian copy of volume 1. As a result the censorship article in volume 3 of *The Jewish Encyclopedia* features an image of the "Alexander III" article from volume 1 of the very same work, now with a large black splotch covering the bottom of the first paragraph.

In the 1930s, there was a palpable shift in the Soviet Union's attack on Jewish and Jewish-related books. Early that decade the Central Committee of the Communist Party expelled and murdered all of its members who belonged to "non-Russian nationalities"—mostly Jews. Thus free of its Jews, the Central Committee instituted an unofficial but strictly enforced policy with regard to antisemitism in the Soviet Union: it didn't exist. In printed literature and other public media, all references to pogroms, anti-Jewish labor practices, and other forms of Jewish oppression were forbidden. Publishers needed government approval before they could release anything, and whenever the censors noticed language even tacitly acknowledging antisemitism, the material had to be edited or its release canceled. Anything deemed "Zionist Propaganda" was subject to the same treatment.

Jewish short stories were removed from anthologies; a math book was censored because it contained an image of two overlapping triangles deemed to be a Star of David; even Vladimir Lenin's 1919 "Speech on the Persecution of Jews" was suppressed because it acknowledged the existence of Russian antisemitism under czarist rule.[13]

By the time the Nazis rose to power, then, a long history of antisemitic assaults on Jewish books had already been playing itself out for centuries. It was a complicated history, manifesting itself in different eras as censorial insult, ruinous theft, or wanton destruction. Sometimes it left Judaism and Jewish culture relatively unscathed; at other times it was devastating.

Christian Europe's practice of burning and censoring Jewish books was aimed at controlling Jews, altering Judaism, and inoculating Christianity against the dangers of Jewish words. The Nazi approach to Jewish books, as we shall see, exhibited none of these characteristics. For starters, and contrary to modern historical memory, the Nazis didn't make a practice of burning Jewish books for very long. After 1933, Nazi policy exhibited a great reluctance to destroy Jewish books at all, and Nazis certainly didn't want to bother censoring them. The sheer volume of the material that the Nazis collected did result in many of the less valuable books going and other youths took an active part in the revolutionary movement of the seventies. Alexander knew and always appreciated the loyalty of the great majority of his Jewish subjects, and on many occasions rewarded them for their services to the country. When the assassination of Alexander by nihilist conspirators became known, the Jews of Russia deeply mourned the loss of the benevolent czar and liberator.

BIBLIOGRAPHY: Demidov San-Donato, *Yevreiski Vopros v Rossii*, St. Petersburg, 1883; Julius Eckard, *Von Nicolaus I. zu Alexander III.* 2d ed., Leipsic, 1881; Orshanski, *Russkoe Zakonodatelstvo o Yevreyakh*, pp. 309-335, St. Petersburg, 1877; *Sistematicheski Ukazatel Literatury o Yevreyakh na Russkom Yazykye s 1708 do 1889*, St. Petersburg, 1893.

H. R.

**ALEXANDER III., ALEXANDROVICH, Emperor of Russia:** Born at St. Petersburg, March 10, 1845; died at Livadia, Nov. 1, 1894. He ascended the throne March 14, 1881, the day after the assassination of his father, Alexander II. The terrible fate of the latter produced an awful impression upon Alexander, but instead of continuing the reforms of the "Czar-Emancipator," as was expected, he at once gave proof of his reactionary tendencies by discharging the liberal minister Loris Melikov, and by his first manifesto, wherein he made it evident that he was determined to maintain his autocratic power against all attacks. In internal politics he followed the advice of his former teacher Pobiedonostzev, and ruled with rigorous absolutism, favoring the principles of the Panslavists. He permitted, and even encouraged, the oppression of the various foreign residents in Russia, and was particularly harsh in his persecution of the Jews. The participation of some Jewish youths in the revolutionary movement of the NIHILISTS was made use of to lead the Russian people to believe that the Jews were connected with the conspiracy which had resulted in the murder of Alexander II. Hostility against the Jews was fostered in order to divert the attention of the discontented elements, and if possible to suppress the revolutionary movement.

Soon after Alexander III. had ascended the throne, anti-Jewish riots (POGROMY) broke out in Elizabethgrad (April 27, 28), Kiev (May 8-11), Shpola (May 9), Ananiev (May 9), Wasilkov (May 10), Konotop (May 10), and, during the following six months, in one hundred and sixty other places of southern Russia. In these riots thousands of Jewish homes were destroyed, many families reduced to extremes of poverty; women outraged, and large numbers of men, women, and children killed or injured. It was clear that the riots were premeditated ("Voskhod," May 24, 1881, p. 75). To give but one example—a week before the *pogrom* of Kiev broke out, Von Hubbenet, chief of police of Kiev, warned some of his Jewish friends of the coming riots. Appeals to the authorities for protection were of no avail. All the police did was to prevent the Jews from defending their homes, families, and property. "The local authorities," says Mysh in "Voskhod," 1883, i. 210, "surrounded the pillagers with an honorary escort, while some of the rabble shouted approval." To a delegation of the Jews of Kiev, Governor-General Drentelen said that he could do nothing for them; "for the sake of a few Jews he would not endanger the lives of his soldiers" ("Zeitung des Judenthums," May 31, 1881). On May 18, Baron Horace de Günzburg was received in audience by Grand Duke Vladimir, who declared that the motive of the anti-Jewish agitation

*His Reactionary Tendencies.*

*Popular Outbreaks Against Jews.*

was not so much resentment against the Jews as a general tendency to create disturbances ("London Times," May 19, 1881). On May 23, a deputation of the Jews of St. Petersburg waited upon the czar at Gachina. It consisted of Baron Günzburg, Sack, Pasover, Bank, and Berlin. The emperor assured its members that the Jewish question would receive his attention, that the disturbances were the work of anarchists, and he advised them to address a memorandum on the subject to the minister of the interior. Both the emperor and the grand duke Vladimir expressed their belief that race-hatred was not the real cause, but only the pretext, of the recent disorders. In accordance with the promise of the czar, an edict was issued Sept. 3, 1881, ordering the appointment of local commissions from all the governments to be under the direction of the governors, for the solution of the Jewish question. But on the same day, General Ignatiev by order of the czar issued a circular to the governors, in which he pointed out that the Jews had been exploiting the Slav inhabitants of the empire, and that this was the real cause of the riots. This contradiction may explain the conduct of Attorney-General Stryelnikov, who during the trial of the rioters before the court-martial at Kiev, instead of incriminating the guilty parties, turned upon the Jews and endeavored to cast the whole blame upon them. These persecutions, added to the distressing economic conditions then prevailing, gave rise to the emigration movement, which soon assumed extensive proportions. The intelligent classes of Russia condemned the medieval barbarities against the Jews, but the anti-Semitic propaganda of the "Novoe Vremya," "Kievlyanin," and other organs hostile to the Jews, did not cease even after the riots. The constant Jew-baiting of Aksakov, Suvorin, and Pichno had its effect on that class of the Russian people which was entirely unfamiliar with Jewish life, and therefore believed all the charges brought against the Jews by the agitators. That the South Russians especially had no cause for complaints against the Jews may be seen from the following statement made by the Russian economist Chicherin: "Those who have lived in Little Russia, which is densely inhabited by Jews, and have compared the conditions of the peasant there with those existing in the provinces of Great Russia, know how exaggerated are the accusations against the Jews. If there is a difference in the condition of these peasants, it is in favor of the Little Russians."

The second series of persecutions began with the riots of Warsaw on Christmas, 1881, and lasted for three days. Twelve Jews were killed, many women outraged, and two million rubles' worth of property destroyed. In the neighboring Lithuanian provinces the disturbances were slight, owing to the precautions taken by Count Todleben, governor-general of Wilna, who was not one of Ignatiev's disciples.

Order was also maintained by General Gurko, governor-general of Odessa, and thus the riots in Odessa and vicinity were prevented from assuming great proportions. In Nyezhin the soldiers, who were called out to quell the riots, killed and pillaged a wealthy Jewish family. Other riots occurred in Kuzmintzy, Plitovich, Klimov, Okhrimotzy, and, on March 23, in Lubny, where three soldiers killed a Jewish family of six. Balta was the scene of another series of riots (Easter, 1882) resulting in the death of eight and the wounding of more than two hundred persons. Over a thousand houses were demolished and property to the value of over one million dollars was destroyed. These disgraceful acts aroused the public indignation of

*Further Persecutions.*

needs of all the Russian Jews. It was not until 1798 that a censor's office was established at Wilna, Karl Tile of Leipsic being appointed **At Wilna.** censor for Hebrew books in that year.

The new office did not, however, commence operations until March 14, 1800; and in the mean while the censorship of Hebrew books, of either foreign or native production, continued to be exercised in Riga, whither the Jewish printing-houses of Grodno, Shklov, Slavuta, Koretz, and Novodvor had to send their works for approbation.

It is interesting to note that the first book to puzzle the official censor as to its being in accord with the designs of the government was an ordinary prayer-book, entitled "Rosh Ḥodesh Siddurim." The most doubtful passages were found in the "Eighteen Benedictions," in "Taḥnun," and in the Sabbatic poem "Iklu Mashmannim": the passages in the first two containing hints about tyrants and the land of exile; while the last was considered immoral on account of its exhortations to feasting and drinking. Elkan did not recommend the burning of the prayer-book; but he advised that the page containing "Iklu Mashmannim" be torn out, and in the other cases that the obnoxious words be obliterated. Of other books that were condemned by the censor the first to fall under the ban was the "Ḥizzuk Emunah," written at the end of the sixteenth century **Confiscations.** by Isaac ben Abraham Troki. In March, 1799, the entire edition of "Niẓẓaḥon," by Lipman Mülhausen, was confiscated, on the ground that it was written as a refutation of the Christian religion.

In 1800 the historical work of Joseph ha-Kohen, "Dibre ha-Yamim le-Malke Ẓarfat," was prohibited because it contained passages disrespectful to Chris-

tians and the Christian religion. The same fate befell the "Teḥinnot Immahot," because the prayers for the New Moon contained allusions to cruel potentates calculated to breed hatred. The history of the Cossack persecutions under Chmielnicki, entitled "Yawen Meẓulah," was prohibited, because of the name יון applied to Russians, and on the further ground that the reading of the book might prejudice the Jews against the natural-born subjects of the czar. The "Or ha-Ḥayyim," by Ya'abeẓ, was prohibited because of one passage stating that God in heaven, unlike the czars on earth, is not influenced by the high social standing of the sinner. Other books, notably "Babe Ma'aseh" and "Imre Yosef," were prohibited on account of alleged coarse or profane expressions in the text.

By the ukase of April 30, 1800, the importation of books in any language was prohibited till further notice, and the Hebrew censors at Riga were dismissed. During the 28 months of their activity in office 126 books were confiscated out of a total of 6,295 which were imported.

With the accession of Alexander I. the importation of books was once more legalized, the censorship being entrusted to the civil governors. This arrangement did not last; and in 1804 a committee of censors was

reestablished in every Russian university.

During the reign of Nicholas I. the censorship of Hebrew books was entrusted to the official rabbi, who, partly through ignorance and **Nicholas I.** partly from fear of the government, **to Alexan-** showed themselves particularly severe. **der III.** Under Alexander II. Jewish publications shared with Russian literature a liberal interpretation of the law with regard to censorship. Since the reign of Alexander III. Russian, and especially Hebrew, literature has suffered much from

---

**THE JEWISH ENCYCLOPEDIA**     Alexander I. Pavlovich / Alexander III., Alexandrovich

and other youths took an active part in the revolutionary movement of the seventies. Alexander knew and always appreciated the loyalty of the great majority of his Jewish subjects, and on many occasions rewarded them for their services to the country. When the assassination of Alexander by nihilist conspirators became known, the Jews of Russia deeply mourned the loss of the benevolent czar and liberator

H. R.

**ALEXANDER III., ALEXANDROVICH,** Emperor of Russia; born at St. Petersburg March 10, 1845; died at Livadia, Nov. 1, 1894. He succeeded to the throne March 14, 1881, the day after the assassination of his father Alexander II. The terrible fate of the latter produced an awful impression upon Alexander, but instead of continuing the reforms of the

was not so much resentment against the Jews as a general tendency to create disturbances ("London Times," May 19, 1881). On May 19, a deputation of the Jews of St. Petersburg waited upon the czar at Gatchina. It consisted of Baron Günzburg, Sack, Passover, Bank, and Berlin. The emperor assured its members that the Jewish question would receive his attention, that the disturbances were the work of anarchists, and he advised them to address a memorandum on the subject to the minister of the interior. Both the emperor and the grand duke Vladimir expressed their belief that race-hatred was not the real cause, but only the pretext, of the recent disorders. In accordance with the promise of the czar, an edict was issued Sept. 3, 1881, ordering the appointment of local commissions from all the governments to be under the direction of the governors, for the solution of the Jewish question. But on the same day, General Ignatiev by order of the czar issued a circular to the governors, in which he pointed out that the Jews had been exploiting the Slav inhabitants of the empire, and that this was the real cause of the riots. This contradiction may explain the conduct of Attorney-General Strylnikov, who during the trial of the rioters before the court-martial at Kiev, instead of incriminating the guilty parties, turned upon the Jews and endeavored to cast the whole blame upon them. These persecutions, aided by the riots. The constant Jew-baiting of Aksakov, Suvorin, and Pichno had its effect on that class of the Russian people which was entirely unfamiliar with Jewish life, and therefore believed all the charges brought against the Jews by the agitators. That the South Russians especially had no cause for complaints against the Jews may be seen from the following statement made by the Russian economist Chicherin: "Those who have lived in Little Russia, which is densely inhabited by Jews, and have compared the condition of the peasant there with those dwelling in the provinces of Great Russia, know how exaggerated are the accusations against the Jews. If there is a difference in the condition of these peasants, it is in favor of the Little Russians." The second series of persecutions began with the riots of Warsaw on Christmas, 1881, and lasted for three days. Twelve Jews were killed, many women outraged, and two million rubles' worth of property destroyed. In the neighboring Lithuanian provinces the disturbances were slight, owing to the precautions taken by Count Todleben, governor-general of Wilna, who was not one of Ignatiev's disciples. Order was also maintained by General Gurko, governor-general of Odessa, and thus the riots in Odessa and vicinity were prevented from assuming great proportions. In Nyezhin the soldiers, who were called out to quell the riots, killed and pillaged a wealthy Jewish family. Other riots occurred in Kurnitzky, Pltovich, Klinov, and March 23, in Lubny, where three soldiers killed a Jewish family of six. Balta was the scene of another series of riots (Easter, 1882) resulting in the death of eight and the wounding of more than two hundred persons. Over a thousand houses were demolished and property to the value of over one million dollars was destroyed. These disgraceful acts aroused the public indignation of

**Soon after** Alexander III. had ascended the throne, anti-Jewish riots (Pogroms) broke out in Elizabethgrad (April 27, 28), Kiev (May 8-11), Shpola (May 9), Ananiev (May 9), Wasilkov (May 10), Konotop (May 10), and, during the following six months, in one hundred and sixty other places of southern Russia. In these riots thousands of Jewish homes were destroyed, **Popular Outbreaks Against Jews.** many families reduced to extremes of poverty, women outraged, and large numbers of men, women, and children killed or injured. It was clear that the riots were premeditated ("Voskhod," May 24, 1881, p. 75). To give but one example—a week before the pogrom of Kiev broke out, Von Hubbenet, chief of police of Kiev, warned some of his Jewish friends of the coming riots. Appeals to the authorities for protection were of no avail. "In Nyezhin the pillagers **Further Persecutions.** with an honorary escort, while some of the rabble shouted approval." To a delegation of the Jews of Kiev, Governor-General Drenteln said that he could do nothing for them, "for the sake of a few Jews he would not endanger the lives of his soldiers" ("Zeitung des Judenthums," May 31, 1881). On May 18, Baron Horace de Ginzburg was received in audience by Grand Duke Vladimir, who declared that the motive of the anti-Jewish agitation

REDUCED FACSIMILE OF A CENSORED PAGE OF THE JEWISH ENCYCLOPEDIA.

---

10. An article on "Censorship of Hebrew Books" from *Jewish Encyclopedia*, vol. 3 (1902), showing the page from the "Alexander III" article as it appeared in Russia the following year.

to pulp mills or incinerators, but the Nazis seem to have destroyed the books only out of necessity, not desire.

In fact Nazi Germany worked hard *not* to destroy Jewish books but to save them. Furthermore the Nazis' Jewish book policy wasn't interested in controlling Jewish behaviors or in getting Jews to convert away from Judaism. Typically the Nazis first deported or killed Jews and then took their books afterward. The Nazis weren't interested in editing or censoring Jewish books; they wanted to study the volumes in their original form. They weren't scared of Jewish books; they were fascinated by them. They wanted to preserve the books as a relic of the great, evil civilization that they were confident would soon be no more. They dreamed of drawing worldwide attention to the content of those books and to co-opt that content into their own historical narrative and worldview.

Earlier antisemites stole Jewish literature from living Jews and sought to destroy it. The Nazis usually stole Jewish literature from dead Jews and sought to preserve it. In this sense the Nazis' dealings with Jewish books represented a revolution in antisemitic dealings with Jewish literature—a radical break with their book-burning, book-censoring predecessors. Their efforts to preserve Jewish literature would have been utterly baffling to European leaders of the past.

One perspective that many individual Nazis did share with some of their predecessors was an understanding that under antisemitic regimes, seizing Jewish books can do great things for one's professional advancement. Jewish apostates to Christianity as well as mid-level church and government officials were almost always eager to cooperate with the ruler's campaigns to confiscate, translate, and often destroy Jewish literature. Similarly, as the following chapters will show, many Nazi officials who looted Jewish books did so out of a fervent desire to get into Hitler's good graces. The more books they looted, these officials hoped, the more impressed the führer would be.

For many centuries, it seems, attacking Jewish books has been a great way to earn "cred" with antisemitic bosses.

Another perspective that the Nazis shared with their predecessors was an appreciation of the power of the written word—an awe of books and their contents. Previous generations of antisemites evidently felt that burning and censoring Jewish books was a way to "save" Jewish souls and convert them to Christianity. The Nazis cared not a whit about Jewish souls, of course, but they too saw in the capture of Jewish books a way to affirm the most fundamental truths of their worldview. The gigantic collection of Jewish literature that they planned to amass would attest to German greatness and its dominance over the late-great civilization of the Jews. Earlier antisemites, in other words, took hold of Jewish books as a way to take hold of Jewish souls. The Nazis, however, took Jewish books to prove that they had taken hold of Jewish civilization as a whole. In capturing Jewish books, both groups hoped to affirm—fundamentally and undeniably—the greatest truths that their worldview had to teach.

# 3

# From Bonfires to Bookshelves

An anti-Semitism based on purely emotional grounds will find its ultimate expression in the form of pogroms. An anti-Semitism based on reason, however, must lead to a systematic legal opposition and elimination of the special privileges which Jews hold. . . . Its final objective must unswervingly be the removal of the Jews altogether.

—*Adolph Hitler, September 16, 1919*

At first, burning Jewish books was easy for the Nazis, but in the long run it proved extremely difficult. Books, they learned, are hard to burn. Tightly bound pages admit very little oxygen between them, and flames touching a book's margin are often turned away before gaining access to the words inside. Even when a book does burn, identical copies elsewhere often survive, and the words live on. Handwritten notes and onetime records can perish easily, of course, but in the age of printing, books rarely go extinct. The operative rule here is what we might call "the Survival of the Printed." Darwin showed that in the natural world it is the strong who can most successfully reproduce, but here we see that in the world of literature it is the reproduced that can most successfully be strong.

As enlightened as their society was, the Nazis of the 1930s seemed oblivious to printed literature's independence and survival powers. Instead, in a vain and perversely quixotic effort to quash the entirety of

11. Bonfire in Berlin, May 1933. Courtesy Bundesarchiv, Bild 102-14597/
Georg Pahl.

Jewish literature, they tried to conquer Jewish books. The Nazis differed
greatly from antisemitic book burners of ages past, of course, but they
tried to invoke those biblioclasts anyway, and they called on modern-day
Germany to continue their predecessors' campaign of book destruction.
Many popes and prelates of previous centuries had done admirable work
in this area, but their successes were pitifully small. Now, modern technology had opened great vistas of possibility. Now, the Nazis realized,
they could finally finish the job.

For his part, Hitler invoked his book-burning predecessors with little
consistency or logic. One day he would identify Aryans as modern-day
incarnations of the Nordic race; the next day he would call them a Teu-
tonic nation; and after that, Caucasians. It was fuzzy history—weak in
its scholarship, but effective in its ability to link modern Germany with
the great European powers of the past. Flooded with such rhetoric, it

12. Sorting books in Reval, Latvia, ca. 1942. Courtesy Yad Vashem Photo Archives.

was only natural that Germany would turn to the incineration of Jewish literature as one of its first tools for advancing the Nazi cause.

## *Books: Deep in the German Heart*

Hitler's invocation of history's book burners was far from happenstance, for German society had been growing increasingly bookish for centuries. The University of Heidelberg was founded as early as 1386 and was among the oldest in the world; soon there were other such institutions in Leipzig, Rostock, and Greifswald. By the early twentieth century there were dozens of universities throughout Germany, many of which had achieved worldwide acclaim. The nation was also home to a pantheon of great writers and thinkers—Martin Luther, Immanuel Kant, Johann Wolfgang von Goethe, and many others. It produced scientists who were among the most respected in the world, such as Heinrich Hertz, Wilhelm Röntgen, and Daniel Fahrenheit. Composers such as Bach, Beethoven, and Brahms set Germany's cultural ascent to music, thus adding their own contributions to the precipitous climb of German national culture.

For centuries, then, Germany prided itself as being a center of Enlightenment and Romanticism, a bulwark of rational inquiry, and an exemplar of true aesthetic refinement. This advanced and knowledge-friendly environment inevitably produced a massive body of literature. And with the rise of the printed book in the late 1500s, print shops and publishing companies sprouted like wildflowers throughout the country. In large cities and small hamlets, bookstores seemed to appear on every corner; all of Germany's urban centers and each of its major universities featured libraries housing remarkable collections of books, old and new. In fact by the outbreak of World War II, there were fifteen thousand public lending libraries in Germany, and together they purchased two to three million books each year; sometimes, especially in the case of best sellers, the libraries would buy more than one hundred copies of the same title.[1]

The city of Frankfurt especially had a long and prominent history as a center for German bookselling and publishing, beginning with the Frankfurt Book Fair, first mentioned, perhaps, in a mid-twelfth-century Talmud commentary by a rabbi named Eliezer ben Natan, of Mainz.[2] The Frankfurt Book Fair is still going strong today, centuries later, as Europe's largest, most prestigious book gathering. It draws thousands of attendees from dozens of countries who, whether or not they are aware of it, gather to buy, sell, and talk books in a place that has been a critical center for the marketing and selling of books off and on since not long after Johannes Gutenberg invented the printing press in 1439 in the town of Mainz, twenty miles to the west. Frankfurt's Municipal Library, founded in the Middle Ages and housed since the early 1820s in a grand, neoclassical building near the city center overlooking the Main River, has long boasted one of Europe's most significant collections of books and manuscripts. And beginning in the mid-nineteenth century the city was also home to the extraordinary private library of Baron Wilhelm von Rothschild, a library that would continue to be an enticing lure to friend and foe alike during the years to come.

Once books made their way into the heart of German culture and identity, the nation had only to make a short logical jump to land on the idea of burning Jewish literature: "Books lie deep in the German heart," went the unspoken reasoning, "so surely the books of other nations and ethnic groups are important to their identities too. Jews are the people of the book, so books must lie just as close to the Jewish heart as German books are to ours." Germans viewed those book-hearted Jews as a dangerous menace to society—a beast that a nation as enlightened and superior as Germany must battle. And if you want to slay any beast, what better way is there to do so than to rip out its heart? Even if what constitutes that heart is merely bound stacks of printed paper.

## Preparing the Pyres

It began with a Nazi propaganda campaign launched even before Hitler became head of state. In 1929 the Nazi party established the "Combat League for German Culture" and two newspapers, *Völkischer Beobachter* (People's Observer) and *Der Angriff* (The Attack). Both organs blatantly denounced "un-German" authors and ideas, particularly those that were Jewish. In 1930 and 1931 Nazis disrupted book readings by Thomas Mann and his daughter Erika. Later in 1931 the rhetoric grew more intense, as *Völkischer Beobachter* published a declaration signed by forty-two scholars calling on Germans to protect their culture against *Kulturbolschewismus*, "cultural Bolshevism," an oft-used Nazi euphemism for Judaism. In April 1932 Joseph Goebbels published a list of authors whom he suggested be lined up against the wall. The *Völkischer Beobachter* published a similar list of its own. During the same month a committee of librarians met to assemble a list of authors—again primarily Jewish ones—whose works they felt should be banned. Largely due to the contributions of a prominent librarian named Wolfgang Hermann, it released a full-fledged blacklist early the following year.

And crackling in the background as these events unfolded was the bright glow of Nazi fire. Fire had long been one of Hitler's favorite motifs, and as his power grew, so too did the use of fire imagery in Nazi rhetoric and ceremonies. The Aryan, he wrote in *Mein Kampf*, is the "Prometheus of mankind, from whose bright forehead the divine spark of genius has sprung at all times." He argued that the beginning of World War I represented Germany's "baptism of fire." One of his own early speeches, Hitler suggested, kindled "a fire . . . from whose glowing heat the sword would be fashioned which would restore freedom to the . . . German nation."[3]

All this fire talk captured Germany's imagination. In fact Nazi gatherings, especially those during the summertime, were rarely without bonfires. The bright flames, the flying sparks, the intense heat emanating from the fire's burning core—all these images and others served as powerful metaphors to galvanize support and enthusiasm for the growing Nazi movement. Consequently the ceremonial bonfires at Hitler Youth gatherings transformed what might otherwise have been simple teenage get-togethers into powerful "religious" rituals. Usually speakers at these events recited "fire oaths"—short, incendiary speeches designed to rile the crowd's passion, enthusiasm, and commitment to the German national cause. For their part, and in true Nordic spirit, the young people in attendance chanted incantations to express their fealty and devotion:

*We are the fire, we are the flame*
*We burn before Germany's altars.*
*We carry the drums across the land:*
*We are the fanfares of the battles*[4]

On January 30, 1933, Adolph Hitler was appointed chancellor of Germany, and the fervor grew even more heated. The SS, the Schutzstaffel, Hitler's paramilitary police, raided bookstores, publishers, and the homes of writers throughout the country to confiscate "un-German" literature. The press seethed with calls for even stricter policies of cultural control. More lists of "dangerous" books appeared in publications all over Germany.

In such a tinderbox, one might think that all it would take to ignite an outbreak of book burnings would be a stray spark—one renegade devotee burning a single book, or one particularly incendiary speech to rile the masses into a fiery fervor. In fact, however, the story of the May 1933 book burnings was just the opposite. The events were carefully planned and choreographed spectacles, meticulously designed for maximum effect.

## The Bonfires

At the time, two of the largest student organizations in Germany bore confusingly similar titles: the Deutsche Studentenschaft (German Student Association, DS), and the Nationalsozialistische Deutsche Studentenbund (National German Socialist Student Federation, NDS). The missions of the two agencies were almost identical, and naturally the groups became rivals, each trying to one-up the other with its many events and activities.

In an effort to gain recognition and favor with the government, the DS designed a publicity stunt that it hoped would garner nationwide attention. In early April the organization announced an upcoming event—an "action against Jewish decomposition of German literature." On April 14 the student group published a statement called "The Twelve Theses" in the *Völkischer Beobachter*. The document, dripping with vitriol, called upon the "German Folk" to ensure the purity of its language and literature. It described "the Jew" as alien, a traitor, and Germans' greatest enemy; it demanded censorship of Jewish books and an end to "Jewish intellectualism and the resulting liberal decay in the German spirit." The antisemitic tract didn't explicitly call for the burning of Jewish books. It didn't need to.

The DS ordered its university chapters to work with local Nazi authorities, instructing them to form "fighting committees" composed of students, professors, and other would-be plunderers. The fighting committees were to collect condemned books, and along the way they were also to plan highly publicized marches for the following month. The DS encouraged students to purge their personal libraries of the banned books and called on lending libraries and bookstores to remove these volumes from their collections as well.

The public denunciation of Jewish literature grew in fervor, and soon a palpable feeling of excitement swept through the country. Teams of looters fanned out through German cities and towns, emptying dozens of Jewish libraries, leaving the once warm, hushed facilities cold and desolate. Shelves that had only recently sagged under the weight of Jewish books suddenly turned bare, often with only a thin outline of book dust as the sole reminder of what they once held.

On the night of May 10, 1933, the fires began. Preparations had commenced earlier that day, as trucks, cars, and even handheld manure wagons brought tons of books to the meeting places. There students and other helpers eagerly unloaded the books and tossed them into large heaps. Some of the volumes were recently printed and of little monetary value—novels, schoolbooks, and newly written works of popular history. Others were centuries old and quite rare, their soft rag-paper pages and ancient words holding up nicely as a testament to the care they'd received through the centuries. As the books flew from the looters' hands, many opened and landed spread-eagle atop the piles, with their pages often crumpling under of the weight of the books dumped on them a few moments later.

The squares and plazas were festooned with Nazi banners and slogans. Some participants brought food and drinks to enjoy before the ceremonies. In larger venues, wires snaked from generators or nearby shops to temporary sound systems erected around the periphery of the rally grounds. The crowds gathered. In Munich, Frankfurt, Heidelberg, and other urban centers, in dozens of small towns dotting the German countryside, and at more than thirty universities throughout the country, people of all ages assembled to watch the spectacles. According to some accounts, the rally in Berlin drew more than forty thousand participants.[5]

As the sky darkened; the excitement grew. Soon there was music—sturdy, boot-pounding songs whose lyrics the crowds sang with beer-hall gusto. After a while speakers appeared and riled the throngs with inflammatory Nazi oratory, their voices crackling over the surrounding loudspeakers. The crowds responded with loud cheers, "Heil Hitlers," and straight-armed Nazi salutes.

The organizers had decided to synchronize the spectacles nationwide; leaders at all of the individual rallies were to hold off lighting their matches until the appointed time. Finally, at eleven o'clock, the destruction began. Often the fires were difficult to start, for books don't burn like kindling—they burn like logs. But eventually flames did engulf the books, illuminating city squares and plazas, shining off the thrilled faces of spectators. Dozens of camera crews from the international press covered the events. Observers recall that the cameras' floodlights and the flames from the burning book pyres lit the gathering places as brightly as the noonday sun.

Some Jews hid at home as their books went up in flames. Others watched from afar and wept.

The book burnings didn't last long. However galvanizing and spellbinding their impact, the ceremonies were, in the end, merely spectacles. The bonfires were of course horribly destructive, but after their first flare-ups they lacked the substance and staying power to continue capturing the hearts of German citizens. By early April, after only about three weeks, the book-burning fervor in Germany had petered out. The force of a great spectacle is similar to that of bright shooting stars—it flashes brilliantly at first but soon disappears into the darkness.

Five years later, in November 1938, the fires broke out again as part of the violence of Kristallnacht, the Night of Broken Glass, a widespread series of pogroms against the Jews of Germany and Austria. And then, once again . . . the fires burned out.

## *Bad Press*

The book burnings in the spring of 1933 did last long enough, however, to draw the attention and condemnation of the international press. The critics had a heyday with it. Exiled German writer Oskar Maria Graf *complained* that his work hadn't made the list of banned books. He'd been "whitelisted," he cried, and he hoped his books would merit burning soon. Emil Ludwig wrote from Barcelona of the satisfaction he would feel when the Nazis burned his works. He couldn't wait to "hear over the radio the crackling flames that are destroying [my] literary labors."[6]

Other critics dismissed the book burnings as ineffective twaddle. Even while the gatherings were still being planned, the *Manchester Guardian* described them as the "most unedifying examples of mob psychology that can be found in any history." The *Literary Digest* observed that the pageantry didn't work. "The elements in Berlin were unfavorable," it reported, "for it rained; the books themselves would not burn easily, and finely bound volumes that were at first dedicated to the holocaust . . . were removed from circulation and preserved under tabu."[7] In fact several observers mockingly noted how difficult it was for the Nazis to get the books to burn. Not only did the bonfires at several venues sputter out in the rain, but because of their resistance to fire, many books escaped the bonfires with only minimal damage.[8]

Still other observers denounced the fires more vehemently. Helen Keller, whose book *How I Became a Socialist* was included on the Nazis' lists, wrote an open letter of condemnation to the students, saying, "History has taught you nothing if you think you can kill ideas." Speaking to a large audience of Jews in New York shortly after the burnings, Major General John F. O'Ryan expressed the civilized world's horror with "the policies of intolerance inaugurated by the Hitler government against the Jewish element of the German population."[9]

Clearly these fiery extravaganzas had not played well on the world stage, and Nazi leaders quickly came to a tacit agreement that their efforts to vanquish the "Jewish menace" would best be aimed elsewhere. The book burnings continued for a few days after the May 10 outburst, but soon they lost steam. Through the mid-1930s the Nazi list of banned books remained in effect and Germans continued to confiscate Jewish libraries, but the looting became stealthier and, for the time-being, more subdued.

Most remaining vestiges of Germany's book-burning frenzy fizzled out in early 1936. That summer the Olympics were coming to Berlin. Germany would be in the international spotlight, and spectacles such as book burnings would portray Germany as a nation of boors and thugs rather than as the civilized *übermenschen* they knew themselves to be. Consequently German leaders conducted a campaign later referred to as "reverse censorship." Antisemitic signs were removed from stores and restaurants, vending machines selling antisemitic newspapers disappeared from the streets, books of hateful Nazi propaganda in shops and libraries were shelved away from public view. As the pre-Olympic fervor intensified, questions of what to do with Jewish books disappeared from common discourse. To all appearances Nazi Germany was the most modern and enlightened of all the world's nations.

Of course, later events would prove otherwise. In 1933 the Nazis had not yet begun their systematic murder of Europe's Jewish people, but they were burning Jewish books. A decade later, however, the Nazis *were* murdering Jewish people—millions of them—but by then they were no longer burning Jewish books. Instead the Nazis were saving them.

These two techniques for dealing with Jewish literature—incineration and preservation—were, in many ways, quite similar to one another. Both strategies acknowledged the centrality of books to Jewish culture and spirit, both reflected the Nazi obsession with Jewish books, and both, of course, were tools that the Third Reich used to debase, oppress, and ultimately murder as many Jews as it could. Nevertheless, the contrast between the May 1933 book burnings and the Nazis' later plans to save, catalogue, and study the very same titles is striking, to say the least. Despite the commonality of their goals, the two policies were, in many ways, polar opposites.

### Antisemitism of Reason

Hitler had planted the seeds of the book burnings' demise early in his career. In fact Hitler's very first written statement of antisemitism—a letter he wrote to "Herr Gemlich" shortly after his release from military service in 1919—called for Germany to adopt an "antisemitism of reason." He complained that, in the past, anti-Jewish policies and ideas were often based on the vagaries of emotion. Such antisemitism, Hitler argued, "will find its ultimate expression in the form of the pogrom."[10] Antisemitism based on the robust strength of German rationality, however, could eventually achieve no less than "the irrevocable removal of the Jews in general." Historically, he argued, well-intentioned Jew haters had tried to seduce Jews into conversion or assimilation. Now, however, scientists had shown that "the Jews are a race, and that any attempt to assimilate them is therefore bound to fail." Consequently, Hitler argued, modern Germany must employ its great intellectual gifts and finally accomplish what antisemites had been trying to do for centuries—get rid of the Jews.[11]

Hitler's idea of an intellectually based antisemitic ideology caught on quickly in the salons, cafes, and beer halls of interwar Germany. Many Germans, particularly the intelligentsia, found Hitler's arguments downright exciting. They agreed that modern Germany should apply its knowledge of history, biology, anthropology, linguistics, and a host of other sciences to its exposition of the Jewish menace. As a result German policy toward the Jews would not be as slapdash or improvised as it had been so often in the past. Instead the antisemitism would be rational; it would be scientific; it would be respectable.

Immediately after Hitler's assumption of power in 1933—just around the time of the book burnings—German universities began hiring anti-semitic scholars to join their faculties. Historians, anthropologists, and other scientists published papers about the racial characteristics of Jews. Schools changed their curricula to better reflect the new antisemitic ideas. German thought was galvanizing around a science of supremacism.

No wonder, then, that the book burnings petered out so quickly. Those were thuggish, mob-like affairs, many citizens felt; they failed to impress the world with the power of the German intellect, and they drew very bad press. With a more sophisticated and enlightened policy, Germany could surely draw the respect of thinking people everywhere.

The cast of characters in this pseudo-scholarly effort was a colorful one. It included, for example, economic historian Peter-Heinz Seraphim, who over the years would serve at the Universities of Königsberg, Breslau, and Greifswald.[12] In 1938 Seraphim published a massive tome called *The Jews of Eastern Europe.* In it he argued that eastern European Jews lived in walled-off ghettos not because that was where the law forced them to live, but rather because that was where they *wanted* to live. Seraphim said that this voluntary isolation served as the Jews' "basis of expansion." Jews, in other words, were secretly gathering and conspiring. Their strategy was to grow stronger, to spread their influence, and eventually to dominate the world—economically, culturally, and even biologically.

Peter-Heinz Seraphim knew his Jewish books. He had traveled extensively in eastern Europe, where he familiarized himself with its many historical and scholarly resources. At one point Seraphim even visited YIVO (the Yiddish Scientific Institute) in Vilna, where, after presenting a letter of recommendation from the Polish government, he was promptly given the grand tour of the facility and full access to its information.[13] Using these and other resources, Seraphim drew heavily on the work of Jewish historians, typically employing questionable methods of scholarship and rejecting the previous writers' conclusions. To many Germans, the mere appearance of *The Jews of Eastern Europe* added scholarly credence to the Nazi enterprise. It was 732 pages long; it contained 197 graphs and charts and more than one thousand footnotes. There were 563 entries in its bibliography, of which 346 referred to Jewish works. At the very least it looked very impressive on the shelf.[14]

*The Jews of Eastern Europe* established Peter-Heinz Seraphim as one of Germany's top experts on Jews and Judaism, and within a few years he had become one of the country's most sought-after speakers and consultants. In early 1941 he wrote several articles rejecting recent suggestions that Germany gather all its Jews onto "reservations" and argued instead for mass deportation. As long as the Jews remained in Europe, he argued, Germany could never safely isolate itself from them. Better to remove them all.

While Seraphim came to his studies of Judaism as a historian, some of the Nazis' other Judaic scholars brought more explicitly religious perspectives to their work. Perhaps the most noteworthy of these thinkers was the prominent theologian Gerhard Kittel.[15] Son of the renowned Old Testament scholar Rudolf Kittel, Gerhard was born in 1888, entered academia as an expert on the New Testament, and served most of his career as a professor at the University of Tübingen. Perhaps due to the influence of his father's Old Testament work, Gerhard Kittel devoted his early scholarship to studying the Jewish roots of Christianity. Unlike many Christian scholars before and since, Kittel saw no benefit in arguing for the superiority of his religion over Judaism. In Kittel's 1914 book *Jesus and the Rabbis*, and later in his 1926 *Problems of Late Palestinian Judaism and Early Christianity*, he argued that it is impossible to understand Christianity without a complete picture of the Jewish context from which it emerged. Indeed, he suggested in the earlier work, the Talmud was in many ways even more instructive than the New Testament in the study of Jesus's parables and other teachings.

But then in 1933 something changed. Within a few months of Hitler's installment as chancellor, Kittel's writings and talks took a decidedly antisemitic tone. In June of that year Kittel delivered a speech in Tübingen during which he analyzed the Nazis' intensifying antisemitic activities from his perspective as a Christian scholar. The important question facing the citizens of Germany, he argued, was not what to do with their Jewish coworkers and neighbors, but rather what to do with the Jewish *Volk*— the Jewish people as a whole. Germans, he argued, should "not first ask what shall become of the individual Jew, but what shall become of Jewry."

To deal with this Jewish collectivity, he explained, the Germans had four possible options: extermination, Zionism, assimilation, and *Gastzustand*. Extermination, he continued, had been tried in the past, and it had never worked—no use trying it again. Zionism would never work, either; there were too few Jews in Palestine, the local Arabs wouldn't stand for it, and the Jews already living there were mostly Socialists and Communists, so they'd never work hard enough to make a go of it. Nor was assimilation a good option; in fact the idea of blending Jews into German culture and society would be even worse than the first two options. Judaism, he argued, represented decadence and depravity— the very worst of Enlightenment ideals. To welcome Jews into the fold would therefore allow secularism, radicalism, and profound disrespect for religion to irreparably contaminate German life.

The only remaining option, Kittel argued, was *Gastzustand*—separating Jews from the people among whom they lived, deeming them "guests" rather than "citizens." By this he was probably not suggesting outright deportation, but rather a blend of cultural and professional exclusion. Jewish professors, he said, should be removed from university faculties, Jewish lawyers and judges disbarred. To preserve German purity, inter-marriage between Jews and Germans should be absolutely forbidden. These changes might be difficult to stomach, he acknowledged, because many Jews have become Germans' friends. But "such considerations must never lead to a sentimental softening and paralysis." Though some might invoke "Christian sensitivity" to argue against his proposals, Kittel retorted that "if the struggle is objectively correct, then the Christian also has a place at the front." To Kittel, it seems, oppressing Jews was not only the right thing to do, it was the Christian thing to do as well.

Kittel continued writing and speaking along these lines throughout the war. Sometimes he used theological arguments to bolster his points, and sometimes his approach was more directly political or archeological. Often Kittel's ideas drew on his thorough knowledge of Jewish texts and world history. In one article he argued that the large noses on a group of ancient statues discovered in England were proof of Jewish expansionism and rapaciousness. In another he suggested that the Talmud encourages Jews to murder non-Jews.

Regardless of what approach he used in his articles, however, Kittel's status as a scholar of religion—not to mention his academic pedigree— brought theological credence to the Nazis' oppression and murder of Jews. Nazi ideology was often anti-Christian, but in Kittel Nazi leaders had a scholar who could appeal to both the academy and the church. *Not* to have used such an invaluable resource would have been foolish, and eventually organs as prominent as Propaganda Minister Joseph Goebbels's *Archive for Jewish Questions* published Kittel's work extensively. "His willful distortion of Jewish texts," says historian Alan E. Steinweis, "provided intellectual cover for genocide."[16]

Other German scholars also brought credence to the German study of Jewish texts. Walter Frank, for example, director of the Reich Institute for the History of New Germany, argued that Jewish studies were vitally important for the Third Reich. Until now, he said in a November 1937 speech, Jewish historical scholarship has been written only by Jews; it manifests Jews' desire to justify their emancipation from the ghettos and infiltrate their way into German society. Only when *Germans* write Jewish history, he implied, will the world be able to get a truly objective view.

Similarly, linguist Franz Joseph Beranek argued in a 1941 book that Germans should reclaim the study of Yiddish. The language, he suggested, is actually a dialect of German; studying it could reveal "the racial and unique cultural foundations of Jewry."[17]

Johannes Pohl had begun his career as a Catholic priest. He wrote his doctoral dissertation on the biblical prophet Ezekiel and studied biblical archaeology at the Hebrew University in Jerusalem from 1934 to 1936.[18] The notorious Adolph Eichmann studied Zionism in 1935 and even traveled to Palestine along with another Nazi official, where he met with Zionist leaders to seek their support in removing Jews from Germany. British officials kicked out the two Nazis almost immediately, but shortly after his return, Eichmann claimed the requisite expertise to deliver a talk at an SS Intelligence seminar titled "World Jewry: Its Political Activity and the Implications of the Activity on the Jews Residing in Germany."[19]

These scholars of Judaism represent only a small percentage of Nazi—or Nazi-influenced—intellectuals studying Jewish sources. Inevitably their emphasis on Jewish books trickled down and worked its way through all levels of German society. For the high-brow academics, the advanced studies of Jewish history and literature provided a new vision of Jewish studies for the German academy—perverse in its obfuscations and ultimately murderous in its effects. For the educated public, the research inspired a wave of nonfiction books, periodicals, and other literature that opened their eyes to the riches of information one could discover between the covers of Jewish books. And for the non-educated masses, the Judaic scholarship yielded a rich body of propaganda—countless films, newspapers, and speeches that would inspire the fervor of German masses as never before.

### Working toward the Führer

Another dynamic at play in the Nazis' decision to plunder rather than burn their Jewish books was the leadership style of the man at the helm.

Adolph Hitler was not a detail man. He rarely showed up at the office until late morning, and often not until two o'clock in the afternoon. Privately his aides complained that it was difficult, if not impossible, to get face time with him, for he typically spoke with only a select few of his most trusted advisors. He did all he could to avoid making decisions, especially those that related to conflicts between subordinates.

When Hitler did issue orders, they were typically verbal and cryptic, and he never liked reading memos and papers. Although it is common to describe the Nazi regime as totalitarian, Hitler rarely exerted total control over his immediate underlings. Instead Hitler left his aides to work out the details for themselves.

By most standards, this style of leadership would seem to have been doomed to failure—as, of course, it ultimately was. During Hitler's reign, however, these practices helped him solidify his power. By remaining uninvolved in the internecine conflicts of Nazi functionaries, Hitler could stay above the fray. After all, Nazi Germany had all but deified him, and for a god, dealing with such minutiae is quite unbecoming.

All Hitler demanded of those around him was their loyalty. Indeed, only those officers whom Hitler saw as unswervingly loyal could maintain their positions. Any hint of infidelity or betrayal would immediately lead to the officer's demise.

It was what one scholar referred to as a "feudal anarchy," and the rules of such a system are vastly different from those of more ordered governments. Rational systems of leadership typically invest power and authority in those who best demonstrate competence and success in their jobs. Under Hitler, however—at least for his inner circle—the only political currency was Hitler's approval. Earning Hitler's trust was all that mattered, and his aides strove to impress him however they could. A Nazi functionary named Werner Willikens described the system in a 1934 speech:

> Up till now everyone with a post in the new Germany has worked best when he has, so to speak, worked towards the Führer. Very often and in many spheres it has been the case—in previous years as well—that individuals have simply waited for orders and instructions. Unfortunately, the same will be true in the future; but in fact it is the duty of everybody to try to work towards the Führer along the lines he would wish. Anyone who makes mistakes will notice

it soon enough. But anyone who really works towards the Führer along his lines and towards his goal will certainly both now and in the future one day have the finest reward in the form of the sudden legal confirmation of his work.[20]

Nazi officials, then, had no option but to scurry about in their frantic attempts to "work towards the führer," and the führer, like spectators at a smash-up derby, sat back and watched the melee with glee. What resulted was a dizzying, complex system of national leadership. In fact from today's perspective, the Nazi organizational chart looks like a Jackson Pollack painting with a German-language overlay. Swirling lines of authority crisscross as if spattered on the page, connecting umlauted names of German leaders with multisyllabic titles of Nazi agencies and an alphabet soup of acronyms that baffle the novice student. One section of the chart often looks just like another.

And wherever pieces of the chart overlapped—wherever multiple agencies did similar or identical work—there was an enormous amount of internecine struggle and conflict. Various security agencies squabbled over administrative and jurisdictional turf. Goering quarreled with Goebbels. A host of generals complained that Hitler's closest assistant, Martin Bormann, was unfairly preventing them access to Hitler when they needed it.

There was scholarly squabbling too, and by the late 1930s there were countless Nazi agencies devoted to studying Jews: Walter Frank's Reich Institute for the History of New Germany, Joseph Goebbels's Institute for the Study of the Jewish Question, Walter Grundmann's Institute for the Study of Jewish Influence on German Church Life, and many others. They were Nazi think tanks—incubators where the new "scholarly" antisemitic creations could be hatched. And of course each of these many agencies needed Hitler's approval if it wanted to keep on its lights.

Hitler wasn't inclined to give them his attention, at least not very much of it. After all, the primary product of these think tanks was scholarship—papers—and Hitler did all he could to avoid reading such material. For an academic institute to impress him, it would need to come up with something better than journals or monographs—it would need a fact or a finding or a feat that would really grab the führer's attention. It might help if the offering was an antisemitic one. Or maybe the agency could simply invoke some sort of large and very impressive number to describe its achievements. However they decided to proceed, the institutes needed to avoid long, boring historical treatises and instead find juicy tidbits that they could package into nice, quick sound bites or slogans. Only then could they hope to draw the approving nod or smile from their leader that they needed. All the while, of course, these agencies needed to remain academic; they were, after all, scholarly institutes, and their work needed to show it. It all made for a very difficult situation. It was essential for the study centers to find academic feats that would impress Hitler, but for Hitler to be impressed, the feats couldn't really be very academic at all.

At the time, Hitler had ordered Goering and other assistants to collect artwork for a huge museum he hoped to build near his birthplace in Linz, Austria. Maybe, reasoned many of the Nazi think-tank leaders, their groups could continue in the same vein and assemble a Jewish library. A really big one.

Why, then, were the Nazis so obsessed with Jewish books? Perhaps it was sheer sadism—they simply wanted to steal the literature of their declared enemies. But there were certainly other reasons as well. The Nazis devoted so much attention to Jewish books because Germans were a bookish people, and they understood the importance of the printed word to cultural identity and ethnic pride. They were obsessed with books because they saw themselves as inheritors of a great tradition of antisemitism, and many antisemites of the past had burned Jewish books. They were obsessed because their country was home to an army of scholars, and those scholars taught them that studying Jews' books could lead to German greatness. Finally Germans were obsessed with Jewish books because their government was an anarchic Hitler cult, replete with scholarly organizations that bickered like siblings competing for their father's attention. Here, however, the agencies were fighting for Hitler's approval; and here the battlegrounds were fields of academia; and here the weapons were not fists and flying toys, but guns, soldiers, and terror.

As the Nazi armies geared up for their eastward invasions of 1939 and 1940, a host of professors and academic administrators arrayed themselves around Adolph Hitler and waited. They waited for some word from their führer—some authorization, some subtle gesture—that might permit to them to amass their collections.

Soon enough, it came. And once it did, the Nazis began gathering Jewish books.

# 4

# Talmud Scholars, Hebraists, and Other Nazi Looters

I made the suggestion to send somebody [to Paris] to examine the
materials, and also to do some research on them.
—*Alfred Rosenberg, Nuremberg, 1946*

By all accounts, Alfred Rosenberg was an unlikely Nazi leader. His name
sounded Jewish; he was born in Estonia, not Germany; he was dour,
humorless, and devoid of charisma; to friends and associates, he was "a
decent man";[1] and he was also a murderer. He was a writer and an editor
but seemingly incapable of expressing himself clearly; he prided himself
as a rational thinker but he was an ardent member of the Hitler cult; he
loved Hitler but never made it into führer's inner circle; he wrote books
and studied books but also stole books and destroyed books. Taken
together, his ideas and actions are a mess of incoherent contradiction,
and yet it is entirely likely that it was Rosenberg's very predisposition to
inconsistency that allowed him to soar to great heights as a Nazi official
and, arguably, as history's greatest pillager of printed words.

From early on Rosenberg seemed to have a passion for study. In his
early teens he explored history and geography; he studied epic tales of
ancient German civilization; he read the work of German philosophers
such as Schopenhauer and Kant. Rosenberg even studied the religions
of India, admiring the country's caste system and lamenting the damage
that the mixture of blood between India's different stratified groups had

13. Alfred Rosenberg. Courtesy Bundesarchiv, Bild 183-1985-0723-500/ Georg Pahl.

wrought on Indian culture. He looked forward to the day when, once again, India would be ruled by its uppermost caste. Mistakenly using a term more properly applied to languages, he referred to the members of that class with a word that he and others would use far more broadly in later years. He called them "Aryans."[2]

One day in 1909, while visiting the home of some relatives, sixteen-year-old Rosenberg—surely bored by the prattle of his older family members—wandered to a nearby bookshelf, where he found a catalogue containing an entry for a volume published a decade earlier: *The Foundations of the Nineteenth Century*, by H. S. Chamberlain. The title fascinated him. "I felt electrified," Rosenberg later recalled. Immediately he ordered a copy of the book, and when the two-volume treatise arrived, Rosenberg dove in and began reading. In a sense he never surfaced.[3]

Its author was Houston Stewart Chamberlain, a British-born philosopher and scientist who wrote extensively about the greatness of the German race. Chamberlain's second wife was the daughter of the renowned nineteenth-century German composer Richard Wagner, whose operatic scores later served as musical background to Nazi rallies, rituals, and raids.

*The Foundations of the Nineteenth Century*, Chamberlain's most famous book, was a paean to the creativity, mental prowess, and physical superiority of Germanic peoples—Aryans. Despite the superiority of the Aryan race, Chamberlain argued, for centuries it had been engaged in an ongoing struggle against the contaminating force of foreign races and ideas. It was Germany that gave the world its greatest ideas, Chamberlain said; German intellect was indispensable to human progress; the German physique represented the human form at its finest. Nevertheless, he continued, Jews, Catholics, and other non-European peoples had striven to destroy German culture and the German race for centuries, and Germany needed a strong leader as well as a strong state to resist these insidious forces.

Reading Chamberlain's book, Rosenberg was transfixed. Here was a full-blown expression of the German nationalism that had so captivated him during his studies. Here was a fulfillment of his people's heroic sagas as they might play out in modern life. Here was a recognized scholar affirming the ideas that had only just begun to crystallize in his teenage mind. "Another world rose up before me," he later recalled. "Hellas, Judah, Rome. And to everything I assented inwardly—again and yet again."[4]

Eight years later while studying architecture as an undergraduate, Rosenberg discovered another piece of literature that would influence him. It was a book by a Christian mystic named Sergei Nilus, and its appendix contained an infamous antisemitic forgery called "The Protocols of the Elders of Zion." Originally composed in the late nineteenth century in Russia, the Protocols were purportedly a secret internal document describing a worldwide Jewish conspiracy to dominate the world. Jewish leaders of all kinds were in on the scheme—bankers, media barons, rabbis, and countless others. It was a complete hoax, of course, but the hoax caught on anyway. Its implicit message was that the Jewish threat needed to be stopped—Jews are dangerous, the menace was growing, and the civilized world should act quickly to quash the sinister plot.

Needless to say, this document also captured Rosenberg's imagination. The world around him was disintegrating; humanity had not recognized the full glory of the German spirit; weakness and immorality prevailed. And now, with the Protocols uncovered, the world understood why. And so could Rosenberg.

In January 1918 Rosenberg graduated with a degree in architecture; his senior project was a design for a crematorium. As he worked on the design, he said, "[i]t turned into a central hall, with Romanesque vaults and a large colonnade, as well as an adjoining graveyard. So far as the actual construction and work were concerned, this problem was not a particularly difficult one. But who, in these days, was able to think of a really great task!"[5] Not long after leaving school, while living in Munich, a friend introduced him to Dietrich Eckart, a well-known writer and editor of antisemitic periodicals. "Can you use a fighter against Jerusalem?" he asked. The question, as it turns out, launched Rosenberg's rocket-like ascent to power.

In Rosenberg, Eckart had found a protégé who was eager to contribute his own literary, pseudo-scholarly fuel to Germany's growing antisemitic fires. Like the work of many well-known writers, the material in Rosenberg's compositions not only expressed his own thoughts, but also gave voice to the spirit of his time. Indeed the essays Rosenberg wrote during the early 1920s would later seem perfectly at home in the libraries of racist Nazi propaganda. "The Russian-Jewish Revolution," he argued, was a destructive axis of power that wrought unspeakable havoc during the 1917 uprisings. His essay "Jews Within Us and Without" described a worldwide Jewish plot to kill Western civilization by removing its soul. Another piece, "Immorality in the Talmud," had a title that spoke for itself. In "The Trace of the Jew in Changing Times," Rosenberg's use of time-worn, antisemitic clichés reached a new zenith for him. As a result of Jewish influence, the article argued, Germans had become victims of anarchy, pernicious religion, and "finance-capital." "The Black, the Red, and the Gold Internationals," he wrote, "represent the dreams of Jewish philosophers from Ezra, Ezekiel and Nehemia to Marx, Rothschild and Trotsky."[6]

Through Eckart, Rosenberg was exposed to a group called the Thule Society, a secretive fraternal organization founded in 1911 on principles of German racial supremacy. Its affluent membership included industrialists, scholars, and adventurers of all kinds. In hushed tones they looked to the future and resolved to restore their beleaguered nation to its former glories. Rosenberg must have loved it! Finally after so many years of loneliness and struggle, he had found his niche. These were his kind of people. From early on many members of the Thule Society had looked to expand its horizons. Operating as a racist, esoteric cabal was pleasant enough, of course, but they wanted to become a political force as well. In January 1919, they founded the German Workers Party (Deutsche Arbeiterpartei, DAP), as an advocate for its values in the public sphere.

Later that year Eckart found that one of his newspapers was struggling. He invited Rosenberg to his home to discuss how they might revitalize it, and during the visit another Eckart protégé stopped by—a thirty-year-old war veteran who was working with Eckart to help the DAP get on its feet. Rosenberg and the other visitor discussed what was a common topic in DAP circles in those early days—the insidious effects of Bolshevism. By most accounts, Rosenberg wasn't overly impressed by the other visitor that day. Over the course of the next few years, however, Rosenberg's feelings about Adolph Hitler would change quite a bit.[7]

In February 1920 the German Workers Party added the words "National Socialist" to the beginning of its name, officially becoming the Nationalsozialistische Deutsche Arbeiterpartei (NSDAP)—or, in shortened anglicized form, the Nazi Party. It had only a few dozen members at the beginning, but in a postwar Germany searching for strength and direction, its membership grew quickly—to six thousand in 1922, and twenty thousand in 1923.[8] Early on Hitler distinguished himself as its most effective orator. Traveling the country to address increasingly large audiences, Hitler described Jews both as miserable parasites and, conversely, as sinister, conspiratorial enemies of the German nation. He called for a vast expansion of German territory. Germany, he argued, needed *"Lebensraum"*—literally, "living room," or space to grow. With such an expanded territorial reach, the superior German race could displace other inferior groups, and Germany could end the overcrowding wrought by the borders imposed on it after World War I.

As a speechmaker, Hitler was able to tweak his facial expressions, gestures, and vocal timbre in ways that stirred his audiences to hysterics, and when his speeches concluded, listeners were often left with tears streaming down their faces, chanting, *"Sieg heil, sieg heil, sieg heil."* The attention these speeches drew extended far beyond the podiums from which Hitler spoke. Increasingly party members looked to him as the heart and soul of the party. It was Hitler who engineered the change of the party's name; it was Hitler who designed the swastika as the party's symbol; and it was Hitler who, on February 24, 1920, proclaimed the party's twenty-five-point platform. Hitler organized a group of party members into a brown-shirted paramilitary organization—the Sturmabteilung, or SA—to provide security at rallies and, later, to harass party opponents and intimidate German Jews. Increasingly, the identity of the Nazi Party and the person of Adolph Hitler were becoming one and the same.

Among the mesmerized was Alfred Rosenberg. When Hitler officially took over as party leader in 1921, he appointed Dietrich Eckart as editor of its newspaper, *Völkischer Beobachter* (People's Observer), with Rosenberg as the assistant editor. Two years later Rosenberg replaced his aging mentor Eckart at the helm. Hitler didn't agree with everything Rosenberg said during those early years, but in general he found Rosenberg's insights and abilities impressive. "Get on good terms with him," Hitler suggested to a young Nazi in 1922. "He is the only man I always listen to. He is a thinker. His large conception of foreign policy will interest you."[9]

In February 1923, one month before Rosenberg became chief editor, the weekly *Völkischer Beobachter* changed to a daily paper. Rosenberg knew that the paper's new publishing schedule would demand that he step up its operations. One day shortly after he was hired, he and Hitler went out on a shopping expedition to buy desks and chairs for the paper's expanding office. Shopping with Adolph Hitler! It was an experience Rosenberg would never forget.

One of Rosenberg's most important contributions to the Nazi enterprise was the veneer of scholarship that he spread over the party's racist ideology. Unlike most other second-level Nazi officials—and indeed unlike Hitler himself—Rosenberg had received an advanced education. As a result he could not only spout bigoted rhetoric along with everyone else, but he could quote Nietzsche and Kant as he did so, making his vitriol sound almost scholarly to countless educated and uneducated listeners alike. Rosenberg was conversant in European history; he had read Marxist literature forward and backward; he had even studied Catholic doctrine, the Talmud, and other classical Jewish texts. During the second half of the 1920s, Alfred Rosenberg became the Nazi's go-to guy on ideology and philosophy.

Sometime back in 1917 or 1918 Rosenberg had recorded some thoughts as to why it was no longer possible to build Gothic-style buildings in the twentieth century. Years later Rosenberg wove that passage and many others into his most massive literary opus—one with a massive literary title: *Der Mythus des zwanzigsten Jahrhunderts: Eine Wertung der seelischgeistigen Gestaltenkämpfe unserer Zeit* (*The Myth of the Twentieth Century: An Evaluation of the Formative Spiritual-Intellectual Struggles of Our Time*). Completed in 1929 and published in 1930, *The Mythus* gives full, in-depth, and often utterly incomprehensible expression to its author's view of racial and cultural history. Rosenberg claimed that it was not a political tract, not a work of science, and not a systematic philosophy. Instead, he claimed, it was a work of literary and artistic analysis. The claim was disingenuous of course. The first two-thirds of the seven-hundred-page book are devoted to his convoluted theories of world history and Germanic art. The remainder of the book describes how these historical and aesthetic trends will contribute to the rise of "the coming Reich," the Reich's religious and educational responsibilities, and its role in international affairs.[10] The work, as we'd expect, is vehemently antisemitic. Anti-Catholic too. And anti-Masonic. And also anti-Marxist. And while we're at it, anti-astrologist. In fact Rosenberg viewed just about any minority group or fraternal organization he could find as part of the sinister plot against German blood and honor.

When Rosenberg completed the manuscript in late 1929, he immediately took it to Hitler for feedback. Then, he waited . . . and waited. Finally after six months, Rosenberg sheepishly asked Hitler whether he'd had a chance to read the manuscript. "It is a very clever book," Hitler responded. "Only I ask myself who is likely to read and understand such a book." Should Rosenberg suppress the work? "Not at all," Hitler said. "It is your intellectual property."[11]

So Rosenberg published it. The *Mythus* came out in late 1930, and it hit the best-seller lists almost immediately. Hitler's *Mein Kampf* had inspired Germans ever since it was first published in the mid-1920s. But although that book obviously contained a great deal of political philosophy and Nazi ideology, it was primarily autobiographical in its approach. The *Mythus*, on the other hand, was a work of scholarship. Here was a cogent statement of Nazi ideology, written by an accomplished scholar who, not incidentally, was close to the führer himself. Here was a thoughtful, well-researched treatise showing by its very heft that Nazism was far more than neatly pressed uniforms and impassioned speeches—it was an expansive philosophy worthy of academic inquiry. By 1937 there were more than half a million copies in print; by the end of the war, more than twice that. Libraries, schoolrooms, and universities all had copies. Most educated German households had the book as well. Nazi officials displayed it on their office bookshelves. In the Nazi literary market, sales of the *Mythus* were exceeded only by those of *Mein Kampf*.[12] "The book," Albert Speer wrote, "is widely regarded by the public as the standard text of Party ideology."[13] And, of course, its anti-Catholic vitriol quickly earned the *Mythus* a place on the Vatican's "Index of Prohibited Books."

The *Mythus* looked great sitting on German bookshelves, and that's exactly where most of its copies remained. Rosenberg's prose was so abstruse, his writing so dense, that most people couldn't get past its first few pages. Even Hitler, though not publicly critical of the book, is said to have described it in private as "that thing that nobody can understand."

Whether or not the *Mythus* was intelligible to its readers, it afforded Rosenberg a level of recognition in German society that he'd never enjoyed before. His timing couldn't have been better. On September

14, 1930, just around the time the *Mythus* was released, the Nazi Party achieved yet another decisive victory in Reichstag elections, and it was clear that Alfred Rosenberg, now firmly established as one of the party's fastest rising stars, would get a significant post in the new government. He was appointed as one of the party's Reichstag deputies, and for more than a decade afterward, his position in the Nazi regime moved slowly and steadily higher as if impelled by a ceaseless goose-step march.

In 1933 Rosenberg became head of the party's Office on Foreign Relations and then deputy of ideology and education. In 1934 he was promoted to the rank of *Reichsleiter* (national leader), the highest political position attainable for everyone but Hitler. The full title of his first *Reichsleiter* position was, like Rosenberg's book, classically Nazi in verbosity, multi-syllabism, and tone: *Reichsleiter* for the Office for Supervision of the Total Intellectual Schooling of the Nazi Party. On July 17, 1941, less than a month after Germany invaded Russia and almost a year into its sweep through eastern Europe, Hitler appointed Rosenberg Reich minister for the Occupied Eastern Territories, a position of enormous military and political power.

Even with the notoriety Rosenberg achieved when he published the *Mythus* in 1930, he still hadn't gotten much recognition for his work in scholarly circles. Rosenberg was, however, a master administrator, and his successes in establishing Nazi academic institutions soon won over many of the Reich's professors. When Rosenberg took his position at the helm of Total Intellectual Schooling of the Nazi Party, he immediately got the operation into shape. He divided it into six departments and gave each section a clear mission and a clear chain of command. Meanwhile the age-old culture of German higher learning disintegrated along with the rest of Weimar Germany under Hitler's growing power. Professors who had once been secure in their academic appointments now had to demonstrate Nazi allegiance in order to keep their positions. Newly graduated PhDs sought positions not on traditional university faculties, but rather within the Nazi political machine. One by one, a cadre of German scholars made their way to Rosenberg. And Rosenberg welcomed them with enthusiasm, throwing them well-paying jobs and promising promotions and opportunities for scholarly recognition as if such kudos were trinkets at a highly regimented Mardi Gras parade.[14]

During the late 1930s, as each rousing speech and each heroic poster rendered Nazi national hopes more vivid, a dream began taking shape in Hitler's imagination. He envisioned an academy that would demonstrate the great achievements of German intellect and culture. The world would stand in awe of this great institution of learning. As an international center of National Socialist research and teaching, it would be massive in its scope. Beautiful too. Perhaps he could build it in Chiemsee, Hitler thought—a beautiful, lakeside Bavarian town in the foothills of the Alps. Architect Hermann Geisler was selected to design the Nazi mega-school, and the plans he developed for what would be known as the Hohe Schule der NSDAP—literally, the High Institute of the Nazi Party—featured a building with a half-kilometer façade and a tower 120 meters high.

Hitler's dream of a gargantuan academic center was part of a larger and growing emphasis throughout the Nazi regime on intellectual and scientific study, and once Hitler rose to power in 1933, the interest continued to coalesce. Eventually it became clear that one goal of this developing academic impulse was to provide scientific justification for the Nazis' racism and antisemitism. The world, many German leaders felt, just didn't get it—they were blind to the essential truths of German racial superiority and the insidiousness and destructive power of the Jewish threat. Eventually there was talk of formalizing the study of Jews and Judaism to explain these truths to the astonishingly naïve non-German world. In October 1935 a group of Nazi scholars—always eager to create new, lengthily named agencies—formed the Reichsinstitut für Geschichte des neuen Deutschlands (Reich Institute for the History of the New Germany). Its director was Walter Frank, a historian who had earned his PhD in 1927 with a dissertation about Adolf Stöcker, a leading late nineteenth- and early twentieth-century antisemitic theorist.

Not to be outdone in the creation of multisyllabic organizations, the Reichsinstitut soon created the Forschungsabteilung Judenfrage (Research Department for the Jewish Question). At its grand-opening gala in Munich on November 16, 1936, one of the speakers was Frank's mentor, longtime antisemitic historian and president of the Bavarian Academy of Sciences Karl Alexander von Müller. During his talk, von Müller gave what was perhaps the first official hint of the coming Nazi pillage of Jewish books. Academic study, he argued, can forge an indispensable weapon for the German nation to employ in its struggle for power. "Owing to the support of the Movement and the State," von Müller declared, "[we are going] to call into being here in the immediate vicinity of the State Library and its treasures which are irreplaceable—also for our work and through a large complementary professional library of our own—a unique scientific library for the [Jewish] question."[15] Von Müller didn't specify how his proposed "scientific library" would obtain its books. For his audience that day, he didn't really need to.

Leading the Research Department was Dr. Wilhelm Grau, who had received his PhD in 1933 with a dissertation on the history of antisemitism. Grau was not only a historian but also an energetic and talented administrator. In a 1936 speech to the Association of German Historical Societies, he described his vision for the department and, in the process, took von Müller's inaugural call for a Nazi Jewish library to its logical conclusion. He explained to his audience that for the department to fulfill its mission, Nazi policy would need to take at least two steps to support the effort: First, the Jewish materials in the Frankfort Municipal Library (Stadtbibliothek) would need to be "designated for a specifically German end," and second, "German archival officials . . . shall be no conservative natures that faithfully preserve intact what has been placed into their hands but they must be conquerors who daringly take hold of what their archives do not possess but should possess."[16] Translation: Germans will need to confiscate Jewish archives.

As all of this unfolded, Rosenberg stayed in the background, watching with growing concern as these new academic institutions grew in stature and threatened to undermine his position as Hitler's "ideologue-in-chief." Seeing Geisler's model for Hitler's Hohe Schule, however, he wondered whether an opportunity might be presenting itself. With Hitler in an institute-building mindset, with German universities opening dozens of new courses on Judaism, and now with these new formalized efforts for the Nazis to study "the Jewish Question," Rosenberg realized that this might very well be his moment. Maybe now was the time when he could finally step ahead of the other scholars and help the führer realize his Hohe Schule dream after all.

To test the waters, Rosenberg appealed to Hitler for authorization to begin putting plans in place for the creation—finally—of the Hohe Schule. The looming war meant that actually constructing the campus would be cost prohibitive for the moment, but at least he could begin setting up the Hohe Schule's organizational infrastructure and construction plans. That way, after the war, the Third Reich would be able to hit the ground running and get it built.

On January 29, 1940, Rosenberg got his authorization in the form of an official statement from the führer: "The Hohe Schule is some day to become the center for National Socialist doctrinal research and education. . . . I order that Reichsleiter Alfred Rosenberg continue [his] preparatory work, especially in the field of research and the establishment of a library. The offices of the Party and the State organizations are required to support his work in every way."[17] Rosenberg, it seemed, had succeeded in stepping over the Reichsinstitut and regaining his place atop the Nazi academic ladder.

His assignment was to go ahead and create the Hohe Schule but to do the work more deliberately and realistically than his pie-in-the-sky predecessors. It was to consist of ten branches, each affiliated with an existing academic institution. Each branch would have its own facilities, its own faculty, and its own support staff. Additionally, of course, each branch would have a library.[18]

## Rosenberg's Looting Begins

Rosenberg's authorization to create the Hohe Schule barely raised an eyebrow at first. In just over a month hostilities would begin, and the nation—in particular the Nazi administration—was already caught up in a frenzied war fever. Nevertheless Rosenberg proceeded with his plans. The first of the ten institutes, he decided, would be the Institut der NSDAP zur Erforschung der Judenfrage (Nazi Institute for Research into the Jewish Question, IEJ). For some time, Nazi officials and academicians had been eyeing the Judaica collection at the Municipal Library of Frankfurt. The collection, estimated to consist of 350,000 volumes, was the largest Jewish library in the world; many of its holdings had been donated by the Rothschild family. Certainly, the thinking went, that library would need to be "nationalized" so that the Reich could get its hands on the priceless treasures. The only question was where the collection should go, and various Nazi agencies hovered like vultures, waiting for the authorization to pounce.

The destiny of the Frankfurt collection quickly became clear—it was headed for the Hohe Schule's IEJ. And since the IEJ was going to get such a huge library, it also became clear that Frankfurt was the most sensible place for the institute to set up shop. As the excitement over the new effort grew, the players soon ignored the fact that they were supposed to still be in the planning stage. To house its operation, the IEJ was given a double house in Frankfurt at Bockenheimer Landstrasse 68–70.[19]

It took Rosenberg almost two years of planning, but finally on March 26, 1941, Nazi leaders from throughout the country gathered in Frankfurt for the official three-day inaugural conference of the IEJ. The attendance roster was a who's who of early 1940s Germany—government officials, military officers, university rectors, and foreign envoys all came to the dedication. In fact, so grand was the celebration that the classrooms and library stacks of the Bockenheimer Landstrasse facility would not accommodate such an affair as this, so the festivities took place in the Bürgersaal,

14. The meeting hall at the Bürgersaal in the Frankfurt city hall, venue of the opening ceremonies of Rosenberg's Institute for Jewish Research. Courtesy YIVO Institute.

a large assembly room in the Frankfurt city hall. As the dignitaries gathered, they saw crystal chandeliers hanging from the high vaulted ceiling above them. The walls were fronted with rich wooden pillars, above which were large paintings showing key events in German history. And for this particular occasion the room was festooned with Nazi banners as well.

For Rosenberg it was a day of triumph. He stepped to the podium for his keynote—a speech that, like the *Mythus*, was likely received with far more awe than understanding. When he finished, the crowd broke into thunderous applause. In his closing speech at the end of the conference, Rosenberg reminded his audience of the Jewish peril. Referring to a family whose assets he'd already targeted, he described the previous twelve months as "a decisive year in which the troops of the Rothschild republic were beaten." Later continuing to develop the same theme, he continued:

In this housecleaning of ours, Mr. Roosevelt, with his Baruchs and his film-Jews, too, will be unable to interfere . . . and the strongest military instrument that history has ever known, the Wehrmacht of Adolf Hitler, will see to it that this last furious attempt once more to put the white race on the march against Europe for the sake of Jewish-finance domination is terminated forever.[20]

Still, there remained the question as to how IEJ was going to fill the shelves of its library. The Frankfurt material was a great start, but it wasn't enough. Rosenberg bought a library here and a few books there, but for several months after Hitler's January 1940 authorization, the deluge of Jewish books he had hoped would soon flow to the IEJ remained only a trickle. Rosenberg wanted more. Much more.

The floodgates were soon to open. In May 1940 Nazi forces invaded France, conquering the country after a vicious six-week battle. When the fighting ended, Rosenberg's staffers throughout the country—particularly in Paris—reported finding many significant libraries and archives that Jews and other enemy groups had abandoned during the hostilities. It was another golden opportunity for Rosenberg. On June 18 he wrote to Hitler's secretary, Martin Bormann, informing him that a great trove of material was ripe for the picking and hinting that he might be interested in getting the führer's permission to confiscate the country's abandoned cultural property. On July 1 he made the request directly, asking for Hitler's authorization to create a task force charged with conducting "a thorough examination of items left behind by Jews and Freemasons that would provide a basis for future intellectual study, as considered necessary for the political, ideological, and academic operations of both the NSDAP and the Hohe Schule."[21] Later he recalled the request in common Nazi doublespeak: "I made the suggestion," he said, "to send somebody there to examine the materials, and also to do some research on them."[22] In late June or early July, Rosenberg received authorization from Hitler to create what was to be known as the Einsatzstab Reichsleiter Rosenberg (ERR)—the Reichsleiter Rosenberg Task Force.

The former newspaper editor now found himself at the head of a major research agency charged with fulfilling one of Hitler's greatest dreams—creating an institution that would serve as a beacon to the world of Nazi greatness and achievement, and to play an essential role in the Third Reich's overall efforts to eliminate Jews and Judaism from the world. His more public title was minister of the Occupied Eastern Territories, and opening the IEJ on the eve of the Nazi invasion of Russia meant that the region under his command was about to extend its eastward reach to include vast territories and millions of Jews.

## Heinrich Himmler and the RSHA

For all of its brutality and violence, the Rosenberg Task Force was, at least on paper, a cultural organization. Although its members wore military uniforms, traveled in army vehicles, and operated under the imprimatur of a man with vast martial authority, its mission was ultimately just gathering material for the Hohe Schule library. The ERR may have looked military, but it operated as part of the Nazi *Party*, not part of the Nazi *army*.

Effectively, the ERR's status as a party entity pushed it to the edges of the Nazi organizational chart. Yes, the ERR was a powerful organization, and it regularly employed its authority with cold, cruel efficiency. Yes, the ERR received great support from the Nazi regime, for its activities reflected and realized Nazi Germany's racist worldview. But as the 1930s progressed, Germany became an increasingly militarized country. Millions of German men donned crisp Nazi uniforms, military music echoed through the streets, the nation galvanized its will and resources for the war everyone knew was coming. In such an atmosphere, it was the army that counted most of all. As much as they may have wanted to be soldiers, the members of Rosenberg's ERR were really just uniformed library procurers. Later, during the war, it was the army that attacked; the

ERR moved in afterward. It was the army that decided where to invade, and the ERR had to operate within the parameters of those decisions. It was the army that took the land and vanquished its opponents; the ERR just got the books and archives.

Nevertheless even though the ERR was relegated to the sidelines, book looting wasn't. Rosenberg and his minions, you see, were far from the only Nazis pillaging Jewish literary material. Rosenberg's ERR had competitors in the business of book looting, some of whom operated at the very center of the Nazi military machine.

The most prominent competitor was the Reichssicherheitshauptamt (Reich Security Main Office, RSHA), an umbrella organization of Nazi agencies brought together into a single national police force by Heinrich Himmler in 1939. Unlike the ERR, the RSHA was composed of agencies from both the Nazi Party and the Nazi army, and its goals were therefore both ideological and military. Unlike other army organizations, the RSHA was not part of the normal command structure of the Nazi army; it was accountable only to Heinrich Himmler, a powerful Nazi military commander and a member of Hitler's innermost circle. Over time the RSHA grew in stature and its areas of activity expanded enormously. Under the aegis of its various organizations, the RSHA provided personal security for Hitler and other top-ranking Nazi officials, it conducted innumerable "counterintelligence" operations against individuals and groups deemed enemies of the Reich, and most horrifically, it oversaw the Nazis' death camps and the murder of millions.

And, as it happens, the RSHA also stole a lot of books.

Heinrich Himmler certainly didn't look like one of the most brutal mass murderers in history. Bespectacled, five-foot-nine, with a high fore-head and the beginnings of a double chin, Himmler looked more like a middle-school math teacher than a killer. From 1919 to 1922, Himmler studied agronomy in Munich, where he met Ernst Röhm, an early member of the Nazi Party and one of the founders of the SA—Hitler's

"Brownshirts." When Röhm invited him to become a member of an antisemitic organization called the Reichskriegsflagge (Imperial War Flag), Himmler joined right up.

Enthralled by the Germanic mythology and fiery rituals, Himmler joined the Nazi Party in 1923 and became a member of Röhm's SA. He participated and was arrested in Hitler's failed Beer Hall Putsch in November of that year. Although he was soon released from jail, his participation was enough to get him fired from his agronomist job and turn him into a full-time Nazi operative. He jumped into his new work with gusto, serving as a party secretary, propaganda assistant, event coordinator, pamphlet distributer, and speaker on behalf of the cause. In 1925 Himmler joined the SS. Gaining Hitler's trust, he was appointed deputy commander of the SS in 1927. Two years later, Hitler chose this rising Nazi star to command the SS.

There were 290 members in the SS when Himmler first took the helm; within a year he had increased that number to 1,000, and the exponential ascent continued apace: 52,000 in 1932, 250,000 when the war began, and about 1,250,000 when it ended.

During the 1930s the chaotic, labyrinthine, and increasingly despotic web of Nazi law enforcement agencies wove its tentacles almost unfettered into the fabric of German society. The English term "police state" made its way into common English usage during this decade. The expression, not surprisingly, was originally taken from a mid-nineteenth-century German phrase meaning the same thing.[23]

As the decade's second half began, the entire, massively growing police structure of the Third Reich had come under the command of Himmler and his assistant Reinhard Heydrich, a superefficient, blond-haired, blue-eyed former naval officer who typified the Himmler-led SS. With the Nazi police state aggressively extending its reach, Himmler and Heydrich found themselves commanding a vast, unwieldy maze of police organizations with overlapping job descriptions and fiercely competitive supervisors. Heydrich spent the spring and early summer of 1939 stewing about how he might tame the unruly beast. Finally on July 5, surely with Himmler's blessing, he issued an order to the heads of the Security Police and the Sicherheitsdienst (SD), the security service of the SS: "In order to achieve a uniform amalgamation of the Security Police and the Security Service, the Main Office Security Police will be transformed into the Reich Security Main Office under my direction."[24] Effectively, Heydrich had outlined a plan under which he—working at Himmler's behest—would direct an organization with almost unlimited policing powers.

## The RSHA's Dr. Six and Office VII

When World War II began two months later with Germany's invasion of Poland, both personnel and financial resources were diverted to the war effort, but Heydrich and Himmler were undeterred. On September 27, 1939, Himmler issued an order turning Heydrich's plan into reality, creating the RSHA. Despite the fact that the outbreak of war left little manpower and money available for anything other than the military, Heydrich got the RSHA up and running in short order. He moved the RSHA into the Gestapo headquarters in Berlin, eventually expanding the office complex to include the nearby Prinz Albrecht Palais, a grand seventeenth-century palace.

Officially the RSHA's responsibilities included intelligence gathering, crime fighting, propaganda, observing foreigners, and monitoring public opinion. More generally, however, the officers of the RSHA understood its mission in political and ideological terms: To maintain the racial purity of the German nation, to eliminate its enemies, and to fulfill—unfailingly and unflinchingly—the will of the führer.[25] The RSHA was part of Germany's security apparatus, but it was not assigned to protect the *state*, nor even to protect German *people* per se. Rather, the RSHA strove to defend *the* German people, the *Volk*, as an ethnic and racial entity.

As the RSHA got its feet on the ground and its huge administrative apparatus began to thrum with activity, the implications of its growing power became clear. Its intelligence gatherers embarked on a systematic campaign to gain information on every enemy group and individual it could identify. Its officers harassed Jews, political dissidents, and other groups. The SS and other RSHA police agencies arrested many leaders of these groups, and as the war progressed, the SS created *Einsatzgruppen*, action groups, to slaughter Jewish and other "enemy" residents of newly conquered communities. As the war progressed, Heydrich turned to Office IV of the RSHA, "Investigating and Combating Opponents," to implement a "final solution to the Jewish problem." Under the leadership of a Heydrich subordinate named Adolf Eichmann, the RSHA rounded up, ghettoized, and gassed millions of Jews in a genocidal campaign of unprecedented proportions and indescribable horror.

Part of the early flurry of activity came out of Office VII, "Ideological Research and Evaluation." This was the academic branch of the RSHA, the department that would bridge the administrative work of the agency—not to mention its oppressive police and intelligence-gathering operations—with the world of academia and modern science. It would not only research the historical and ideological background of the Nazis' enemies, but it would also provide background information to support prosecutions of individuals accused of crime and subversion.

To manage Office VII, Heydrich chose a man named Dr. Six, Franz Alfred Six, who, though only thirty years old, seems to have been made for the job. Six had studied sociology and political science at Heidelberg University, where he received a doctorate in 1934. His thesis, "Die Presse der nationalen Minderheiten im Deutschen Reich," described what the Nazi party could learn from its methods during the 1933 elections. In 1935 Six joined the SS and began working for the elite SD security service. There he joined other scholars in giving scientific "cover" to Nazi activities and, more fundamentally, in defining the role that scholarship would play in the life of Nazi Germany. Scholarship was important in the Third Reich of course, but not for advancing and defining German policy and practice. Instead, the "fundamental principle of science" was the German state itself. Scientific research and inquiry were always—*always*—to be subordinate to the state, not the other way around.[26]

Shortly after joining the SD, Six took a full-time position at its head-quarters. He was assigned to the SD's Press Office, where he projected German totalitarian ideas from Berlin out to every region of the country. He trained SD staff to submit reports on *all* printed literature released *anywhere* in the country; nothing was to be published without being duly noted in the SD's files. He also created archives on all "enemy" groups, first to create profiles and deeper understanding of them and later for the more "practical" purposes, such as helping equip the Gestapo with information to aid their campaigns of arrest, deportation, and ultimately murder.

Throughout his rise, Six maintained his academic affiliations. After receiving his PhD, he received a position as a lecturer in journalism at the University of Heidelberg and in 1938 became a professor at Königs-berg University. When he moved to the capital in 1939 to work for the SD, he took a position at the University of Berlin, where he established an Institute for Foreign Studies, the better to gather information about countries soon to be conquered by the Third Reich.[27] His growing stature within the Reich enabled him to hire his own staff, denounce his enemies into administrative oblivion, and pave the way for his rise in the regime.

Franz Alfred Six considered his work at the RSHA to be a crucial element of Nazi ideological warfare. All subversive groups, he argued, were allied in a vast conspiracy to undermine the Reich, and lurking behind the entire cabal was Germany's true enemy: the Jew. Obviously the Jew needed to be eliminated along with all of his other co-conspirators. Doing so would demand full knowledge of the Jewish menace—its history, its philosophy, and enormous libraries documenting its present-day institutions and individuals. As an expert in journalism, as an accomplished scholar of culture, and with his expertise navigating the maze of Nazi bureaucracy, nobody was better equipped to take on the job.

So, Dr. Six got to work.[28] By the time Six took his position with the

RSHA, the organization had already accumulated a large number of Jewish books—130 tons that it had "secured" as soon as the Nazis took power, and another 300,000 or so volumes that it had looted during Kristallnacht. That September, it would get many more volumes after the Nazi army conquered Poland. Seeing these literary riches, Franz Alfred Six set about creating the RSHA library to prove the Nazi contention regarding the existence of an international Jewish conspiracy once and for all. He ordered all the books shipped to Berlin, hired a group of librarians and a staff of SS workers to begin the massive task of sorting through the books and organizing them into a usable library, and he brought in a team of scholars to join him in studying it. His resources were almost limitless; most of the costs of his operation were covered by Adolf Eichmann's illegal slush fund of money confiscated from Jewish deportees. "In other words," historian Dov Schidorsky has observed, "the library's expenses were covered by its victims' own money."[29]

For Franz Alfred Six, this was a golden opportunity to prove what he had been arguing all along. He dove into the books and surfaced with reams of maps and diagrams "proving" the existence of the Jewish/Bolshevik/Catholic/Nazi-enemies-of-all-kinds conspiracy to rule the world. At first Six couldn't conscript any Jewish laborers to staff the library. Such workers were available to him of course, but RSHA personnel argued that the SS staffers would refuse to work with Jewish crews. Finally, however, in 1941 the work involved in maintaining the enormous collection outgrew RSHA resources; they had plenty of manpower but not enough people with the Jewish knowledge to sort through the books.

A scholar named Ernst Grumach was selected to head a team of eight other Jewish librarians and scientists to work at the RSHA's Berlin library facility. The team, which would later grow in size to twenty-four workers, was assigned not only to identify and sort the books, but also with the far more grueling tasks of packing them, loading them into trucks, cleaning the facility, repairing bomb damage, and much more. They worked fourteen to sixteen hours a day, always under the constant harassment of their Nazi overseers. Grumach worked tirelessly to keep the names of his crew off the deportation lists. Alas, it was to no avail. In the end, only Grumach himself and another worker named Berthold Breslauer—both of whom were married to non-Jewish women—survived the Holocaust.[30]

Franz Alfred Six was, in many ways, a Nazi from central casting. Self-assured and boastful, a tyrant with his staff, and obsequious with his superiors, Six's overall book-looting agenda was largely and tragically successful. The material he gathered provided the Gestapo with information about Jewish communities, biographies, and other invaluable tools that helped them carry out their plan to murder Europe's Jews. More fundamentally Six's work created a sense of intellectual credibility and a veneer of scholarly achievement for the RSHA and other Nazi organizations.

Alfred Rosenberg. Heinrich Himmler. Franz Alfred Six. These were the three Nazis, with their academic credentials, bookish habits, and attraction to "scholarship," who, operating through a pair of powerful Nazi Party organizations, the ERR and RSHA, conducted the largest, most ambitious book-looting operation in human history—one designed to plunder a continent.

After the guns of war had fallen silent and the stolen books of Europe's Jews lay horizontal in massive jumbled piles throughout Europe, Col. Robert G. Storey, American prosecutor at the Nuremberg war trials, described these literary materials and the plight they were about to encounter when the war began: "Envision Europe as a treasure-house in which is stored the major portion of the artistic and literary products of two thousand years of Western civilization. . . . Further . . . envision the forcing of this treasure-house by a horde of vandals bent on systematically removing to the Reich these treasures."[31] It was an apt description. After herculean administrative feats and years of preparation, the Nazi removal of these treasures had begun.

# 5
## *Pillage*

We were scared. We thought they had come to take us away. . . .
But the Germans just took all the books . . . and left.
—*Avraham Negrin, president of the Jewish community of*
*Larissa, Greece, on events of July 1942*

Many of the texts that the RSHA and the ERR, Alfred Rosenberg's task
force, looted from Europe had been created in distant lands, in ages long
past. The provenances of some involved great tales of adventure and
survival even before the books fell into the hands of Nazi henchmen.
One manuscript in particular was a medieval Egyptian edition of a text
that had first been composed in the second century BCE. The manuscript had spent many centuries in a *genizah*, a dark, attic-like room in
Cairo, heaped together with thousands of other texts and fragmentary
documents, before making its way to France and eventually into the
ERR piles of plunder. For most of that time scholars knew that the text
it contained had once existed, but nobody had seen it for centuries.

What saved the text, and indeed what allowed it to reappear after it
had been lost almost one thousand years earlier, was the great value that
Judaism sees in the written word. As explained in chapter 1, Jewish law
considers written texts so sacred that it forbids the disposal of them,
insisting that they be "interred" in a *genizah*, instead of thrown away.

On May 13, 1896, Rabbi Solomon Schechter, then the only Jewish faculty member at Cambridge University, was running errands in downtown
Cambridge when he ran into his good friend Mrs. Agnes Lewis. Mrs.

Lewis told him that she and her sister, Mrs. Margaret Dunlop Gibson, had just returned from a trip to the Middle East, where they had purchased some old Jewish manuscripts. Accomplished amateur scholars versed in Hebrew, Arabic, Greek, Syriac, and many other languages, the sisters had been able to identify most, but not all, of the old documents. Would Rabbi Schechter be interested in coming over to help?

Of course he would! Schechter headed straightaway to Castlebrae, the Gibson-Lewis mansion, where he sat with the sisters at their dining room table and began paging through the ragged bundle of papers. Some of the manuscripts represented rare versions of the Jerusalem Talmud and were quite valuable. The collection seemed to have come from Fustat, the oldest neighborhood of Cairo. Schechter had heard rumors of a sizable *genizah* there; in all likelihood, that was where the sisters' dealer (or the dealer's supplier) had gotten the documents. Then Schechter came to another manuscript, and his heart skipped a beat. It was a tattered page with two partly faded columns of Hebrew writing. Schechter suspected—and later confirmed—that the manuscript was a page from the original Hebrew of the book of Ben Sirah, also called Ecclesiasticus.

It was an astounding discovery. Ben Sirah is an ancient book of Wisdom Literature (similar in some ways to the biblical book of Proverbs) that for a variety of reasons hadn't made the cut into the Hebrew Bible; Protestant Scripture left it out as well. By the early Middle Ages, however, Catholic scholars such as Saint Augustine had identified passages in the work that resonated with Catholic theology and included it in their Bibles. The version they included, however, was based on later Greek translations of the work. The original Hebrew had last been seen by the Babylonian sage Saadia Gaon, whom we met in chapter 1, and Saadia Gaon had died in the year 952. Since then the original Hebrew of Ben Sirah had been lost to history. Or so everyone thought.

After Schechter and the sisters announced their find, librarians around Europe dove into their own piles of old Jewish manuscripts in search of

Ben Sirah. Within a few weeks, librarians at Oxford's Bodleian Library announced that they had identified several additional Ben Sirah manuscript pages, some of which came from the very same copy as the one that Schechter had identified at the home of Mrs. Gibson and Mrs. Lewis.

Schechter traced the manuscript to the *genizah* at the Ben Ezra Synagogue in Cairo, Egypt. A few collectors and manuscript dealers had already discovered the trove, and a handful of its contents had hit the manuscript market—Schechter himself may have even seen a few of them. For the most part, however, nobody had paid it any attention. Now Schechter paid attention. As soon as he could, Schechter traveled to Cairo and secured permission to enter the *genizah*. There, to his astonishment, he found a pile of almost three hundred thousand ancient and medieval manuscripts. It was a discovery of literary treasure unparalleled in scope and magnitude before or since.

Schechter packed up almost two hundred thousand of the manuscripts to take back to Cambridge for further study, where he hired a team of scholars and assistants to help him sort through the material. The additional staffing not only allowed more manuscripts to come to light, it also allowed Schechter to search through the crates for manuscripts that were of particular interest to him. In short order, he too found several more pages of Ben Sirah.

Although Schechter had removed a massive amount of material from the *genizah*, he left behind some one hundred thousand manuscripts that didn't interest him. Other collectors and dealers descended on the synagogue, hauling off the last of the Cairo Genizah's contents by 1911. Among the manuscripts that Schechter left behind were still more pages of Ben Sirah in its original Hebrew.[1]

One of those pages made its way into the hands of Baron Edmond James de Rothschild. Unlike other members of his prominent banking family, Edmond de Rothschild was far more into collecting and philanthropy than he was into business. He was an ardent supporter of Zionism, he had an astounding collection of art, and his library—particularly his collection of Judaica—was second to none. Among its many treasures were fifteen hundred manuscripts from the Cairo Genizah, one of which was our page from Ben Sirah.[2] Rothschild donated a significant portion of his Judaic library to the Alliance Israélite Universelle, a Paris-based organization devoted to protecting Jewish communities around the world and to promoting Jewish education. When World War II began, the Alliance's library consisted of fifty thousand volumes (of which twenty were incunabula) and about eighteen hundred manuscripts, including that trove from the Cairo Genizah.

On August 7, 1940, barely a month after Germany conquered France, agents of the ERR entered the eight-story library of the Alliance Israélite Universelle and got to work packing up its precious collection. They cleared the shelves and placed what they grabbed into fourteen hundred book crates; they found and removed a secret safe containing three hundred manuscripts of different kinds, and they also looted the Cairo Genizah manuscripts.

A new, dark chapter in the epic story of the Ben Sirah manuscript had begun. Inscribed in the Middle East many centuries earlier, in time it became faded and tattered, and eventually it was placed in the Cairo Genizah chamber with thousands of other Jewish documents. There it remained until the late nineteenth century, when a collector or dealer removed it and the manuscript eventually found its way to an ornate Parisian palace belonging to the wealthiest Jewish family in the world. Later it was donated to the library of one of the world's leading Jewish organizations. And now the Nazis had it.

In the summer of 1940 France opened like a treasure chest before Alfred Rosenberg's eyes. As we saw earlier, the Nazi campaign against Jewish books had begun even before Hitler's rise to power in 1933, exploded in a spate of book burnings immediately afterward, and then exploded again as part of the violence of Kristallnacht in November 1938. But in a civilized country like Germany, campaigns of rapacious pillage and genocidal murder must grow slowly. Confiscating a collection here and impounding a library there might have been okay before the war, but now the fate of Europe's Jewish literary collections would be decided by men like Rosenberg—men whose goal was nothing less than acquiring *all* of Europe's Jewish books. How was Rosenberg to get his hands on them? For an answer to that question, he would have to wait.

Alfred Rosenberg's hands were particularly tied in Germany itself; his authorization to claim Jewish books was limited to the occupied territories, which meant that he couldn't loot the material within the Reich's borders. For the time being he'd have to content himself with book-rich France and elsewhere. On May 10, 1940, Germany invaded France, defeating its army by late June. At the time France was home to about 350,000 Jews.[3] Now, with Germany in control, its large Jewish communal and organizational libraries were Rosenberg's for the taking. Furthermore Jews throughout the country were fleeing their homes or going into hiding, and more often than not, they left their books behind. Finders, keepers. And as an added benefit, the Freemasons were also laying low, and Rosenberg was convinced that they and other ostensibly innocent organizations were actually part of the Jewish-Bolshevik conspiracy bent on destroying the Aryan race. Rosenberg spent the summer getting his ERR machine up and running. He appointed Baron Kurt von Baer as head of the ERR's operations in Paris, and soon the ERR established a French national headquarters and four regional offices in the city. With the help of the Gestapo and other police organizations, Rosenberg and his men branched out from there. They spread through the country in search of artwork, books, archives, and other cultural treasures. Using information gleaned from police address lists, storage inventories, and documents of French shipping companies, they searched castles, warehouses, farms, and private homes—anyplace where they might find some of the precious loot they sought.

Despite their totalitarian approach, Nazi civilian and military leaders needed to maintain at least a pretense of legality as they went about their pillaging. Often such legal cover came easily. For example, Nazi policy deemed all "abandoned" property to be the property of the state and thus fair game for Rosenberg and his task force. As a result the chateau of a Jewish resident of Bordeaux who fled to the United States for safety, or the home of a Parisian Jew who had been arrested on his daily errands, or the offices of a small Lyon business whose Jewish owner had gone into hiding were all legally deemed state property, as were the items within these places, giving Rosenberg and other Nazi looters free rein to take what they wanted.

It was a magnificent banquet of riches, and the ERR sidled up to the table and heaped its plate high. Along with 50,000 volumes from the Alliance Israélite Universelle, they plundered 10,000 from the city's prominent rabbinic seminary, L'Ecole Rabbinique. The ERR took 4,000 volumes from an umbrella group, the Fédération des Sociétés Juives de France (Federation of Jewish Societies of France), 20,000 from the Lipschuetz Bookstore, and another 28,000 from the private collection of the Rothschild family. Later sweeps of the city's private homes in the city yielded thousands more books, enough to fill 482 crates.[4]

The ERR pillagers also helped themselves to a priceless haul at the Chateau de Beaumesnil, in Normandy. The seventeenth-century baroque edifice, surrounded by well-groomed walkways, manicured gardens, and a moat, was home to Hans Furstenberg, a wealthy Jewish banker and bibliophile. Not only did the palace house Furstenberg's 16,000-volume library of priceless first editions, incunabula, and fine bindings, but by the time of the invasion it also held material from the Bibliothèque Nationale and the Archives de France as well. The curators of those collections had asked Furstenberg to hold parts of their collections; keeping the material out of Paris, they hoped, might keep it out of Nazi hands.

It didn't work. In the fall of 1940 a crew of ERR officials drove past the Beaumesnil gardens, traversed the moat, and entered the palace.

15. Books discovered concealed in an Amsterdam synagogue.
Courtesy Yad Vashem Photo Archives.

They packed up its libraries and shipped the books to a central storage
facility. Some of the material was never recovered.[5]

As Nazi forces swarmed through France in the spring and summer of
1940, so too did they march into the Netherlands. Germany conquered
Holland's grand cities and its windmill-powered farms, and here too the
ERR swept down on the country's Jewish books. They took *millions* of
them. In Amsterdam alone the haul included 25,000 volumes from the
Bibliotheek van het Portugeesch Israelietisch Seminarium, 4,000 from
the Ashkenazic Beth ha-Midrasch Ets Haim, an unknown number of
antiquarian treasures from the private collections of Sigmund Seeligmann, and fully 100,000 from the Bibliotheca Rosenthaliana.[6]

Some of the ERR's greatest hauls were valuable not because of their
quantity, but because of the matchless nature of the collections they took.
For example, in the fall of 1940 the head of Rosenberg's operations in
the Netherlands, Oberbereichsleiter Schimmer, brought a group of ERR
soldiers to the Spinoza Society in The Hague and the Spinoza House in

Rijnsburg, and they packed the "Spinoza Library" into eighteen shipping crates. Baruch Spinoza (1632–77), widely considered to have been the father of modern Jewish thought, owned a handsome collection of 159 volumes: Aristotle, Machiavelli, Rabbinic literature, and more. When he died, a notary catalogued the 159 volumes in his library, and the collection was promptly sold at auction. Later, in 1900, a Dutch philanthropist used the old inventory to re-create the collection; he purchased identical printings of the books that appeared on the list, thus amassing a *facsimile* of the Spinoza collection. Schimmer somehow missed the "facsimile" detail and seems to have thought that the books he and his soldiers removed were the very same ones that had once belonged to the philosopher. "Not without reason," he reported, "did the director of the Societas Spinozana try, under false pretenses which we uncovered, to withhold the library from us."[7]

The books weren't Spinoza's, but they were old, and they were valuable. And now they joined millions of others in the growing pile of Nazi loot.

As the ERR machine roared up to full speed, the RSHA accelerated too. While the ERR was confined to conducting its operations outside the Reich and in the occupied territories, the RSHA was under no such limitation. As a result the RSHA—particularly Dr. Six and his Department VII—implemented an extensive book-looting campaign within German borders and beyond. More than one hundred sizable collections fell prey to the RSHA book behemoth, and probably many other smaller ones as well. They took more than two hundred thousand volumes from twenty-six different collections in Berlin, tens of thousands more from nine collections in Breslau, and thousands more from eleven libraries in Frankfurt. There were also collections from smaller communities, such as Ulm, Glogau, and Trier. In short, the RSHA's sweep through Germany denuded the nation of its Jewish books, leaving behind only a skeleton of empty bookshelves as testimony to the great literary collections that once enlivened its many Jewish communities.[8]

Many entries in the catalogues of looted work assembled after the war are both tantalizing and tragic in their vagueness. For example, one entry describes a looted collection from Mayence that contained memorial books and other precious material dating back to the late thirteenth century:

*Bibliothek der Israelitischen Religionsgemeinschaft,*
*owned by the Jewish Community.*

Valuable library with rare documents and some mss.

Outstanding is the *Nuernberger Memorbuch* [Neurenberg Memorial book]; first entry: 1296.

Included collection of Rabbi Dr. M. Lehmann.

Sources: *Menorah* (Vienna), 1927.

Siegmund Salfeld, "Das Martyrologium des Nuernberger Memorbuchs," in *Quellen zur Geschichte der Juden in Deutschland* (Berlin 1898), vol. 3.[9]

Some of the material that the ERR, RSHA, and other Nazi organizations looted during the war was later recovered; much of it was not. If their goal was to preserve Jewish cultural treasures, they failed, for much of what they collected was subsequently lost. If their goal was to destroy Jewish culture, they failed at that task too. Most of the works they sought to possess for themselves now survive in the hands of others.

## For Our Youth

For most German Jews, books were the least of their worries. Living under the specter of arrest, deportation, and death, they were usually worried far more about their basic survival than the fate of their libraries. On their way to the train stations, they often locked their front doors, leaving behind most or all of their worldly possessions—their furniture, clothing, kitchen utensils, rugs, linens, financial records, lamps, family photos, knickknacks . . . and the contents of the bookshelves lining their walls.

Wolfgang Lachmann was one of those whose books were left behind, but he hardly remembers them. He was born in Berlin in 1928 and was only five years old when the Nazis came to power. His parents, like many German Jews, were avid readers, and over the years the Lachmann family accumulated a nice collection of several hundred books. At first Wolfgang had a pretty normal middle-class German childhood—school, a dog, a bike, and summer vacations with his family. His maternal grandfather had fought for Germany during the First World War at Verdun. Lachmann's father joined the army himself just before the war ended, and after his military service concluded, he became a businessman and remained a proud and patriotic German until the day he died.

Things began to change for Wolfgang and his family in the mid-1930s. Like the other Jewish kids, when the Nazis came to power he had to drop out of his neighborhood public school and attend a school for Jewish children on the other side of town. After Kristallnacht, November 1938, things became especially difficult. "My father's business was all smeared up on the outside with 'Jewish Store' kind of a thing," he told an interviewer for the U.S. Holocaust Museum in 1992. "It was painted with big letters and people were standing outside and discouraging customers from going in."[10]

The following summer Wolfgang's mother fell ill with what turned out to be leukemia, and she died a few months later. He and his father moved to his maternal grandmother's home, whereupon his father contracted tuberculosis and died in 1941. The following January, Wolfgang's grandmother received a letter ordering her and the other residents of her home—that is, Wolfgang—to report to a local synagogue about ten days later. Each member of her family would be allowed to bring one suitcase weighing no more than thirty kilograms, about sixty-six pounds. As they prepared to leave, Wolfgang's grandmother filled out a form listing everything in the home—two armchairs, seven pillows, twelve glasses, balcony furniture, a stamp collection, and 350 books. With the exception of a French dictionary, the eight-page document did not list any details about the individual volumes in the Lachmanns' home library.[11] Later, as he and about one thousand other deportees left the synagogue to board the trucks waiting outside, the principal of Wolfgang's elementary school stood at the door handing out hard candy to everyone who passed by. To Wolfgang's surprise, the principal remembered him.

The chronology of Wolfgang's life for the next several years is one that is both tragic and sadly typical to students of the Holocaust: the Riga Ghetto, a few small concentration camps, Bergen-Belsen; starvation, loss, and despair; liberation in April 1945. Eventually he moved to the United States, changed his first name to Walter and dropped an *n* off of his last name, got married, had a family, and started a business.

In 2008 an article appeared in the German magazine *Der Spiegel* announcing that a team of librarians in Berlin had discovered that, scattered in their collections, were thousands of books that had once belonged to Jewish families who had left Berlin during the war. According to library records, Berlin's Jews had "gifted" them to the state on their departure from the city. Reading the article in Orange County, California, Rabbi Lawrence Seideman came across a detail that quickened his pulse. Immediately he picked up the phone and called a friend of his. "Walter," he asked, "who is *Wolfgang* Lachmann?"

"Why, that's me," said the voice on the other end of the line. "It was my name before I came here from Germany."

The detail that caught Seideman's eye was an account from Detlef Bockenkamm, a curator at Berlin's Central and Regional Library, describing his discovery of a Jewish children's book: "One was titled *For Our Youth: A Book of Entertainment for Israelite Boys and Girls*. The book contained the handwritten dedication: 'For my dear Wolfgang Lachmann, in friendship, Chanuka 5698, December 1937.' Bockenkamm has

16. Walter Lachman, reunited with a book that was looted from his home when he was a child. Courtesy Walter Lachman.

been unable to find out what happened to the boy."[12] Seideman shared the article's description of the children's book with his friend Walter . . . Wolfgang, who immediately cried out, "That's my book."

Walter Lachman had no specific recollections of that particular volume—he had received it from a teacher when he was nine years old and, in all likelihood, had placed it unused on the shelf and never gave it a second thought. In 2009 he was scheduled to travel to Berlin to be reunited with his childhood book. However, the previous week his wife had fallen and injured herself, so Lachman sent his daughter to receive the copy of *For Our Youth* on his behalf. Aside from the standard-issue cap he had kept with him from his days in Bergen-Belsen, the book his daughter handed to him upon her return represented his only physical connection with his life in Germany.[13]

## The Mini Italian Bible

The Jewish community of Rome, Italy, is the oldest in Europe; Jews have lived in the city ever since the second century BCE. For most of that time they lived in the shadow of the Vatican and consequently encountered oppression of all kinds: poll taxes, humiliating dress codes, expulsions, torture, forced conversions, and murder. This oppression would reach its zenith, of course, during the years of World War II.

The history of Roman Jewry, however, was not simply a two-thousand year crescendo of oppression—far from it. There were many good times too. Though a large number of Jews arrived as slaves during the second century CE, many early popes tolerated and even provided active support to Rome's Jews. In the Middle Ages the city was home to prominent Jewish sages, poets, and philosophers. As we have seen, Rome was also an important center of Jewish printing and publishing for centuries. The city was home to Jewish print shops as early as 1469, and many of those early books still exist today. In 1492 thousands of Jewish refugees from Spain found safe haven there. Around them were magnificent Christian domes, pillared palaces few Jews would enter, and ruins of a civilization once bent on destroying their own. And yet, even as they faced persecution, these Jewish refugees made the city their home and often thrived. By the late 1930s the city was home to twelve thousand Jews.[14]

During the war the two significant Jewish libraries in Rome were both housed in the same building—the Central Synagogue. On the third floor was the library belonging to the Italian Rabbinical College. Most of the stacks were open to the students, who used the volumes regularly, and a Jewish librarian who visited Rome at that time doubted that its books were of much monetary value.[15] The books in that seminary library were, however, the primary tools of instruction for the country's Jewish religious leaders, and they were thus of great value indeed.[16] On the second floor of the synagogue building was the Jewish Community Library.

Unlike that of the seminary, this library's collection was not open to the public. In 1893 one of Rome's historic synagogues had burnt down, and the destruction of its priceless antiquities became a tragic reminder of the literary treasures that Rome's Jewish community needed to preserve. Immediately they gathered the books from five local schools into the library that now sat above the synagogue.[17]

In 1934 a scholar named Isaia Sonne catalogued part of the collection, and the list he assembled illustrates how truly priceless it was. The library held incunabula, early publications of the famous Sonsino Press, antiquarian books from other Italian cities such as Venice and Livorno, not to mention books from beyond Italy's boarders—from Constantinople, Salonika, and elsewhere. It held priceless manuscripts, palimpsests, archival material, and much more. Sonne's catalogue was seventy pages long,[18] but it included only part of the collection—there were about seven thousand books in all.[19]

At least one book in the seminary's library *was* of historic and monetary value. It was a small Bible, pocket-sized really, about four by seven inches. The book was published in Amsterdam in 1680, and the ivory-colored leather in which it was bound had scalloped over the years, giving it a wizened, wrinkled appearance. On the spine was a sticker—clearly printed long after the book itself—with the words "Biblioteca di Collegio Rabbinico Italiano" and handwritten shelf markings inside an ornately designed box around the edges. Inside the right cover was a bookplate bearing a similar design.

Although Italy had long been rife with antisemitism, the deportations and mass murder of the Holocaust came late to the country. In the early years of the war Italy strove to maintain its independence from Germany, and as a result Mussolini and other Italian leaders refused to allow the country's Jews to be deported to Nazi death camps. But the summer and fall of 1943 were a time of chaos in Italy: Mussolini was overthrown and arrested; Italy's new government signed an armistice with the Allies; Germany rescued Mussolini from prison and reinstated him to power.

17. A seventeenth-century Bible returned to the Jewish community of Italy. Courtesy Unione delle Comunità Ebraiche Italiane (Union of Italian Jewish communities).

Mussolini, resolved to show his allegiance to his Nazi patrons, decided to give the Reich full access to its Jews.

In late September Herbert Kappler, head of the Gestapo's unit in Rome, called in the leaders of the local Jewish community and informed them that he could guarantee the safety of Rome's twelve thousand Jews for the reasonable fee of fifty kilos of gold—the equivalent of about $56,000, or about $4.50 per person. Not realizing that their deportation orders had already been signed, and not seeing that they had any other choice, the Jews of Rome quickly gathered the money and made the payment on September 28. They breathed a sigh of relief. Rosh Hashanah was to begin the following night, and having paid their ransom, they might be able to celebrate the new year in peace.

On the day of September 29 the synagogue staff arrived at work and thankfully began what they thought was to be a normal day in the office. Soon, however, a military convoy consisting of several trucks and two tanks rumbled up to the building. Forty soldiers climbed out of the trucks; officers, translators, and machine-gun-wielding guards stationed themselves around the building.[20] The officers knocked on the door of Ugo Foà, president of the Jewish Community of Rome. There were rumors, they told him, that Roman Jews were collaborating with the enemy and hiding anti-fascists in the synagogue. They had orders to conduct a search immediately.

Without delay, the officers entered the synagogue and conducted their "search"—quite a thorough one in fact. They broke into the synagogue's charity boxes, destroyed one of its arks, and threw two Torah scrolls to the ground. Adding to the desecration, the soldiers also carried away several boxes of archival material, which, among its historical records, held the contact information for almost every Jew in Rome.[21]

The Gestapo soldiers and officers who entered the synagogue that afternoon were bent on little more than destruction, intimidation, and the gathering of names of Rome's Jews for future deportations. On the following day, however—the first day of Rosh Hashanah—two ERR officers showed up to inspect the second and third floors of the building, particularly the libraries. They returned the next day for a closer look and informed Foà that he was to provide them with the catalogues of the books in the two libraries—the ERR needed the information for their "studies." On October 11 the ERR officers returned yet again, this time with a man the local Jews understood to be a German scholar with expertise in book publishing. Giacomo Debenedetti, a witness of these events who survived the war, later provided a vivid description of him:

> Like the others, from head to toe he is all uniform—that close-fitting fastidiously elegant abstract, and implacable uniform, which, tight as a zipper, lock in the wearer's body and, above all, his mind. It is the word *verboten* translated into uniform; access forbidden to the man and to the personal experiences he has lived through, to his past, and truest *uniqueness* as a human being on this earth; access forbidden to the sight of anything but his *present*, stern, programmed, unyielding.[22]

After yet another inspection of the library, this tightly uniformed officer and his colleagues informed Foà that he and his fellow Jews were to consider the contents of both libraries as officially impounded. No books or archival material could be removed, and anyone caught violating the order would be subject to severe corporal punishment. From the synagogue they called a shipping company to make arrangements for the material to be removed.

Ugo Foà and the Dante Almansi, president of the Union of Jewish Communities, wrote a letter to local fascist authorities appealing for intervention. Their efforts, unfortunately, were of no avail. Two days later a man from the shipping company arrived at the synagogue to begin arranging for the shipment of the books. By October 14 all of the material from the Jewish Community Library and some of the material from the Rabbinical College was packed and loaded into three train cars for shipment.

One of the boxes in that shipment most likely contained the small Dutch Bible printed in 1680; perhaps it was crammed into a crate with other, less valuable volumes, perhaps the soldiers could see its value and gave it a box of its own. Regardless, it, along with thousands of other books from the Roman Jewish libraries, was now in the hands not of Jews devoted to studying them, but of Nazis—Nazis who claimed to be devoted to studying them as well.

Two days later, beginning at 5:30 a.m., Nazi soldiers rampaged through Rome, gathered all the Jews they could find, and sent them to Auschwitz. Many Jews escaped, but more than a thousand did not, and they were murdered soon after they arrived at the camp.[23]

Late that December, Nazi officials went through the abandoned Rabbinical College to pack and ship the remaining books. Nobody is certain what happened to the books of the Roman Jewish libraries. The most widely accepted theory is that most of them fell into Soviet hands after the war and promptly melted away into the holdings of state-owned libraries throughout the Soviet Union.[24]

That's why it was such a surprise when, on May 10, 2005, at a symposium in Hannover, Germany, about the looted libraries from World War II, Frederik J. Hoogewoud, a librarian from the Bibliotheca Rosenthaliana in Amsterdam, called forward Dario Tedeschi, an attorney who was there representing the Jewish community of Italy. They were in a conference room at the Wilhelm Leibniz Library, brightly illumined by sunlight streaming through its large plate-glass windows. Hoogewoud had just given a talk about the fate of some of the looted material when he called Tedeschi forward and presented him with one small volume, ivory-colored, with a scalloped cover. It had been printed 325 years earlier, coincidentally in Amsterdam, where it had landed after the war. Nobody knew exactly how it had gotten there, but now it was time for the book to travel from Amsterdam to Rome once again. It was time for the book to go home.

## Books from the Jerusalem of the Balkans

From the City of Seven Hills our attention turns to the east—across the boot of Italy, across the Adriatic Sea, and across the Aegean Peninsula. Soon we find ourselves in a bustling portside city, the medieval ramparts of its old fortifications now surrounded by red-tile rooftops, domed church steeples, and the chockablock apartment buildings of a modern Greek metropolis. We have arrived in Salonika, a city whose thriving, centuries-old Jewish community has earned it the all but official appellation of "the Jerusalem of the Balkans."

By the time of the war, Salonika had long been one of the largest and most highly cultured Jewish communities in the world—home to accomplished Jewish merchants, high-ranking Jewish officials in the secular government, and many renowned rabbis and other Jewish intellectuals. Its Jewish cemetery was the largest in the world, and on the eve of World War II the community consisted of about fifty-five thousand Jews. Jews composed such a large percentage of the city's total population that stores in the city closed on Saturdays rather than Sundays.

In 1917 a massive fire swept through the city, destroying many of its neighborhoods and synagogues, and devouring countless irreplaceable books and manuscripts in the process. As a result, Salonikan Jewry cherished its written words even more dearly in the decades to come. With such a rich literary life, it should be no surprise that Salonika was also home to a lot of Jewish books. And as a place with so many Jewish books, it should be no surprise that it was a prime target for the ERR and other Nazi book-looting organizations. As early as May 1941 Rosenberg had ordered teams of ERR officials to sweep through Greece and collect its literary treasures. It was here that Johannes Pohl got his start in the field of Jewish book looting. By November a unit of more than thirty ERR officers, with the full support of the SS, had taken rare books, manuscripts, and other cultural treasures from forty-nine synagogues, bookshops, organizations, and more than sixty private homes.[25]

The extent of the pillage is perhaps best described by Rabbi Isaac Emmanuel in a memoir he wrote about his experiences after the war:

Some time after the invasion, there arrived in the city a delegation from the "Rosenberg Unit," one of whose members was Dr. Pohl, director of the Hebrew Faculty at the University of Frankfurt. He went through libraries and private homes and looted many priceless books (he was knowledgeable, for example, about books on Judaism and the history of Salonikan Jewry. He came to the home of my father, the wise and righteous Samuel [may God avenge his blood], to see his library and he took whatever he saw fit). After him came another researcher, Hans Heinrich, and the two of them emptied Salonika of all of the valuable books belonging to dozens of scholars and wealthy individuals, an ancestral legacy. Among the noteworthy books that disappeared on this occasion from the Jews of Salonika were about ten thousand volumes of rabbinic responsa, Jewish legal literature, the significant library of the revered Rabbi Chaim Chabib, which included several handwritten manuscripts belonging to him, and the rabbinic library belonging to the descendants of Rabbi Nahmias, several priceless books in Ladino that remained in Jewish homes that were in middle-class neighborhoods in Kalamaria and in [the] Baron Hirsch [neighborhood], neighborhoods that were not burnt down in the year 5677 (1917), and the library that was renovated by Rabbi Nehama. Even if we take into account only the various manuscripts and the Ladino literature that they looted or completely destroyed, this is an enormous loss, whose value is impossible to calculate (all of this spiritual treasure was destroyed along with its owners). . . .

The community was forced to pay the living expenses of the members of the Gestapo, the Rosenberg Unit, and forty Jewish collaborators who were brought from Germany in order to assist in the pursuit and oppression of the city's Jews.[26]

In other places, the looting was befuddling as well as frightening. For example, Avraham Negrin, president of the Jewish community of Larissa, Greece, tells what happened to the Jewish books in that community:

"On a Shabbat morning in July 1942, while we were praying in the *Kehal*, the Germans came in and took away our books. Our *Chacham* Yitschak Cassuto cried out, quoting the Psalms [94:1]: 'O Lord God to whom vengeance belongs; O God to whom vengeance belongs, shine forth.'

"We were scared. We thought they had come to take us away, just as they had rounded up Salonika's Jews in 1942. But the Germans just took all the books from the Talmud Torah and left."[27]

And so it went. In town after town, city after city, country after country, Nazi conquests led to the opening of invaluable cultural treasures to Nazi thieves bearing in their uniforms and official-looking paperwork the imprimatur of one of the twentieth century's mightiest nations. Teams of looters would go into newly conquered towns to collect all of the Jewish books they could find. Often with the help of Jewish conscripts, they would sort through the material to select what was most valuable and destroy the rest.

It had taken centuries for the Jews of Europe to fill their bookshelves. It was taking far less time for the Nazis to empty them.

Overall, the rules of Nazi looting were markedly different in eastern Europe than they had been in the west. In France, Holland, and other western lands, the ERR obtained lists of deported and otherwise departed Jews from local authorities, entered their homes, inventoried the goods, and made off with their haul. Comparatively speaking, this was polite looting. Civilized. In western Europe the Nazis conducted their looting efficiently. They stole Jews' books with the sophistication of a modern megastore accounting department, though of course with the scruples of a looting Mongol horde.

In eastern Europe the situation was different. For one thing, most organizations in these lands were run by the state; there were far fewer private schools and libraries. In fact all Soviet libraries had been nationalized during the 1920s and 1930s, when the Soviet government had taken the material and sold off the most valuable books to collectors and dealers in the west.[28] Looting in the Soviet Union, therefore, was a government-to-government affair, uncomplicated by screaming children, teary-eyed parents, and all the other unpleasantries involved in stealing from private citizens. There were some confiscations from individual communities in the Baltic states, such as Latvia and Lithuania, but on the whole the ERR confiscations in the east were from large libraries that had belonged to national governments for many years.

But not always . . .

## Solly and Cooky's Math Book

Books open the world to us. Each page can describe times and places and realities utterly unknown to readers beforehand—the whir of electrons around a nucleus, the strategic movements of Napoleon's troops, a phantasmagorical tale of knights and dragons and wizards. Books, we readers know, can be marvelous at describing not only the here and now, but also the there and then. They can bring us more fully into the world and also help bring us to worlds both real and imagined that are very different from our own. And it is this very ability—the ability that books have to pull us away from the local and out of the present—that made them so popular during the Holocaust. Books could be an escape, and as a result, during World War II Jews reached for their books with ravenous hunger.

In the early 1940s a young Lithuanian Jew named Solly Ganor saw his mother display just such a hunger. Ganor had been born in the town of Heydekrug near the German border in 1928, and his family had moved to the larger city of Kovno when Hitler came to power in 1933. In 1941, as part of the Nazi effort to render the Jews of eastern Europe more easily accessible and easily murderable, the Jewish section of Kovno was established as a ghetto, eventually becoming a temporary home to tens of thousands.

Like countless others, the Ganor family lost its home and had to move into the overcrowded ghetto. And like so many others, they left behind extended family, friends, career, and community in the widespread upheaval of war and murder so rampant in Lithuania beginning with the Nazi invasion of 1939. Several relatives were deported and never heard from again. Friends died of starvation and disease. Solly's brother Herman was killed in a provisional concentration camp not far from Kovno.

Solly Ganor's mother, however, had one means of escape from the growing darkness—books. Specifically, she turned to a ten-volume anthology featuring the works of Tolstoy, Pushkin, Dostoevsky, and other Russian literary greats. The books, bound in red leather with gold-embossed lettering, were among her most cherished treasures. "Like me," Ganor later recalled, "she escaped from her grief by reading. She would sit almost motionless for hours, only moving two fingers to flip the pages."[29]

Not surprisingly, the Nazis would not allow her to have the books for long. On February 27, 1942, the ERR executed a "Book Action" in the Kovno Ghetto. An order went out demanding that all books be brought to a two-story house serving as an assembly point, where Jewish conscripts who knew Hebrew had been put to work sorting through the material to identify the books valuable enough to save.[30]

Tearfully Solly's mother helped him load her ten volumes into a makeshift sled so that he could take them to the appointed spot. Fourteen-year-old Solly, however, wasn't as ready to cooperate. He and his friend Cooky found an abandoned house at the outskirts of the ghetto and hid the books there instead. Some of Solly's neighbors were eager to get rid of their books too, and soon the boys had gathered several hundred volumes—books in Hebrew, Yiddish, Russian, and other languages. When Solly tapped into a contact he had at the German collecting point, he was able get his hands on still more books, and the size of their library grew to about one thousand volumes. It represented the Babel of eastern European Jewry, gathered together as contraband on several carefully hidden shelves in Kovno.

Originally the boys collected books for their own use—he and Cooky, he recalls, each read about a book each day. In short order, however, word of the boys' collection spread, and other kids approached them with books of their own to trade. Evidently Solly and Cooky weren't the only budding clandestine librarians in the ghetto.

At school, Solly and Cooky studied carpentry under their favorite teacher, Mr. Edelstein. A shy and kind man, Mr. Edlelstein had somehow managed to maintain a positive outlook on life despite the fact that in the shtetl where he grew up, the Nazis had recently locked up all the Jews in the local synagogue and burned them alive. None of Edelstein's relatives had survived.

Although he was hired to teach carpentry, Edelstein also taught his students mathematics and other forbidden topics, sometimes throwing in a Zionist lesson as well. One day Edelstein approached Solly with a request. He had heard that his young student had access to books. Might Solly be able to get his hands on some mathematics textbooks? If he could procure some, Edelstein told Solly, he would be very grateful. Solly got right on it, and the next day he handed a forbidden math book to his teacher. Edelstein's face lit up. "Do you know what a treasure this is? Look! It is in Hebrew and was printed in Tel Aviv. Where on earth did you get it?"

The ensuing events unfolded with sickening predictability. When Solly left school that afternoon, he saw Edelstein bargaining for food with a Nazi guard. The guard spotted the book and drunkenly yelled at Edelstein. An SS officer pulled up, examined the book, and demanded to know where Edelstein had gotten it. The beating began. Solly, standing just ten yards away, made momentary eye contact with Edelstein; imperceptibly Edelstein gestured to Solly that he should leave. Solly ran, turned a corner, and heard a gunshot. Looking back, he saw Edelstein fall to his knees. The SS man aimed the gun and fired again. Edelstein fell to the ground and lay still.

"Me and my stupid books!" Solly lamented in a memoir he wrote four decades later. "For the first time, I realized the danger I exposed everyone to with my foolishness. I wouldn't listen and now my teacher was dead. To this day, I remember his feeble gesture waving me away from there. All he had to do is point in my direction to save himself, but he wouldn't do it."[31] Edelstein was buried in an unmarked grave. When the weather warmed, Solly planted some peas at the site. "To my surprise," he recalled, "they grew into bushes and eventually bore fruit, which Cooky and I shared. I knew that Mr. Edelstein wouldn't mind."[32]

At the ERR and RSHA collecting points across Europe, the books rolled in. They came by the box at first, but soon the boxes gathered in precarious heaps and were moved from place to place on pallets, and eventually the pallets outran their usefulness. When the books were coming in at a more measured pace in Germany, France, and Holland, the Nazi book-gathering agencies tried to catalogue them. But as the eastern European collection program grew, the books burst out of their shelves and overflowed in a deluge across warehouse floors. Cataloguing such a fast-growing collection would have been impossible, and storing them neatly on bookshelves would have been akin to gathering the floodwaters of a hurricane in drinking glasses. Even trying to do so would have been pointless and downright foolish.

What were they to do with this massive and rapidly growing mountain of literary material? Where were they to put it? For Rosenberg, of course, the original idea was to gather the books and archives as materials for the Institute for Research into the Jewish Question that the führer had authorized him to open in Frankfurt. But the institute existed only on paper. It didn't yet have anything even remotely resembling a functioning facility where it could store its library and archival material. In fact during World War II, Frankfurt was hardly the kind of place that any-one with half a brain—perhaps an apt description for Rosenberg and his associates—would want to build anything. And the same was true for most cities in Germany. Rosenberg's counterparts at the RSHA and other Nazi looting organizations faced the same challenges. The great academic institutions of their dreams didn't exist yet, but the libraries of those nonexistent institutes had millions of books. Clearly Rosenberg and the others would need to figure out how to store the books until after the war.

Since Rosenberg's first major acquisitions came from the Rothschild Library in Frankfurt, and since the plan was for the research institute to be headquartered in that city after the war, Rosenberg's staff sent most of the Jewish books to Frankfurt. At first. But then, in 1943, Allied forces bombed the city, and it no longer was a safe storage site for the Nazis' growing pile of literary loot.

They looked to Hungen, a small city about thirty miles to the north-east of Frankfurt. Hungen's fourteenth-century castle, renovated during the 1870s, was well situated for the task at hand. It was close enough to Frankfurt to be convenient, yet far enough away to escape the bombs and other depredations of war that might imperil the collections. The half-timbered, Bavarian-style castle was vacant, and it was right near the rail line running through town. It was perfect.

So, beginning in 1943, the ERR shipped the bulk of its Jewish books to Hungen. By the end of the war the ERR had shipped a few million volumes there.[33] Its Masonic material, on the other hand, went to a nearby hunting lodge in Hirzenhain or directly to the RSHA for them to dispose of as they wished. Not only had Frankfurt suffered from the ravages of Allied bombing, but so too had the ERR headquarters in Berlin. When its leaders realized that Berlin wasn't a safe place to store books either, they turned eastward again, more specifically to the southeast. The Silesian city of Ratibor, now called Racibórz, was also a convenient site for their storage needs. Not only was it closer to the eastern looting

18. Schloss Hungen. Courtesy Freundeskreis Schloss Hungen.

sites, but like Hungen, it too was situated with easy access to rail lines. And of course, since it was in the east, Rosenberg and his ERR officials had free rein when it came to choosing buildings for their facilities.

As in many of its activities, the ERR moved into Ratibor with gusto. In May 1943 it set up an office in a building that had once been a bank. In mid-August, an advance team of four officers arrived in the town and arranged housing for twenty people. Furniture arrived—looted furniture, of course—and in short order barges carrying six thousand crates of books and other confiscated material arrived at a nearby river port. It took seventy freight cars to carry the shipment from the docks to the Ratibor storage facilities.

The ERR set up its headquarters in the local Franciscan monastery and then took over some nearby barracks for office space and additional storage. Still more storage was designated at a former bathhouse that had also been a Jewish center. More offices went into the library, and the

ERR turned a warehouse into a movie theater. The local synagogue had been badly damaged in a 1938 fire, but the ERR renovated it to house a large portion of its library holdings, particularly those from the Soviet Union. Additional material went into a large building on the main market square that had once been a Jewish-owned department store.

Evidently Ratibor itself wasn't big enough for what the ERR needed, so it took over facilities in other parts of the region. They stored the deluge of books in a cigar factory in nearby Paulsgrund, a cigarette factory in Kranstdädt, and castles in or near the towns of Tworków, Gratenfeld, Schillersdorf, and Oberlangendorf. One of their most important sites was the castle of the Princes Von Pless, in the city now known in Polish as Pszczyna, which became an ERR branch office and collecting point. Some members of the family that owned the castle were invited to continue living there as cover; evidently they were never told the true nature of what was going on in their home.[34]

Once the ERR set up shop in Ratibor, the city become the central sorting point for all of its steadily growing collections headed to the Hohe Schule: 61 cases of priceless works from the library of Baron de Rothschild, looted in early September 1943; 1,940 from the opulent Château de Ferrières, in Ferrières-en-Brie, France; another 22 cases from Elene Droin-Rothschild; 16 from an attorney named Albert Wahl; and the list goes on.

The former synagogue served as the repository for most of the books from the east, but other buildings took the piles of archival material: 394 crates from Mogilev, 17 wagonloads from the Lenin Library in Minsk, scholarly material from Smolensk, and other collections from Kiev, Riga, and Kharkiv. We tend to think of depositories of this type of material as single buildings, hidden warehouses. With regard to Ratibor, however, such an image would be on far too small a scale. From 1943 until the end of the war, Ratibor was, in many ways, a hidden city of archival and bibliographic loot. Books there filled castles, warehouses, former religious and cultural centers, and other buildings too numerous to list.

Additional buildings provided lodging for the staff, recreational facilities, and other infrastructure necessities. It was a city of literary jewels, and its rulers were Alfred Rosenberg and a team of Nazi soldiers.

If that weren't enough, the ERR also took over the monastery in the Austrian town of Tanzenberg. There, by the end of the war, it had assembled six hundred thousand of its finest books—volumes that it had set aside for the Hohe Schule library—rare volumes from various Rothschild libraries, incunabula from other German and French collections, priceless material from Soviet collections. Unlike Ratibor, the Tanzenberg material had generally been vetted and was stored there by virtue of its high value and desirability.

Like the ERR, the RSHA had its own set of castles and other repositories where it sent its own books. It left about half the collection in Berlin, where much of the material was destroyed by Allied bombs before the end of the war. Of the Jewish library material that the RSHA removed, a large portion of it was allotted to four castles in the Sudetenland (more or less the modern-day Czech Republic): Niemes, Böhmish-Leipa, Neu-Pürstein, and Neufalkenberg.[35]

The RSHA had one additional repository on its list of major Jewish book destinations, only this one wasn't a magnificent palace or mountaintop monastery; it was an overcrowded, walled-off slum where 140,000 Jews lived, most of whom died before the end of the war.[36] The Nazis first formulated their plans for the Theresienstadt Ghetto in October 1941, and by the following May the operation was up and running. The idea was for the small garrison town first built in the eighteenth century to serve as a collecting point for Czechoslovakian Jews. There they could be housed, given a few morsels of food, and later sent to the extermination camps to be murdered. Additionally Theresienstadt could provide cover for the Nazi extermination of Jews; it could be a "model Jewish settlement" and thus preserve the Reich's image in the court of world opinion.

In building this "model community," the Nazis had a lot to work with.

Among the Czechoslovakian Jews sent to live in Theresienstadt were a good number of artists, writers, and scholars. As a result, a rich cultural life arose in the ghetto despite the miserable conditions in which its residents lived. There were several orchestras, an opera, and different types of theaters. There were clandestine religious activities. Each week there were dozens of performances and lectures for the high-minded and low-browed alike.

And there was also a library. It started small—six staff members and one room with stacks holding about four thousand books. Most of the books were RSHA loot: Judaica and Hebraica sent to Theresienstadt after it was no longer safe in Berlin. Many of the other books came from the ghetto inmates themselves. The Nazis searched prisoners on all of Theresienstadt's incoming and outgoing transports—those coming in with new prisoners, and those leaving with downtrodden others bound for the death camps. Invariably, most new prisoners brought one or more of their favorite books with them, hoping in vain to be able to read the books while living in the ghetto. These volumes too ended up in the library.

The Jews of Theresienstadt devoured the books. Czechoslovakian Jewry was, as a whole, a modernized and highly assimilated community when the war began. Many of its members had never studied anything about Judaism before, let alone learned the Hebrew of its ancient texts. The Holocaust, however, shook everything up. Ghettoization had turned the world of these acculturated and assimilated Jews upside down. In Prague or Bratislava, a Jew could easily hide his or her ethnic and religious background. Here in the ghetto, however, one's Jewishness was not only public knowledge, it was also the defining factor in one's life . . . and perhaps in one's death. Rather than reject it, Jews by the thousands turned to their Judaism with eager passion and read everything they could on Jewish subjects.

Soon the library outgrew its one-room facility, and in June 1943 a reading room opened. Books by the thousands rolled in. People flocked to the library. Their reading appetites were voracious. There was a banquet of literary riches available to them, and they couldn't get enough. Soon, a checkout system was put into place. To get a library card, a patron had to pay fifty ghetto Kronen (the money was worthless anyway) and prove to the librarians that they had received a higher education (most had). Since it was hard for some ghetto residents to get to the library facility, a bookmobile system was created, which brought boxes of thirty books to various parts of the ghetto. There were book groups, small libraries set up in group homes around the ghetto, technical and professional libraries, and a well-utilized children's library of thirty-five thousand volumes. It took fifteen librarians and dozens of support staff to oversee the collection.

Inevitably some books disappeared. Paper was a precious commodity in the ghetto, and desperate prisoners often repurposed the pages of library holdings into the fuel and toilet paper they so urgently needed for their very survival. Still, the Jews of Theresienstadt yearned to read. And with such an intense demand for literature, not to mention a growing population, it soon became hard for readers to get hold of the books they wanted. One inmate named Rudolph Geissmar gave voice to this frustration in part of a poem he wrote in the camp titled "Dedicated to the library":

> I am lying abed and would like to read something
> And have already submitted several requests
> And each time you were accommodating.
> But what I got I had already studied before.
> Be once more nice and send me something
> Because here a body has time. . . .
> But please no thin and lightweight books.
> No, rather something to chew on, heavy and hard.
> . . . at least something serious and good.
> I place my wish confidently in your hands.

*And obediently and in good mood look forward*
*To a well-meaning gift.*

Theresienstadt was a show camp—gussied up for visiting foreign dignitaries and inspectors not only with a beautiful library, but also with orchestras, nice schools, and spacious barracks. But during the final months of the war, after the inspectors had left, transports left the camp carrying most of Theresienstadt's inmates to their deaths at Auschwitz and other death camps. By the end of the war, there were one hundred thousand books in the Theresienstadt library, and the collection was overseen by a single librarian, Emil Utitz, and his assistant, Käthe Starke.[37]

By then, of course, there were no readers.

How many books, all told, did the Nazis loot? The number is astoundingly difficult to calculate. In Poland the Nazis pillaged more than 100 libraries, stealing more than a million books in all, 600,000 from Lodz alone. They took 700,000–800,000 in Belgium and the contents of more than 200 libraries in Belarus. It's easy to get lost in the numbers. The first postwar catalogue of all the looted books came out in 1946. It listed 704 separate collections, including the number of volumes thought to be in many of them, but the numbers for many others were unknown. At the end of the war, there were 10–12 million volumes in the Soviet Union and anywhere from a few hundred thousand to a few million at each of several different collecting points in western Europe. In the end we'll never know exactly how many books the Nazis stole—"tens of millions" is about as accurate as we can get.[38]

By means of comparison, the Library of Congress in Washington DC currently holds about 35 million books in its collections. It is entirely possible that the number of books that the Nazis stole from the Jews of Europe was larger than that. In fact it could have been far larger.

# 6
## *Resistance*

Books don't just grow on trees.
—*Zelig Kalmanovitch, 1946*

The Nazis weren't able to get hold of all of the books. Some slipped through their fingers, and some of the slippage happened because of secret plots afoot during the war to save Jewish books. These plots came both from Jews who refused to let their books fall into Nazi hands and from non-Jews who wanted to protect Jewish books from the Third Reich. Some were large-scale attempts to save massive amounts of literature, and others were aimed at saving one book or maybe a single collection. One of the great lessons of postwar Holocaust studies is that not all Jews marched silently to slaughter—many resisted. Similarly not all Jewish books flowed effortlessly to the ERR and RSHA coffers. Some resisted the pillage.

While some of the efforts to keep Jewish books out of Nazi hands succeeded, others failed, and many of the successful ones were able to protect the literature only until it fell prey to bombings or, ironically, was destroyed in cleanup efforts when survivors of the war removed the rubble that had once been their homes and communities.

One place where there were particularly courageous efforts to save Jewish books was the large Jewish ghetto in Vilna, Lithuania.

## The Paper Brigade

The "Jerusalem of Lithuania" counted among its former and current residents scores of renowned thinkers, the most famous of whom was

19. Shmerke Kaczerginski sorts books at YIVO in Vilna during the war. Courtesy Yad Vashem Photo Archives.

the outspoken eighteenth-century critic of Hasidic Judaism Elijah ben Shlomo Zalman Kremer, more commonly known as the Vilna Gaon. Vilna was home to poets and scientists and merchants, political activists and dreamers of all kinds. It was also a center of Jewish printing, and among its many printers were those of the Romm family, whose late nineteenth-century edition of the Talmud established a worldwide standard for the complex page layout of that sacred text. In Jewish Vilna, Yiddish was the Jewish lingua franca. The city had Jewish boxing leagues, Jewish labor unions, and Jewish pickpockets—with countless Jewish pockets to pick. In 1931 there were fifty-five thousand Jews in the city, 28.2 percent of the entire population and growing. When the Nazis entered the city a decade later, its Jewish population had risen to eighty thousand.[1]

One of Vilna's greatest legacies can be traced to a pamphlet written by a young Jewish historian named Simon Dubnow in 1891. Titled *On*

*the Study of Russian Jewish History*, the tract opens with the words of
Cicero: "Not to know history means to forever remain a child." Dubnow
called on the Jewish people collectively to take Cicero's admonition to
heart. He observed that the Jews of eastern Europe were ignorant of their
own great past, and he bemoaned the extent to which the memory of
that past had already been irretrievably lost to time. In Cicero's terms,
he argued, eastern European Jews had become immature children.

What made Dubnow think that Jews were so ignorant of their history? Exhibit A was the way the Jews of Russia and Poland treated the
literary records documenting their history. He realized that Jewish
communities everywhere were rich with paperwork of all kinds. There
were birth and marriage records, newspapers, stacks of letters, and in
particular *pinkasim*—books of communal minutes recording the tax
assessments, historical events, disciplinary actions, and other events large
and small of Jewish communities throughout eastern Europe. Political
groups, synagogues, arts organizations, schools, labor unions, and all the
others—they all had archives. Dubnow saw all this material as archival
gold. Alas, he cried, the papers "are lying in attics, in piles of trash, or in
equally unpleasant and filthy rooms. . . . [The] manuscripts are rotting
away. . . . Year by year, they are disappearing and being lost to history."[2]

Dubnow's antidote to this lamentable situation was at once simple
and grand: Keep files. Gather the papers. Organize them. Preserve them.
And in so doing, document the history of the great cultural drama
called eastern European Jewry. Dubnow harped on the idea—preserve
the literary records of our culture!—and slowly over the years it caught
on. Finally, in 1925, the *Yidisher Visnshaftlekher Institut* (the Yiddish
Scientific Institute, or YIVO) opened its doors in Vilna. Its aim was to
preserve the books and papers of the Jews of eastern Europe and thus to
prevent the Jewish people from the eternal "immaturity" against which
Cicero warned. In the year YIVO opened, its six-member advisory panel
included personages no less than Albert Einstein, Sigmund Freud, and,
of course, Simon Dubnow.

Dubnow's ideas, we should note, didn't just catch on—they *really* caught on. In the twenties and thirties, eastern European Jewry collected all the papers it could. At YIVO the process was systematized and professionalized, but it also caught on in less scientific ways throughout the land. The region's scholars and poets poured enormous energy into historical documentation. In cities, towns, and the countrysides of eastern Europe, there could be found *zamlers*, collectors of Jewish books and papers. Their work and their passion became the stuff of legend. In the words of historian David Fishman, "A virtual cult of documentary collection existed in Jewish eastern Europe between 1925 and 1939, with Vilna YIVO as its temple."[3]

But it wasn't just YIVO. Vilna was also home to Khaykl Lunski's forty-thousand-volume Strashun Library. Additionally small shtetls dotted the countryside around Vilna—towns such as Vabolnik, Kupishok, and Birzh—and most of these communities had libraries and records of their own. With the new rage in records collecting, the sea of Jewish paper whirling around and into Vilna swelled to record volumes.

As a result, Vilna and its environs were easy targets for the ERR looters. A week after the city fell into German hands, an ERR official named Dr. Gotthardt arrived and began gathering information. He visited the city's synagogues, libraries, and museums and assessed the literary pickings that would be available when his team arrived. The Strashun Library, he saw, was located inside the boundaries of the ghetto and was thus surrounded by teeming crowds of starved and bedraggled Jews whom the Nazis had packed into that small neighborhood as tightly as they could. The YIVO Library, on the other hand, was outside the ghetto walls, but even it seemed inadequate to the task. They would have to find a better place.

Sorting, however, would come later. For now Gotthardt needed to gain a more complete picture of what he had. He "hired" three scholars to compile lists of the valuable holdings at the Strashun. One of his conscripted workers was Khaykl Lunski; another was a prominent folklorist, a former director of YIVO named Noyekh Prilutski; and the third was well-known journalist and museum director Elijah Jacob Goldschmidt. The three men compiled their lists. Later that summer Gotthardt returned to Berlin, Prilutski and Goldschmidt were murdered, and Lunski, in a manner of speaking, was released.

What the Germans learned, evidently, was that in deciding to loot the books of Vilna, they had taken on a huge job. This was not a matter of going into the home of a wealthy collector to pack up his library, nor was it even like raiding the collection at a small-town yeshivah. There were *millions* of Jewish books in Vilna and countless tons of archival material. To process such a huge amount of loot, they would need large-scale systems, assembly lines of pillage, and a knowledgeable person at the helm to run the whole operation.

Most mornings beginning in the spring of 1943, Dr. Johannes Pohl walked up the steps of the Vilna University Library, his shiny black shoes clacking a rhythm against the pavement with each step he took. Once inside, he made his way to a large room furnished with bookcases along the walls and rows of long tables across the floor. Books filled the shelves; books teetered over the tabletops in tall, precarious stacks; boxes were stashed wherever there was room; and filling those boxes were books waiting to be sorted. Pohl was undoubtedly pleased to find that the dozen Jews selected to serve him had already arrived and gotten to work. He sat at his desk, opened a folder, and turned his attention to the morning reports.

Johannes Pohl, a senior Nazi officer and scholar of Jewish studies, had been appointed to lead a special detail charged with sorting through the millions of books that had once belonged to the Jews of Vilna and other nearby communities. Just like books gathered for the bonfires a decade earlier, the Jewish volumes in Pohl's processing center had also arrived in trucks and wagons. But under his leadership, they were shelved for study in an expansive library reading room rather than heaped into piles for immediate destruction.

Heading the team of conscripted Jewish workers under Pohl were two prominent intellectuals: Herman Kruk, former director of the Vilna Ghetto library, and Zelig Kalmanovitch, a historian of eastern European Jewry. Their crew was instructed to open the book crates, sort through the contents, and set aside the most valuable 30 percent for shipment to a storage facility in Frankfurt. The remaining 70 percent would go to a nearby pulp mill and be destroyed.

Pohl configured the process so that it worked with scientific efficiency. Under the watchful but crafty eyes of Kruk and Kalmanovitch, each worker played his or her role as if part of an assembly line. One worker uncrated the books, another placed them spine-up on the tables, another removed the empty crates to make room for full ones, and so on. (Pohl was probably oblivious to the fact that some of the confiscated books never made it through the process, but instead were spirited off to hiding places in attics, cellars, and hand-hewn caverns throughout the city.)

Johannes Pohl and his conscripts processed hundreds of thousands of books in their spacious library sorting center during the two years it operated. Although they certainly overlooked at least a few valuable treasures, much of what they saved was, like many works burned in the 1933 fires, priceless and irreplaceable: old Bibles, rare rabbinic works, hard-to-find Yiddish novels, and much more.

We can imagine Pohl glancing up on one of those mornings and seeing the busy whir of activity in his looted-book assembly line, deeply satisfied that everything was running so smoothly. The workers were behaving, his stock of Jewish books was flowing steadily; everything was moving with the efficiency that this important project demanded. He had no thoughts of empty libraries, ransacked homes, or destroyed lives that morning. To Johannes Pohl, the day was off to a great start.

Not long after Johannes Pohl got his Vilna operation (which included three of his own Jewish studies specialists) up and running, Herman Kruk recounted the recent events in his diary with a certain resigned fatalism. "After several conferences with my superiors," he wrote, "it becomes clear that the following materials will pass through my hands: the Ansky museum, the YIVO, the Children's Library, the libraries of the Jewish secondary schools, the stock of the Kletskin Publishing Company, and others. Meanwhile, my new boss has gone to Berlin. He will return in a few days, and then everything will be decided. Meanwhile, the Strashun Library is in the university building. The holy books from the Gaon's Prayer House, from the Old Prayer House, from the Glazier's Prayer House, and others have been sent there."[4]

Under the bright lights of the university library's sorting room, the forty thousand volumes of the Strashun Library passed before the eyes of Herman Kruk and Zelig Kalmanovitch. The two scholars were charged with the task of identifying the books that were the most valuable. These were to be catalogued and preserved; the others were pulped. It was a "selection," a holocaust writ small, an eerie literary counterpart to the horrors being perpetrated on millions of Jews in nearby death camps.[5]

Send the books to the pulp mill, or give them to the Nazis? The Jewish literati conscripted to work in Pohl's sorting room couldn't stomach either option. From the beginning, Kruk and Kalmanovitch sought ways to save the books not only from destruction, but also from the grubbing hands of their Nazi conquerors. The ERR agreed to send a few of the books to the ghetto library—a workable, albeit temporary fix that saved a small handful of books. Beyond that, however, what were they to do? How could they save the books? They needed to identify and hand over at least some of the treasures, otherwise the scholars would be removed from their positions and effectively consign all the books to seizure or confiscation. Nevertheless, with each treasure they catalogued, with every rare volume they identified for their Nazi overlords, Kruk and Kalmanovitch felt as if they were betraying their people and all that they held dear. "Kalmanovitch and I don't know whether we are grave diggers or saviors," Kruk wrote. "If we'll manage to keep these treasures in Vilna, it will be to our great merit. But if the library will be sent out, we will have been accomplices."[6]

The books continued to roll into their sorting room at the university library, and sorting them was a monumental task. Looming over their work, however, was the pending arrival of the YIVO library. The collections arriving from the Lithuanian countryside contained precious material, but most of the confiscated libraries were relatively small, the books sometimes of great sentimental value to their owners but of little monetary worth or scholarly importance. The YIVO material, however, was amassed and curated far more systematically and with an eye to its historical consequence. By design it represented the finest collection of eastern European literature under one roof anywhere. Sorting through it would be not only a monumental task, but also heartbreaking for scholars who had grown to treasure its holdings so dearly.

As it turns out, the YIVO library never would arrive at the university. When ERR officials took possession of YIVO in March 1942, they quickly realized that shipping its entire library to the university, only to then discard all but the most valuable of its contents, would have been horribly inefficient. Instead the ERR decided to broaden its Vilna book-sorting operations and open a processing center in YIVO itself. Kruk and Kalmanovitch were authorized to expand their team and promptly recruited forty additional workers to supervise the sorting efforts at YIVO.

Spearheading the efforts would be two poets—twenty-nine-year-old Abraham Sutzkever, and thirty-two-year-old Shmerke Kaczerginski. Like other members of the Vilna Jewish intelligentsia, Sutzkever and Kaczerginski had spent many hours at YIVO before the war, and they loved the place. It was, after all, the largest repository anywhere of their own cultural world. There was a large Yiddish map of the world hanging over the main staircase, emblazoned with the words "YIVO and Its Affiliates across the Globe." There was row after row of neatly organized bookshelves. And, most important, many memories; it had been a place of camaraderie for them and many other historians, writers, and poets who used the facility and shared a passion for Yiddish and the world to which it gave voice.

Since early in the war, the Nazi army had been using the YIVO facility as a military barracks and had dumped its library books into the basement to make room for the bunk beds and mess hall. When the ERR's literary conscripts entered the building, they found it in shambles. Where once there were neatly arrayed bookshelves, now there was empty space, the books haphazardly piled in the basement. Where once there was a lively spirit of learning and conviviality, now there were the sounds of Nazi boot heels echoing through largely empty hallways. And where once the YIVO world map hung proudly for every visitor to see, there now hung a banner of an eagle carrying a swastika-adorned wreath in its talons.

Almost immediately, YIVO became the primary sorting center for the ERR book-looting operations in and around Vilna. From Vilna itself, from Kovno, and from scores of smaller communities in the surrounding countryside, the books came. Here the instructions were even more specific than they had been at the university. The most valuable 30 percent of the material was to be retained; the remainder, destroyed.

Thus did several dozen Jewish book sorters—among them, poets, novelists, historians, and other scholars—find themselves forced to decide on the fate of their region's Jewish literature, book by book. As each children's schoolbook, or volume of Talmud, or well-thumbed romance novel came before their eyes, the decision was the same Sophie's choice as their counterparts had faced at the university. Here the stakes were far less tragic than those of the mothers forced to decide which of their children to save, but the decisions were gut-wrenching nonetheless. Which of the treasures would get to survive, and which would not? How could they possibly decide?

The process commenced. At YIVO the books flowed into stacks and over tables and into boxes and out the door. "The Jewish porters occupied with the task are literally in tears," Kruk wrote in July 1942. "It is heartbreaking to see this happening." The following month he wrote, "YIVO is dying. Its mass grave is the paper mill."[7]

Fortunately, however, "destroy" or "relinquish" weren't the sorters' only alternatives. From the time their work began, the laborers sought other, more palatable options that might allow them to save the books and keep them out of Nazi hands. One option was simply to stall. Whenever their Nazi overseers weren't looking, the Jewish workers stopped sorting the books and began reading them instead—sometimes aloud, in impromptu poetry and prose recitals. After the war, Sutzkever and Kaczerginski each published volumes of poetry that they had written during the Holocaust. They wrote most of the poems while "slacking off" from their assigned tasks at YIVO.

Sadly the workers couldn't stall forever, so they needed to figure something else out. Maybe there was a way to get the books out of Nazi hands and back into Jewish ones. YIVO, they reasoned, was outside the walls of the ghetto—the sorters received special permission to leave the ghetto to go to work each day. Maybe, if they could just sneak the books back into the ghetto, then they could hide the volumes in safety until after the war.

Thus began what would soon be known as the Paper Brigade. As they sorted through the books at YIVO, the workers would designate the least valuable ones for the pulp mill and some of the more valuable ones for the Nazis. But when they found a *really* valuable book, the workers would do what they could to secretly hide it in their clothing. At the end of the workday they would head back to the ghetto, walking as nonchalantly as possible in their book-laden pants, jackets, and skirts. If the guard on duty when they arrived at the ghetto gate was Jewish, they could usually walk past with no problem. If the guard was a Nazi, however, the Paper Brigade brigands would find ways to stash their loot with non-Jewish friends outside the ghetto until they could safely retrieve it. Occasionally Nazi guards caught the workers returning with their contraband books. Beatings ensued, and the workers were warned of far more dire consequences should they ever try to sneak books into the ghetto again.

Kruk, Kalmanovitch, Sutzkever, and Kaczerginski were joined by six others in the smuggling campaign: Uma Olkenicki, Rokhl Pupko-Krinsky, Ruzhka Korczak, Naomi Markeles, Dr. Yaakov Gordon, and Dr. Daniel Feinstein. Later, Kalmanovitch recalled that other Jews in the ghetto thought they were crazy. "*They* were smuggling foodstuffs into the ghetto, in their clothes and boots. *We* were smuggling books, pieces of paper, occasionally a *sefer Torah*, or mezuzahs." How, these critics wondered, could the Paper Brigade possibly justify taking such risks at a time when people's very lives were so endangered? Kalmanovitch's reply was straight and to the point. "Books," he said, "don't grow on trees."[8]

For the most part, the Paper Brigade succeeded in getting safely inside the ghetto gates with their reclaimed loot. Book by book, overstuffed pant leg by overstuffed pant leg, sagging shirtfront by sagging shirtfront, this group of scholar-smugglers was able to spirit books that the Nazis stole back from the YIVO collecting point to the relative safety of the Vilna Ghetto. Once, Sutzkever got permission to bring wastepaper from YIVO to the ghetto so that he could use it in his household oven. The "wastepaper" he brought with him included a diary of Theodor Herzl, manuscripts and letters from Leon Tolstoy, Sholom Aleichem, and other writers, drawings by Marc Chagall, a handwritten manuscript of the Vilna Gaon, and other priceless treasures. Needless to say, Sutzkever didn't end up burning the material in his oven.

Getting the material inside the ghetto gates was only half the battle. Once the contraband books and papers were in Jewish hands, the Paper Brigade needed to figure out what to do with them. They sent children's books to the many grade schools that were secretly operating in the ghetto. A munitions manual went to a ghetto partisan group, enabling it to build its first arsenal of weapons. Polish material went to members of the Polish underground. And some of the more valuable books didn't even make it back to the ghetto at all; the Paper Brigade entrusted them to non-Jewish friends living outside the ghetto walls for safekeeping until after the war.

One hiding place—perhaps the safest—was an underground bunker built by a Jewish partisan commander named Gershon Abramovitsch. Sixty feet underground, fitted out with ventilation and electric lighting, Abramovitsch had originally built it as a hiding place for his paralyzed mother, but he agreed to stash the Paper Brigade's loot there as well. One day in March 1943, perhaps after one of his many trips down into Abramovitsch's subterranean bunker, Sutzkever took out a sheet of paper and penned a poem called "Grains of Wheat." In the poem, he described an ancient pharaoh, ordering that grains of wheat be placed alongside him in his crypt. Nine thousand years later the seeds are discovered, and lo and behold, they blossom and yield produce even after so many centuries underground. Words, Sutzkever suggested, have the same power to bear fruit even after being entombed in darkness for many years.

*And like the primeval grain*
*That turned into a stalk—*
*The words will nourish,*
*The words will belong*
*To the people, in its eternal walk.*[9]

Sutzkever buried volume after volume of Jewish literature in dirty tunnels and caverns beneath the Vilna Ghetto. One day, he hoped—even if he wouldn't live to see it—they too would be discovered and belong to his people in its eternal walk.

The pharaohs' seeds, Sutzkever had learned, could grow even after being entombed in the ground for thousands of years. Might these seeds—the books he was hiding in the ground beneath the Vilna Ghetto—also grow when they were brought to the light of day?

Sutzkever concealed some of the material in the walls and floors of his own apartment, and he found other such hiding places as well. In one of the great ironies of this convoluted story, Kruk was able to hide some of the material in the Strashun Library, thus bringing the books for safekeeping to the very place from which many of them were originally stolen. Still, for all of the Paper Brigade's efforts, its work was going far too slowly. With the deluge of books flooding into YIVO and the other collecting points every day, the small handful of them that they were able to smuggle back into the ghetto amounted to barely a trickle.

Soon another option presented itself. If the Paper Brigade couldn't smuggle the books out of YIVO to the relative safety of the ghetto, maybe the books could be rescued inside the walls of YIVO itself. Sutzkever noticed that the architecture of the YIVO building afforded the Paper Brigade ample room for a book stash beneath the beams and girders in the attic. All he and his cohorts would need to do would be to distract the guard who kept watch over them as they did their work—a deaf, uneducated Pole named Virbilis.

To the Paper Brigade's great fortune, Virbilis didn't like being uneducated, and when Drs. Gordon and Feinstein offered to tutor him in math during his lunch breaks, the guard readily took them up on their offer. Each day at noontime Virbilis's lessons commenced. As they did, so too did the work of the Paper Brigade. Quietly, furtively, while Gordon and Feinstein kept Virbilis distracted, the other members of the Paper Brigade moved as many books as they could from the YIVO sorting rooms to the attic hiding places above. They conducted their work at a frenzied pace, for none of them knew how long they would be able to continue. What they did know was that abandoning their efforts would almost certainly lead to the destruction of the precious literary treasures that paraded into YIVO each day.

Packing books wasn't all that the Paper Brigade did during the times when they could escape Virbilis's gaze. Often, when the German overseers left the building, the Jewish workers stopped sorting the books, and the readings began. Usually it was Sutzkever, reading from his favorite Yiddish poets. The poetry was easily available of course; one of the world's greatest Jewish libraries lay in piles on the tables before them. These moments "brought solace and forgetfulness for a time," wrote

Rokhl Pupko-Krinsky in a postwar memoir.[10] To the writers, scholars, and other Jewish literati enduring the misery of their forced labor, such moments of solace and forgetfulness were a ray of sunshine.

Virbilis, deaf to what was really going on, never complained. Every day the workers were careful to tidy up before they left. If for some reason they never returned to the YIVO building, they wanted to be sure that the Germans would remain oblivious to what they had been doing.

One day while sorting through a pile of books, they came across a leather-bound volume that none of them noticed before. It was the visitors' book from YIVO—thousands of signatures of people who had been in the library before it had fallen into Nazi hands. Leafing through its pages brought back a flood of memories. So many visitors . . . it was such a vibrant place . . . look, there's the signature of a friend of mine. Kalmanovitch, ever optimistic, assured his fellow Paper Brigade members that the book would survive the war. "Don't worry," he said, "it will not be lost. The Germans will not succeed in destroying everything. They're on the run themselves right now. Whatever they have stolen will be found after the war and taken from them." The men and women standing around the book paused. Then, one by one, they added their names to the list of their predecessors. Sutzkever signed his with the last stanza of one of his most popular ghetto poems, "A Prayer to a Miracle":

> You're here, you're here! You're a living kernel
> Wrapped in a dead shell like an egg.
>
> You're here, you're here! And you'll be a help to me
> While my pain will warm you.
> I'm naked in the freezing cold. And see, I warm
> Your dead shell: have pity, have pity![11]

Rokhl Pupko-Krinsky's signature was terser. "*Morituri vos salutant*," she wrote. "We who are about to die salute you."[12]

On Wednesday, July 28, 1943, Sutzkever once again snuck away from his work to write. There in the YIVO sorting room he was surrounded by the written words of his people—words that enlivened him beyond description. And just beyond the walls of the room where that surreal book rescue was taking place was the growing presence of death itself. Reflecting on the words amid the ashes of those who wrote and cherished them, Sutzkever invoked an image from medieval Jewish poetry, referring to words as pearls—burnt pearls, this time—upon the charred remains of the person who once wore them.

*And no one—not even I—shredded by time*
*can recognize the woman drenched in flame*
*for all that remains of her now*
*are those grey pearls*
*smoldering in the ash.*[13]

Two weeks later, on September 12, Sutzkever, Kaczerginski, Rokhl Pupko-Krinsky, and Ruzhka Korczak were able to escape into the surrounding woods and join up with partisan groups.[14] Later that month Nazi forces liquidated the ghetto, and along with thousands of others, the other members of the Paper Brigade are believed to have been brought to the nearby resort town of Ponar, where they were lined up alongside large pits and shot.[15] These members of the Paper Brigade were buried in mass graves near Vilna. In the very same ground, not far away, lay grains of wheat by the thousands, preserved in the soil only by virtue of the brigade members' devotion and courage.

On July 13, 1944, Soviet troops liberated Vilna from its Nazi captors. As the Red Army marched into the war-torn city, they were accompanied by two bedraggled survivors of its Jewish ghetto, Abraham Sutzkever and Shmerke Kaczerginski. The destruction that Sutzkever and Kaczerginski found was astonishing. The ghetto had taken heavy artillery fire, most of its buildings turned to rubble. Of the fifty-seven thousand Jews who had lived in the ghetto during the Nazi occupation, only two to three thousand had survived. Those who did used what little energy they could muster to search for friends and relatives.

Sutzkever and Kaczerginski, of course, also had something else on their minds—and what they saw only added to their devastation. The YIVO building had been completely destroyed by artillery fire, its attic and its precious contents burned to ash. Just a few days earlier someone had discovered the materials that Kruk had so carefully hidden in the Strashun Library. The books and papers were thrown into a pile and burned in a bonfire. Some of the private hiding places, however, had held, including Abramovitsch's underground bunker. Twenty tons of YIVO material turned up on a platform at a nearby paper mill; the war's end had saved it from destruction—barely. Another thirty tons were found at a local garbage facility, having also been saved at the last moment by the caprice of diplomatic and military maneuverings.

Immediately Sutzkever and Kaczerginski moved into salvage mode. Less than two weeks after Vilna's liberation they opened the Commission to Collect and Systematize Jewish Culture, an organization whose dry name presaged the Soviet bureaucracy that would soon destroy it. Initially the organization's headquarters was in the young men's apartment, which proceeded to become the gathering place and mailing address for Vilna's few bewildered, dazed, and grieving Jewish survivors. Soon, however, the commission outgrew that small apartment and moved to the only other facility it could find—the bombed-out remains of the ghetto library on Strashun Street. The only usable part of the building was the section that the Gestapo had turned into a prison during the war. Once thousands of books had been lovingly cared for in those rooms. Later the Nazis removed those books so that they could use the space to torture Vilna's Jews, many of whom had once sat at the very spot to read books from the library. Now, this site was the center of the efforts to reclaim the written and printed legacy of Vilna Jewry.

And perhaps, from somewhere far beyond the bewildering horrors

20. Ruins at YIVO after the war's end. Courtesy Yad Vashem Photo Archives.

of this world, a hint of a smile crossed the tear-stained face of Khaykl Lunksi.

Soviet officials stonewalled the commission staff, blocking their efforts to garner the resources they needed to gather the material. Kaczergin-ski, realizing that there were thirty tons of books and archives at the nearby garbage platform, dashed out to the pile, grabbed a handful of its treasures, and returned to town to plead with local officials for help in saving the material. By the time he returned the next day, the pile—all thirty tons of it—was gone. Soviet authorities ended up assigning a staff of three workers to conduct the salvage operations, but even this tiny staff was harassed to the point of paralysis by the KGB.

In late 1945 Kaczerginski resigned his post, left Vilna, and eventually ended up in Argentina. In 1948 he published a collection of poems and songs written in the ghettos and camps; still today it remains the largest and most significant collection of its kind. Sadly, in 1954 Shmerke Kaczerginski was killed in a tragic plane crash. He was forty-six years old.[16]

Abraham Sutzkever testified at the Nuremberg war crimes trials in 1946, and the next year he moved to the Land of Israel. There, for more than a half-century, he continued writing poetry and working indefatigably as an advocate on behalf of Yiddish language and culture. Throughout Sutzkever's long life, words invigorated and exhilarated him. "If I didn't write," he once observed, "I wouldn't live." Abraham Sutzkever died in Tel Aviv in 2010 at the age of ninety-six.[17]

In the end a good deal of the looted material did survive. Sutzkever, Kaczerginski, and others smuggled out what they could when they left Vilna and forwarded their material to YIVO, by then headquartered in temporary facilities on Lafayette Street in Manhattan. But much of it remained in Vilna, where the KGB eventually impounded it and dumped it into a Lithuanian "book chamber" located in the basement of a former church, whereupon Soviet authorities ordered the supervisor of the book chamber, Dr. Antanas Ulpis, to destroy the material.

Little did anyone know, however, that Dr. Ulpis disobeyed his orders. Instead he quietly arranged for the books to be catalogued and then held onto them in his subterranean book chamber for more than forty years without telling anyone. It wasn't until 1988 that the material was discovered, and another group of books turned up in 1993. In 1995 and 1996 the books were shipped to YIVO in New York, where they remain today.

### The Guttmann Books

The discovery of Vilna's surviving Jewish books was greeted with universal celebration throughout the Jewish world. Sometimes, however, books coming to light long after the Holocaust caused controversy and conflict even amid the satisfaction that came with knowing that they survived. Such was the case with the Guttmann Collection.

I hasten to add that perhaps this group of books shouldn't have been called the Guttmann Collection. Maybe they should have been called the Jewish Theological Seminary Collection. Or maybe the Hebrew Union College Collection. Or maybe just the Hochschule Collection. That was the problem: when books emerge from chaos, it's not always clear who owns them. And sometimes the chaos can simmer unnoticed for many years.

Very few people knew about the chaos surrounding these particular books until April 13, 1984. That day, a brief article in the *New York Times* announced, "A 15th-century Hebrew manuscript Bible from Prague, richly illuminated, will be auctioned by Sotheby's on June 26." The three-volume work, written in the 1480s, had been the subject of a year's research on the part of Sotheby's Judaica expert George Snyder. He found that the Bible had a long and eventful provenance, with the list of its many owners over the centuries including renowned scholars Moses Mendelssohn and Leopold Zunz. "In the 20th century," the article cryptically concluded, "the work changed hands several times. Mr. Snyder said that the identity of the owner was unknown and that all negotiations had been conducted through agents." The Bible was expected to fetch a price of about $500,000.[18]

Immediately the announcement set off alarms throughout the Jewish book world. A Bible such as this was of enormous value not only monetarily, but also in terms of what it represented—one of the earliest printed Jewish books in the world. Abraham Geiger, one of the Bible's owners, had died in 1874 and had spent the final years of his life as a faculty member of the Hochschule für die Wissenschaft des Judentums (Higher Institute for the Scientific Study of Judaism), the liberal rabbinic seminary in Berlin that he helped create. His personal library had become part of the Hochschule's collection, and the Hochschule's collection was one of the major libraries that the Nazis had plundered during the war.

In all likelihood, then, the Bible had been taken from the Hochschule. Perhaps it was taken when the Nazis looted the rest of the seminary's books and had somehow stayed under the radar for four decades. Or maybe someone had hidden it from the Nazis and had been holding onto it ever since. The Hochschule, of course, no longer existed, but many other institutions had since taken up the mantle of high-level scientific Jewish learning that the Hochschule had first pioneered. Some of these institutions had received the Hochschule's books after the war, and some had even gone to great lengths to save the lives of its teachers and students *during* the war.

If this had been a Hochschule book, suggested some Jewish bibliophiles, it really should have belonged to the Jewish people as a whole and housed in a library where everyone could study it. Instead someone else had the book—perhaps an individual, perhaps an institution. Who was this mystery seller? How did he, she, or it get the book?

One of the first people to come under suspicion was Ismar Elbogen, a leading member of the Hochschule faculty who had escaped Germany for the United States in 1938 and taught at several liberal institutions of Jewish study until his death in 1943. But it turned out that Elbogen hadn't taken any books with him when he left Germany. In fact there was some indication that Elbogen had deputized another scholar to bring books to Israel when that scholar moved there in 1939. That scholar was never identified, but, evidently, when he arrived he told the director of the library at the Hebrew University in Jerusalem that Elbogen had given him permission to use the materials for his own research, after which he was to deposit them in the library, where they could be properly preserved and made available to students and researchers.[19]

To complicate matters, it turns out that the Prague Bible wasn't the only valuable book from the Hochschule library about to go up onto the Sotheby's auction block on June 26. In fact, there were a total of sixty-two such books and manuscripts scheduled to be sold. In addition to the Bible, one of the most valuable books was a manuscript of a fourteenth-century *machzor* (Days of Awe festival prayer book) from Catalan. The collection also contained an early sixteenth-century Hebrew dictionary, an eighteenth-century Passover haggadah, and even a late thirteenth-century biblical commentary by the famed sage Rabbi Shlomo Yitzchaki—Rashi.

It was becoming increasingly clear that these books had all come from the Hochschule. But how? Where had they been since the war? Who owned ("owned"?) them? Having originally come from the Hochschule, it would seem that the Jewish people owned them—collectively. But what did that mean? If "the Jewish people" were their owners, where should the books be housed, and who should take care of them? And if the Jewish people owned them, how could the Jewish people get them from Sotheby's? Once again the world was faced with the same question that arose immediately after the war: Who had dibs on the literary remains of European Jewry?

The outcry began. The Jewish Restitution Successor Organization—the international group founded to restore heirless property to Holocaust survivors—publicly requested that Sotheby's divulge the owner's name. The Anti-Defamation League of B'nai B'rith did the same.[20] The Reform movement's Central Conference of American Rabbis, meeting in the Catskills that week, called on its leadership "to take all necessary steps to stop this sale until the ownership of these books and manuscripts is clearly established and publicly revealed for all to know."[21] Dr. Alfred Gottschalk, president of the same movement's Hebrew Union College–Jewish Institute of Religion, said that HUC-JIR wouldn't purchase the items even if it could. The sale, he argued, is "tainted." He told a reporter that "our belief is that these books came from the Hochschule to this country for safekeeping. My hunch is that the original owners are no longer alive, and people are now using these books to profit personally from them. I think that's outrageous."[22]

The Conservative movement's Jewish Theological Seminary evidently did not share Gottschalk's compunctions about bidding on material of such doubtful provenance. As the auction drew near, JTS made a last-minute push to buy the collection's two most valuable pieces for itself. Surely JTS realized that if no Jewish library were to purchase the material, the books could very possibly remain in private hands and slip into obscurity once again. Plus, it is entirely possible that what motivated the seminary was simply its desire to expand its collections. After all, librarians like putting nice books into their libraries, and these were about as nice as they got.

Just four days before the scheduled auction, on June 22, JTS succeeded in arranging for a private, pre-auction purchase of the collection's two most valuable items for the bargain-basement price of $900,000—money rumored to have been given to them by Ivan Boesky, whose later dealings and dabblings with other "books" earned him lasting infamy. Various organizations implored the New York attorney general's office to arrange to have a legal kibosh put on Sotheby's upcoming sale of the treasures. In the end their efforts failed, and the ensuing auction brought in another $1.23 million.

Still the legal wrangling continued, and still the big question of the entire episode remained unanswered: Who had brought the books to auction?

The attorney general demanded proof that the seller—whoever that was—had been the legal owner of the books when Sotheby's sold them. Sotheby's got an affidavit from the owner, and the attorney general released it with all identifying information redacted. The owner claimed that Heinrich Veit-Simon, chairman of the Hochschule's board, gave him the books and said they were his for keeps if he could smuggle them out of Germany, which is just what he did.

Attorneys showed the redacted affidavit to Lewis Strauss, who had been a student at the Hochschule from 1937 until 1942. Strauss in turn, wrote an affidavit of his own. "Based on my knowledge of the events during the last year of the Hochschule," Strauss said, "I am convinced that the only person who could have signed [the seller's] affidavit was Alexander Guttmann."[23]

Alexander Guttmann, then in his early eighties, was a professor emeritus of Talmud at the Hebrew Union College–Jewish Institute of Religion in Cincinnati, and he owed a lot to the school where he worked. In 1940, a decade before its merger with the Jewish Institute of Religion, HUC arranged for Guttmann and seven other scholars to emigrate from Germany to the United States and assume positions on its faculty. Governmental red tape, travel plans, and housing arrangements had all made it an expensive proposition to bring these young professors across the Atlantic. Furthermore, HUC didn't really need these scholars on its professorial roster at the time, and their heavily accented English proved to be a liability in their attempts to connect with the young seminarians in their classes. Nevertheless, HUC leaders foresaw the looming darkness in Germany and, aware of American Reform Judaism's deep roots in Germany and the Hochschule, felt that they had no choice but to rescue the imperiled scholars. Without a doubt, hiring them was the right thing to do.[24]

Alexander Guttmann, then, owed much to the Hebrew Union College—perhaps his very life. Now, however, forty-four years after his rescue, it began to look as if Guttmann may have exploited HUC's kindness. After all, the Hochschule's books rightly belonged to the liberal seminaries that were carrying its torch in post-Holocaust America or at the very least to the Jewish people as a whole. If Guttmann had kept these treasures for himself, that would have made him a thief—a thief who stole from the very institution that had once saved his life. And the fact that these books were worth *a lot* of money only made it worse.

In an August 14 article in the *New York Times*, Guttmann denied that he was the one who had put the books up for sale, but the following day he issued a statement through his lawyer affirming that he was indeed the mystery bookseller. In 1939, Guttmann said, he learned that he would be getting a visa and promptly spoke with Heinrich Veit-Simon about how to prevent the treasures of the Hochschule library from falling into Nazi hands. They agreed that the books needed to get out of Germany and that Guttmann was the man to take them. To remove such valuable works without the Nazis' knowing about it was very dangerous, of course, and consequently, Guttmann explained, "Dr. Veit-Simon emphasized that because of the enormous risk, any such books or manuscripts that I did remove and thereby save from the Nazis would belong to me."

On Veit-Simon's instructions, Guttmann continued, the Hochschule's librarians gave him the books, which he then brought home and hid under some garbage in his basement. As the date of his departure approached, Guttmann submitted to the Gestapo a list of other far less valuable books that he was planning to bring with him to America. Perhaps sensing that some mischief was afoot, the Gestapo decided to watch him as he packed the books into two large boxes. After the first day of work, he hadn't finished packing them, so his Gestapo overseers sealed the room holding the partially packed load of books and went home. Then late that night, Guttmann explained, he climbed onto an outside terrace and snuck into the sealed room. There, by flashlight, he removed some of the books on the official list and replaced them with the treasures he had gotten from the Hochschule.

Still, Guttmann's visa was delayed for another year, and during that time the books sat in a warehouse in Bremen awaiting his departure. After the war broke out, Guttmann learned that he would need to repack the treasures in a smaller box. He and his wife did so, and it was only by a stroke of luck that they escaped detection by the Gestapo supervisors.

Guttmann insisted that the books were rightly his; Veit-Simon had said in no uncertain terms that he could keep them. He acknowledged that they were valuable, but this alone didn't mean that he was greedy. "I am now 82 years old," he said. "I have lived a life as a scholar and teacher and have always led a modest life style. It has been our plan to use the proceeds to live on, to pay medical expenses, to make contributions to Jewish institutions, and to leave something to our four children and our grandchildren so that they might have an easier life than ours."[25]

Needless to say, Guttmann's claim set off a flurry of legal wrangling.

Jewish librarians and Hochschule veterans claimed that Veit-Simon would never have given Guttmann the books *for keeps*. On loan until they could get somewhere safe? Maybe. But for good? Never. The attorney general pointed to the Hochschule's bylaws, which said that a transfer of Hochschule property needed to be authorized by three board members. Could Guttmann document that he had such authorization? Sotheby's countered that in this case the burden of proof was on the attorney general to show that Guttmann *didn't* have the authorization. And the attorney general wants *paperwork*? Sotheby's exclaimed. We're talking about a Jewish organization in Nazi Germany, for goodness sake. Very few of its *people* survived, and the attorney general wants paperwork?!

In the end the case never went to trial. Instead, on June 23, 1985, all of the warring parties announced that they had come to an agreement: JTS would return the two books it purchased from Sotheby's and receive a full refund; those two books would be resold for $900,000—the Bible to Yeshiva University, and the *machzor* to the Jewish National and University Library in Jerusalem; the remainder of the books would be sent to public institutions as determined by the Jewish Restitution Successor Organization; Guttmann and his family would receive $900,000.[26]

In the wake of these events, Alexander Guttmann lost his teaching privileges at HUC-JIR. He died in Cincinnati in 1994.

The terms by which Guttmann received these books remain unclear. We do, however, know that Veit-Simon did pass books to other scholars leaving Nazi Germany in trust—not in perpetuity—with the idea that they would one day end up safely stored in libraries and available to students and scholars. Perhaps there was unclear communication between the two men, with what Veit-Simon intended as a book loan understood by Guttmann as a book gift. Perhaps Veit-Simon felt that Guttmann was taking on more risk than the others who were removing books and really did mean to give these treasures to Guttmann. Or perhaps Guttmann was just lying.

What is certain, however, is that Guttmann secretly held books at his home for more than four decades and thus deprived the world of their treasures. And it's also certain that he received $900,000 from them in the final settlement. What is also certain is that Alexander Guttmann rescued dozens of priceless Jewish books from Nazi Germany and that he did so at great peril to his own safety. These books, most of which are centuries old, now sit safely on the shelves of libraries around the world only because of the risks that Guttmann took to preserve them. Without his daring act of subversion, it is possible—if not likely—that they would have disappeared forever.

There are many villains in the story of Nazi book looting: Alfred Rosenberg, Reinhard Heydrich, Johannes Pohl, Franz Alfred Six, and the Nazis' many minions of well-organized thieves. So too are there many heroes, such as Abraham Sutzkever, Shmerke Kaczerginski, and others. But then there's someone like Alexander Guttmann, a man who doesn't fit neatly into either of those categories. Perhaps we should see him as occupying a gray area in between hero and villain, or perhaps, in the end he actually fits into both categories. In the end such judgments yield little benefit. Whether what motivated Guttmann was goodness or greed, virtue or villainy, the part that he played in the centuries-long epic of the Jewish printed word was one of preservation. Now, at least partly because of him, the treasures live on.

## The Sarajevo Haggadah

Dervis Korkut had good reason to fear Gen. Johann Fortner, and as a resident of wartime Sarajevo, Korkut would have been wise to cooperate as much as he could with the general's orders. It was early 1942. The Nazis had already occupied Yugoslavia for almost a year, and during that time Fortner himself had overseen brutal massacres of Serbs, Jews, and members of the partisan Resistance. On this day Fortner had come to the Bosnian National Museum with one goal in mind. As always, he expected that his orders would be obeyed.

Fifty-four years old and nattily dressed, Korkut hardly looked like a man who would cause any trouble; he was, after all, just a scholar, and apparently an unassuming one at that. Dervis Korkut's research and writings spanned a wide range of topics, from architecture to alcohol abuse, and seemingly everything in between. He was also proficient in at least ten languages. Among his many areas of expertise, Korkut took a special interest in the cultures of minority communities of his native Bosnia. That is why, in 1940, the proudly Muslim scholar responded to the growing antisemitic fervor in his country by publishing a paper titled "Antisemitism Is Foreign to the Muslims of Bosnia and Herzegovina."

As the museum's librarian, Korkut might have avoided any direct dealings with Fortner that day, leaving such matters to his higher-ups. Alas, it was not to be. The director of the museum, a prominent Croatian archaeologist, didn't speak German, and had asked Korkut to act as translator during Fortner's visit. When Fortner arrived, the three men sat down in the director's office. There were some opening pleasantries, which Korkut translated as pleasantly as he could, but soon Fortner got down to business. "And now," he said, "please give me the haggadah."

The haggadah that Fortner had so politely "requested" had drawn growing scholarly attention in modern times, and its biography—if a book can be said to have a biography—is an astounding story of survival.

A haggadah is a prayer book that Jews use at their Passover seders, and its pages are often subject to the ravages of spilled wine, dribbled *charoset*, and other such assaults. As a result, *haggadot* tend not to last very long. This haggadah, however, is the exception.

It is a magnificent little book. Measuring about 6½ by 9 inches, its pages feature the traditional Hebrew text within vivid and shimmering illuminations in bold colors—lapis blues, malachite greens, and others. Many pages are adorned with gold and silver leaf. And a few of the folios, like most other *haggadot*, carry the traditional haggadah food stains. Several of the illuminations show pictures of Jewish life in medieval Spain and have led scholars to conclude that the book was written sometime during the mid-1300s—a century before the advent of Jewish printing.

21. Dervis Korkut.

22. A facsimile edition of the Sarajevo Haggadah. Photo by Shoshana Glickman.

Nobody knows for certain how and under what circumstances the book that would one day be known as the Sarajevo Haggadah left Spain, but it's probably safe to assume that its owners took it with them when they left in 1492—the year when, with the stroke of a pen, Ferdinand and Isabella expelled the country's enormous Jewish population. What is known is that by 1609 the book had made its way to Venice. During that year, a Catholic censor named Giovanni Domenico Vistorini inspected the book and gave it his priestly, censorial seal of approval. "Inspected by me," he wrote in Latin at the bottom of the last page. At the time many priests working as church censors were Jewish-born converts to Catholicism.

The story of the haggadah then fades into mystery for a couple of hundred years. The Bosnian National Museum purchased it from a family named Kohen in 1894. It was sent to Vienna for evaluation, where experts proclaimed it a masterpiece. Sadly, a curator assigned to crop the pages botched the rebinding process, discarded the book's original bindings, and replaced them with cheap modern cardboard.

In response to Fortner's request for the haggadah, the museum director raised his eyebrows. "But General, one of your officers came here already and demanded the haggadah," he explained. "Of course, I gave it to him."

Fortner was incredulous. "What officer?" he retorted.

"Sir," the director respectfully informed him through Korkut's translation, "I did not think it was my place to require a name."

As the frustrated Fortner departed, the director and his librarian-translator may have had to suppress mischievous smiles. What they knew—and Fortner didn't—was that as Fortner conducted his clipped, polite conversation with the director and Dervis Korkut, the famous Sarajevo Haggadah that he had come to confiscate was in Dervis Korkut's pants.

Korkut and the director had devised the ruse just moments before Fortner arrived that day. When the general called to say that he was coming over, Korkut pleaded with the director for permission to spirit the haggadah off to a place where it would be safe from Nazi book-grubbing hands. The director, astounded at Korkut's audacity, warned the librarian that hiding the book would mean risking his life. Korkut insisted: he was the librarian; it was his responsibility to protect the books entrusted to him.

The two men hurried to the basement. The director opened the safe holding the Sarajevo Haggadah, removed it from its cardboard case, and handed the small book to Korkut. Carefully Korkut placed the book in the waistband of his pants, buttoned up his jacket, smoothed out the bulges, and the two men went upstairs to smile at the general.

As it turns out, priceless books weren't the only thing that Dervis Korkut hid from the Nazis. Several weeks after he concealed the haggadah, he was approached by the custodian of a nearby building. With him was a bedraggled, half-starved young Jewish woman named Mira Papo. Early in the war Papo had fled Nazi oppression in Sarajevo and joined up with a group of Communist partisans in the woods. Recently, however, Josip Tito had purged Papo's group, and having barely escaped, she had come back to Sarajevo in a desperate search for sanctuary.

Korkut didn't even pause to think about it. He brought Mira home, introduced her to his wife, and sheltered her for the four months it took to get her forged identity papers and an even safer place to live outside the city. Dervis Korkut died of natural causes in 1969, and it wasn't for thirty years that the world learned the heroism he demonstrated in saving Mira Papo's life. In 1999 the Israeli government officially named Dervis and Servet Korkut as "Righteous Among the Nations." Their names are now inscribed and honored in the "Garden of the Righteous" at the Yad Vashem Holocaust Memorial in Jerusalem.[27]

## The Adventures of Fifi

The wedding of Hans Augusto Reyersbach and Margarete Elisabeth Waldstein took place in Rio de Janeiro, Brazil, on August 16, 1935. The two German-born newlyweds waited for several months before traveling from their Brazilian home, and when they finally left for Paris, they probably didn't know that they'd be in France for more than four years. And they certainly would never have guessed that their stay in the country would end with a frantic seventy-five-mile ride on cobbled-together bicycles, a furtive train trip along the French-Spanish border, and boat rides to Lisbon, Rio de Janeiro, and finally to New York, all the while carrying in their small suitcases handwritten manuscripts of books that would later be read by millions.[28] It was, to say the least, one doozy of a honeymoon.

Hans Reyersbach was born in in Hamburg in 1898, where, like most young Jewish boys, he received a traditional Jewish education at a local gymnasium. He served in the German army as a medic during World War I, and afterward, living in Munich and Hamburg, he supported his on-again, off-again college education by working as a lithographer and graphic designer for a company that made circus posters. In 1925 Reyersbach moved to Rio, where he got a job as an accountant in his brother-in-law's import-export firm.

Margarete Waldstein was eight years younger than Hans, but their families had known each other in Hamburg, so the two had probably met when they were children. She too had received a good, liberal education in Germany, but she had been far more purposefully focused on her artwork than the man she would marry. In the late 1920s she studied at the Bauhaus and several other German art schools, and eventually her watercolors were featured at a successful exhibit in Berlin. She studied photography and advertising, and surely in response to her family's urging, she traveled to Rio de Janeiro in 1935 to work with Hans Reyersbach. Even before the couple married later that year, they had succeeded in opening the city's first advertising agency.

When the Reyersbachs arrived in Paris for their honeymoon, they, like many visitors to the city, were immediately enchanted by its elegance, beauty, and excitement, so they decided to stay. To put food on their table, Hans illustrated several children's books and even received a patent for cut-out-and-fold animals that he was able to release as books too. The Reyersbachs settled in the Parisian neighborhood of Montmartre, where in 1939 they collaborated on a children's picture book called *Raffy and the Nine Monkeys* (*Rafi et les 9 Singes*); Margarete wrote the stories, Hans provided the illustrations. Later that year, as Germany's invasion of Poland marked the beginning of the war, the couple sought refuge from Paris in a castle called Chateau Feuga in the southern part of the country. There they began work on a story about the youngest, cutest, and most mischievous of the nine Raffy monkeys, Fifi.[29]

Eventually Margarete and Hans returned to Paris, where they continued working on *The Adventures of Fifi*. But then, in May 1940, Germany invaded Holland and Belgium, and it had become clear that France was not a safe place for a young Jewish couple to live. Hans gathered spare parts and cobbled together two bicycles. Margarete packed some personal items, gathered the preliminary Fifi drawings, and off they went. With German planes flying overhead in preparation for the army's entry into Paris two days later, the Reyersbachs joined the flood of refugees heading out of the city, pumping and pedaling their way south for three days with the first pages of *Fifi* bundled together in their packs.

Eventually, the Reyersbachs made it to Orleans. From there they boarded a train for Bayonne, bicycled to Biarritz, and thus continued through Spain and into Portugal, carrying *Fifi* the whole way. At one point an official stopped the Reyersbachs and, hearing the couple's German accents, suspected that they might be spies. Searching their bags, however, what he found was not secret codes or surveillance devices, but pictures of a cute little monkey, so he sent them on their way.

From Lisbon the Reyersbachs sailed back to Brazil and eventually on to New York, where they arrived in October 1940. As immigrants, Hans and Margarete decided to change not only their own names, but also the name of their yet-to-be-published fictional monkey. Hans Augusto and Margarete Reyersbach became H. A. and Margret Rey, and their monkey Fifi became the legendary Curious George.

Is Curious George Jewish? Are the books describing his adventures Jewish books? On the one hand, it would certainly be an exaggeration to say that the Reys' purpose in writing these stories was to tell a Jewish tale or provide their readers with hidden Jewish metaphors. The Reys were trying to make a living, and Fifi/George was a charming and enjoyable vehicle for them to do so. On the other hand, however, when we read these stories in light of the historical context in which the Reys wrote them, it is difficult *not* to see something of their own world come through. George, after all, is an innocent and exuberant protagonist who is eager to learn, and often can't help but save the day. The people around him nevertheless see him just as a little primate, subhuman, cute at best, and ultimately unworthy of the respect that we wise readers know he deserves. Would it be too much to suggest that a little bit of the world history as lived by the Reys slipped into the character and stories of Curious George?

If only real history came to endings as sweet as those in the Curious George books. If only the millions had had a Man in the Yellow Hat to save them from the jungle.

# 7

## Rescue

"Priceless Treasure Hidden by Rosenberg Is Found in Old German Castle."
—*Headline in* New York Herald Tribune, *April 16, 1945*

It is a moment that only the tumult of war could have made possible. The date is April 9, 1945, and the setting is Schloss Solms-Braunfels, a large, turreted castle, strong and fortified as it sits on a hilltop overlooking the small town of Hungen, Germany. It is a fairy-tale castle—the kind that usually has bats and cobwebs. In three days Franklin Roosevelt will be dead, in three weeks so will Adolf Hitler, and in just under a month the war will come to its official conclusion. But somehow that doesn't seem to matter here in this fortified manse. The walls of this castle, you see, are very, very thick.

The owner of this medieval fortress is Princess Luise Anna Ernestine Margarete Elisabeth Maria Gabriele von Solms-Braunfels.[1] She is away in Upper Bavaria just now; about a year ago she had no choice but to flee when the authorities discovered that she had been helping local Jewish families.[2] Despite the fact that Princess von Solms-Braunfels is absent, her husband for some reason has been allowed to stay. His name is James Pitcairn-Knowles. He is eighty-two years old, a Scotsman, onetime aspirant to the priesthood, and now a portrait painter.[3] Years from now, a biography of him will be entitled *The Unfinished Monk: The Life & Work of Reclusive Artist James Pitcairn-Knowles.*

The reclusive portrait painter—if such a thing is possible—lives in the castle with his butler, a man named Alfred Theissinger. Theissinger looks older than his eighty years, which may be why an account that will soon be written of this day will put him at eighty-seven. Evidently he has lived and worked in the castle for a long time, for he has been entrusted with the keys to the basement, and the basement holds great treasures. For Alfred Theissinger, life in the echoing halls of Schloss Solms-Braunfels is surely a quiet contrast to one of his previous positions. Thirty-two years ago he worked as a first-class steward on a large British steamship. Ordinarily this would been a somewhat routine job, but on the final fateful night of his employment on that ship, Theissinger found himself running to his passengers' cabins—to the Guggenheims' and the Strausses' and others'—pounding on their doors, imploring them to don their life jackets and move to the deck quickly. Theissinger got off the ship safely that night; many of the other passengers on the *Titanic* weren't so lucky.

From the time of the princess's departure until just recently, James Pitcairn-Knowles and Alfred the Butler have lived alone at Solms-Braunfels—just the two old men and a large police guard-dog to keep them safe from intruders. And with the war raging around them, the home's arched walkways, old staircases, and gloomy rooms have come to dwarf the doddering octogenarians more and more with each passing day. Recently, however, Pitcairn-Knowles has agreed to take in some long-term guests: a Swedish doctor, two Swedish baronesses, and a handful of other foreign dignitaries who sought refuge from the Allied bombings in the nearby countryside. On sunny days, the group can sometimes be spotted taking their rationed meals in the courtyard of the castle. From outside the castle walls and beyond the village boundaries sounds of tanks and artillery roar across the countryside and rattle the teacups in their saucers.

There is also another key player here, but this one hasn't come onto the stage yet. He is Lt. Robert Schoenfeld, currently of the U.S. Army, formerly of Brooklyn, New York, and before that a resident of lands not far from Schloss Solms-Braunfels.

Schoenfeld and his soldiers motored into town today, and as the young lieutenant led his men up the winding road toward the castle, it's quite possible that he marveled at the twists and turns that his life's path had taken to get him there.

Born in Lemburg, Poland, in 1913, Schoenfeld's family had moved to Vienna when he was a year old. Growing up, Robert was a good student, and after he graduated from high school he continued his studies, eventually earning a doctor of law degree from the University of Vienna. This was in the late 1930s, however, and as the situation for Viennese Jews darkened, the Schoenfelds soon realized that of them all Robert was the most vulnerable to Nazi persecution, so they arranged for his departure. He moved to Switzerland and then arrived in the United States in September 1939. Within a few months his parents and sister joined him, and the family moved into a small home in Brooklyn. Life in that outer borough was difficult for Robert and his family. He would have liked to have worked as an attorney after he arrived, but Robert's Viennese law degree wasn't valid in New York. Instead, when his father opened an electrical supply business, Robert helped run the store. Thanks to the Nazis—indeed, thanks to Europe in general—Robert had been plunked down into a loud city of foreign language and customs, far away from the friends, family, and comforts of his home in Austria.[4] Robert swore that he would never return to Europe again.

Then the war began. And then the United States got involved. And in July 1943, when the army learned that Schoenfeld was proficient in six languages, he received a lieutenant's commission and was sent overseas as an intelligence officer. "We are all thankful," his mother said, "that at least one of us was going to be able to repay the great debt that we owe to America."[5] Schoenfeld himself was overjoyed too. He'd promised never to return, but there he was, back in Europe, no longer an attorney, no longer the keeper of a small electronics store, but now an army officer, a fighter, wearing the uniform of the greatest military power in the world.

Schoenfeld has received word that there are plundered books and archival material in the castle, and he along with his small detail of soldiers have come to check it out. Reaching the palace with his men behind him, Schoenfeld knocks on the gate, and Alfred Theissinger appears behind it. Theissinger is cooperative. The Americans have all but won the war now, and resistance would do little but destroy the fragile pastoral quiet of the palace and its grounds.

Upon entering, Schoenfeld and his men see that the Nazis have taken possession of the castle, moving Pitcairn-Knowles, Alfred the Butler, and their guests into a few small rooms to clear space for the huge caches of loot that they have stashed in the home. The castle's office is packed tight with countless newspaper files, periodicals, and books. Lining the walls are rows of bookcases holding well-organized deposits from Frankfurt's Museum Jüdischer Altertümer (Jewish Antiquities Museum). Something about those shelves strikes the men as strange. Taking in the magnitude of the literary horde, it is a few moments before they realize that the books on those organized and categorized shelves are the only organized and categorized books in the whole place. Most of the books are sitting in messy stacks, stashed in crates, or carelessly thrown into piles.

Then Theissinger leads Schoenfeld to the cellar. After filing down the stairs, the men come to a locked door. Theissinger pulls out a large key ring; it jangles; he opens the door. Inside are nine metal trunks. Theissinger walks to the nearest one and opens it up. Schoenfeld's eyes widen. Inside are rare Jewish books from the Institute de Bibliographic in Paris. Off to the side is a metal cabinet, also locked. Theissinger opens this too, and when Schoenfeld sees its contents, he can barely contain his excitement. Inside are beautifully bound, centuries-old Judaic books, old illuminated manuscripts, and incunabula. The cabinet, Schoenfeld discovers on closer inspection, holds some of the most valuable pieces of Jewish literature from the Rothschild Library in Frankfurt. Actually, to be more precise, the cabinet holds some of the most valuable items of Jewish literature in the world.

As it turns out, the castle isn't the only building in Hungen holding

Jewish loot. There are seven other repositories as well. In the vault at the Hungen Savings and Loan, in a singing-society building, in some tin sheds at a brickyard on the outskirts of town, in a local church, and elsewhere, American soldiers turn up massive amounts of things that Nazi Germany had stolen from its victims. There is artwork, Jewish and Christian ritual items, and archival material from France, Russia, Scandinavia, and elsewhere. But most of all, there are books. Untold numbers of them. Some of them, like the Rothschild material, are priceless. Some of the other material is of great value, too—Torah scrolls and other rare material that didn't quite make it to Rothschild status. It looks as if some of those rare items have recently been re-looted. Soon-to-be-vanquished Nazi troops evidently wanted a share of the riches for themselves and have left torn scrolls lying out in the brickyard behind them.[6] To the soldiers walking through Hungen's castle and other repositories, the books seem innumerable. Later estimates will put the count at around 1.5 million volumes.[7]

High above this unfolding scene, overlooking the soldiers and the battle-scarred German countryside in the distance, storks roost on the central tower of the castle.[8] But with the war drawing to an end, with the screams of the innocent and the echoes of the bombs still cascading through the hills, these storks are silent. It will be some time before they can herald the beginning of new life once again.

Today you can visit the half-timbered castle in Hungen that once housed millions of stolen Jewish books. Maintained by a committee of local volunteers, its restored rooms, courtyard, and grounds are now used for concerts, art exhibitions, and other cultural events. On the "History" page of its website, there is a timeline. Its final two entries read:

1870: Last renovation.

Until about 1970: Various usages . . . parts of the castle were later used as a retirement home, as a dormitory for Turkish guest workers.

1870. 1970. Nowhere does the website mention the events that occurred during the intervening hundred years.[9]

## *The Monuments Men*

At the heart of the American army's efforts to preserve Europe's cultural treasures during the war was an unlikely cadre of soldiers who composed the Monuments, Fine Arts, and Archives (MFA&A) program. They were a motley crew of artists and historians, archivists and archaeologists, conservators and curators, chosen from the highest ranks of their fields of expertise. Some were bespectacled, some were bald, and some bore paunches uncommon in the battle-hardened ranks of the U.S. military. Nevertheless, they had been entrusted with a task that even the most secular-minded of them might have regarded as sacred—preserving the great cultural heritage of the European continent.

From early in the war, historians, curators, collectors, and others in the art world had grown deeply concerned about the fate of Europe's cultural treasures. Galvanizing their efforts, they asked Harlan Stone, chief justice of the Supreme Court and a patron of the arts himself, to send a memo to President Roosevelt suggesting the establishment of a governmental commission devoted to preserving Europe's artworks and historical monuments and to salvaging and returning those treasures already taken by Axis powers.[10]

The bureaucratic wheels of government rolled slowly in response to Stone's request, but military realities in the spring and summer of 1943 made the pressure to preserve these treasures grow particularly intense. American forces were busily preparing for their July 9 invasion of Sicily and for their conquest of mainland Italy the following September. Experts and amateurs alike knew that those lands were slathered with cultural treasures of unbelievable beauty and unspeakable value. From the top of the Italian boot down to its toe and across the Strait of Messina into Sicily were many of the greatest cathedrals, monasteries, and palaces that humanity had ever created. Inside many of them were priceless artistic treasures: Michelangelos, da Vincis, and Botticellis. Even its plaza fountains and village churches were often home to priceless works of art. The American army was poised to slam Italy hard. Surely some of the treasures would be destroyed in the battle, but maybe there was a way to minimize the destruction; maybe the army could save some of the treasures.

That June, President Roosevelt authorized the creation of the American Commission for the Protection and Salvage of Artistic and Historic Monuments in War Areas, chaired by Supreme Court Justice Owen J. Roberts. Thankfully it soon took on the far more easy to remember nickname, the Roberts Commission.

Headquartered at the National Gallery of Art in Washington DC and carrying the imprimatur of the nation's foremost art experts, the Roberts Commission was able to set up liaisons with the Departments of War, State, and others in the art community to chart a strategy to preserve Europe's cultural treasures. Of course such a setup meant that it had to conduct its work from afar. The Roberts Commission was able to succeed greatly in articulating government policy and coordinate between the various parties involved in the effort, but it soon became clear that preserving Europe's artwork was going to take much more. To succeed, the commission would need "boots on the ground"—an on-the-scene cadre with the expertise needed to deal with the works that the artistic community so desperately wanted to save. As a result the Roberts Commission was instrumental in forming the Monuments, Fine Arts, and Archives section—MFA&A—widely known as the Monuments Men. Attached to as many combat units as their numbers would allow, these uniformed curators and professors faced the seemingly impossible task of saving paintings, statues, and important works of architecture even as the bombs of war exploded around them. Wherever possible, they implored military rulers to spare targets of significant artistic value. They dug through the rubble of bombed-out palaces and churchyards in search of surviving artistic treasures. They set up security systems to prevent American soldiers from taking the artwork home as souvenirs. They established collecting points to process stolen and salvaged material. They catalogued whatever they could.[11]

In the spring of 1945, as Allied troops rushed through Germany and other former Nazi territories, they found only a tiny vestige of the brutal resistance left. Battalions of enemy soldiers melted away into villages and countrysides; townspeople greeted conquering Allied soldiers not with vicious opposition, but with tentative smiles and offers of help; the din of wartime Europe grew quiet, leaving vast piles of rubble in its wake. The Third Reich was crumbling. Finally on April 30 Hitler committed suicide, and by May 8 it was over.

The American army didn't go home immediately, of course; there was a military occupation to set up. There were the Nazi army to disband, war criminals to prosecute, and vast expanses of territory to secure. Now the job was no longer one of conquest, it was one of occupation—the occupation of a continent devastated by six years of horrific destruction and death.

Immediately, the Monuments Men beheld the enormity of the task before them. The Nazis had looted a lot of artwork—private collections, museums, churches too numerous to count. Upon arriving, Allied forces discovered some of the artwork stored in caves and mineshafts deep beneath the ground, in magnificent palaces, and sometimes in warehouses. But there were smaller storage places as well. There were hundreds of small castles throughout Europe where the Nazis had stored material. There was artwork in farmhouses, chapels, libraries, and community centers. It was a vast wilderness of wartime destruction, and the Monuments Men had come to mine the artistic gold hiding in its soil

Complicating matters, the Monuments Men soon realized that Nazi looting was hardly limited to artwork. During the war Germany had also pillaged furniture, archives, textiles, jewelry, and household items. Dealing with the massive volume of wartime plunder was a task whose enormity beggared description. Fortunately, however, the discovery of a great deal of this material came pretty easily. For starters, in many towns there were castles that had been abandoned by their owners during the war and commandeered by the Nazi army—it was usually a safe bet that at least part of those castles had become repositories for Nazi loot. Also, the locals in these formerly German-held territories were eager to please the conquering Allied forces, and the Monuments Men usually had little trouble getting local citizens to lead them to stashes of material.

For obvious reasons, it was the art that most interested the Monuments Men. They were art experts for the most part, and their discoveries of large caches of Vermeers, Rubenses, and Picassos had a way of dwarfing all of their other finds, even when on closer inspection those other finds were of great value too. Usually when the Monuments Men came across a trove of loot, they gave great care and attention to the artwork and carefully set aside all of the other material for later processing. They certainly took seriously the discoveries of books, but massive piles of Yiddish novels and children's Hebrew reading primers were hardly what received their attention. Indeed, most of their memoirs contain excited descriptions of the artistic treasures they discovered, but only passing mention of the books.

One of the other reasons that the Monuments Men focused on art so much more than books was simply a function of language. The "language" of painting and sculpture is universal, and certainly the art-experts-turned-Monuments-Men were fluent in it. The books, however, were written in a Babel of tongues in which few of them were proficient. Was a Hebrew Bible from Vienna a rarity or simply one more book in the mountain of literature that the Nazis stole? Did the handwritten inscriptions inside the cover of the old volume of Talmud come from a great sage who once owned it, or were they simply idle doodlings of a bored student?

To the Monuments Men, the artwork was gold. The books were assemblages of secret code—a given volume might have been valuable, but probably wasn't. Focusing on the artwork instead of the literature was a far more efficient use of their time. Soon it became clear that the

American army would need collecting points of its own for this material and that some of these warehouses should be devoted especially to books. In the meantime the Monuments Men would give the lion's share of their energy to the art.

And so it went. In city after city, hamlet after hamlet, American troops spent the spring of 1945 sweeping into areas that had only recently been part of the Third Reich. There they discovered troves of priceless artwork, golden jewels, valuable furniture, and precious religious items. And they also found books. A lot of them.

# 8

## Restitution

Divine Providence really smiled upon me and caused me to be
sent to Germany to serve in Offenbach and be part of the "greatest
book-restitution in world history."
— *Seymour J. Pomrenze on his work at the*
*Offenbach Archival Depot*

In late February 1946, Capt. Seymour J. Pomrenze rode in a U.S. Army
motorcar through Frankfurt, Germany. A blizzard howled through the
city that day, and through the snow Pomrenze could see bullet-ridden
walls and the bombed-out remains of the war-torn metropolis.

His driver was Lt. Leslie Poste, a thirty-eight-year-old librarian and
archivist whom the army had charged with the task of processing books
and archival material taken by the Nazis during the war. Poste told Captain Pomrenze that their destination was Offenbach, a small city just
across the river from Frankfurt. There, in an old warehouse once owned
by the I. G. Farben chemical company, was a collecting point where the
U.S. Army gathered looted books and papers that they and other Allied
forces had discovered at war's end. There was, Poste explained to his
passenger, a *lot* of material to process.

What Poste probably didn't mention was that the choice of this particular building as a storage center for Jewish books was an ironic one.
Until recently, its former owner, I. G. Farben, had produced components
of Zyklon B, the cyanide-based gas the Nazis used in Auschwitz and
other death camps to murder millions of Jews.

23. Capt. Seymour Pomrenze. Courtesy American Jewish Historical Society, New York, and Newton Centre, Massachusetts.

24. Books waiting to be sorted at the Offenbach Archival Depot. Courtesy Yad Vashem Photo Archives.

Poste reviewed the chain of events that had brought the books to Offenbach: the book burnings; the creation of the ERR; the terror and calamity of the Nazis' theft of Jewish books; the regional collection centers in Brussels, Belgrade, Kiev, and elsewhere; the Germans' last-minute attempts at the end of the war to consolidate their collections and protect them from Allied bombs. Poste explained that after the hostilities concluded the previous year, Allied forces had discovered these treasures and shipped them to the Rothschild Library in Frankfurt. But the enormous volume of material soon rendered the Frankfurt facility inadequate, so the books had been shipped over the Main River to this old—and far roomier—warehouse in Offenbach.

Leslie Poste, an educated librarian, would become an accomplished scholar during his postwar career. But he was out of his league in Offenbach. Processing such a massive hoard of material demanded administrative skill, the ability to cut through tangles of military red tape, and a voice that carried enough authority to move mountains. Mountains of *books*, that is. Poste had assembled only a small staff, he had not established any restitution procedures, and he was overwhelmed to the point of paralysis. To date, a great deal of material had entered the Offenbach facility, but none had left

Unlike Lieutenant Poste, however, Seymour Pomrenze seems to have been made for this task. He was born in the Ukrainian capital, Kiev, in 1915 or 1916 (the specific date of his birth has been lost), and after Pomrenze's father was killed in a pogrom in 1919, his mother brought young Seymour and his older brother Chaim to the United States. They settled in Chicago, which was home to a large Jewish community, including several Pomrenze relatives.[1]

Seymour's mother grew ill shortly after the family's arrival, so his aunt and uncle became his primary caregivers. Under their guidance, Seymour was raised as an observant Jew, and from an early age he distinguished himself in his Jewish studies. By the time he was fourteen, Pomrenze was tutoring Jewish boys to prepare them for their bar mitzvahs. Soon, he was teaching in Chicago's Hebrew schools and even directed some of them for a short time. After high school Pomrenze attended the Lewis Institute (now part of the Illinois Institute of Technology) and then earned a master's degree in Jewish history at the University of Chicago. He was also working toward a doctorate, but while doing research in Washington DC, he ran out of money and took a job at the National Archives and Records Administration.

Soon the war began, and everything changed. Pomrenze joined the army in the spring of 1942 and was commissioned as an officer the following April. He served at domestic posts for a while and then went to Burma, India, and China on intelligence-gathering missions for the Office of Strategic Services (OSS). Shortly after the war ended, in December 1945, Pomrenze—now a captain—was called to Europe. There were colossal hoards of German archives to be organized, and knowing his background, Pomrenze's superiors appointed him to be part of the

American archival team. The assignment would not last long. Sorting through the German archives, Pomrenze didn't realize that, like particles of space dust coalescing to become a planet, Europe's looted Jewish books had been swirling toward Offenbach ever since the war ended the previous May. Soon Pomrenze would fall into the orbit of this massive literary accretion of literature, and in some ways he would never leave.

By 1945, details of the Holocaust were emerging in full and horrifying detail. Millions of Jews had been murdered; European Jewish culture was utterly decimated; most survivors were clothed in tatters, skeleton-like from starvation, and in desperate need of help. One of the many agencies reaching out to these refugees was an American group called the Joint Distribution Committee (JDC). As it sent the survivors food and clothing, the JDC, like many other Jewish groups around the world, became aware of the enormity of the looted book collection that the Allied armies had recovered after the war. Perhaps, thought the JDC, those books could be sent to displaced persons (DP) camps and be made available to Holocaust survivors and other refugees. The JDC asked Koppel Pinson, a Jewish historian at Queens College, to travel to Offenbach and evaluate the collection.

Pinson was friendly with Chaim Pomrenze, and Chaim had mentioned that his archivist brother Seymour was stationed in Germany. Pinson passed the information on to the early organizers of the Offenbach Collecting Point, and almost immediately Seymour Pomrenze received his orders. He was to leave his German archives assignment and travel to Offenbach with all due haste. "Where is Offenbach?" Pomrenze wondered. "Why there? What am I to do there? [And] who got me into this mess?"[2]

As he and Poste pulled up to the warehouse, Pomrenze may have glimpsed some bookcases through the doorway or perhaps large stacks of crates on sagging pallets outside. But when he entered and beheld the full scope of the building's contents, what he saw astounded him. It was "a seemingly endless sea of crates and books," Pomrenze later recalled. Books that once composed thousands of libraries throughout Europe, volumes that had belonged to countless individuals and families—indeed the literary legacy of an entire civilization—had come to rest in this one run-down building outside Frankfurt. "I thought what a horrible mess!" he recalled in a 2002 lecture. "What could I do with all these materials? How could I carry out my assignment successfully?"[3]

As astonishing as the size and the scope of the collection were to Captain Pomrenze, he was also mindful of the human tragedy that it represented. Later he recalled his feelings on walking into the I. G. Farben building. "I felt faint," he recalled. "In one corner I saw Torah scrolls piled in huge heaps, one on top of the other, some on the ground and some on makeshift shelves. In my mind's eye, I envisioned the Nazis breaking into synagogues and Jewish homes, murdering the families and stealing the objects lying before me. I was stunned . . . I wanted to cry."[4]

Another discovery astounded Pomrenze too: nothing was happening. His own assignment was identical to that of Leslie Poste: to "protect and restitute" the seized books. But only a half dozen workers were staffing the Offenbach operation, and around them sat an untended chaos of literature. None of it was *moving*. None of the books were going back to their rightful owners. They were just sitting there.

"It was easy to determine that the OCP [Offenbach Collecting Point] was not effectively managed," he recalled. It was a sleepy organization. "How was I to wake up this activity? How was the mission to be carried out successfully?"[5] Within a few days, Pomrenze figured out what he needed to do. "It seemed as if Divine Providence really smiled upon me and caused me to be sent . . . to Germany to serve in Offenbach," he recalled.[6] This was a job he was made for.

First, Pomrenze realized, he needed to quash his inner librarian. To deal with a collection of this size, he couldn't focus on its individual volumes. As enticing as each of the books might have been, he knew that here his guiding philosophy needed to be the same as it was when he was an archivist—to process the material as a giant collection, not as individual volumes. To get lost in the beautiful title pages and handwritten marginalia that would captivate later readers was a luxury that Seymour Pomrenze simply could not afford. Then he turned to the particulars. He laid out an organizational chart detailing the work of administrative staff, operations workers, and liaisons with restitution officers from other countries. He hired almost two hundred workers—mostly German civilians—and transported them to Offenbach. He built them a kitchen; he trained the staff; he established security procedures. He also cleaned up the decrepit facility, installing heat and electric lighting, fixing the windows, and putting up permanent shelves for the books. To cap it off, he installed an American flag and watched with special pride as it was raised each morning. It didn't take long before German children in Offenbach would greet Pomrenze, "*Jawohl, jawohl*," as he walked by. "You see," he later recalled, "they knew who was boss."[7]

And although he was far too classy to say it aloud, Capt. Seymour Pomrenze also felt a sense of triumph as he watched his operation unfold. There he was, an officer in the U.S. Army, a commander, smack-dab in the heart of a country that only a year earlier had been actively killing his people. Now it wasn't the jackboots who were in charge. He was! The Jewish kid from Kiev and Chicago! These two hundred German workers—former subjects of the Third Reich—were now working under *him*. The reversal of roles certainly didn't undo the evil that the Germans had wrought, but it was gratifying to finally turn the tables. And the fact that he and the Germans he supervised were working to achieve a measure of justice and dignity for the Jewish people made the whole thing even sweeter.[8]

On March 2 Col. James R. Newman, of the Office of Military Government, United States (OMGUS), issued a directive ordering that the collecting point in Offenbach be officially designated the Offenbach Archival Depot (OAD). The OAD and its director were to work with restitution officers throughout the European theater "and assist them in making available for restitution, books and such other properties as are clearly identifiable as to country of origin." It was also to "make recommendations as to the disposition of such books and properties as are not identifiable as to country of origin." The directive authorized Pomrenze to hire staff, supply transportation and maintenance, and "supervise the storage, warehousing, boxing, crating, and shipping of all books and other properties formerly administered by the Offenbach Collecting Point."[9] The new orders not only authorized Pomrenze to manage the staff and facilities of the OAD, it also established him as the army's point man with regard to book restitution. Now, *all* recovered books would come to Offenbach; now, he could call up the resources he needed to systematize restitution work for the entire U.S. military operation in the American Zone; now, he had formal recognition as an archivist from the army, and thus could more easily implement his plan.

### Sorting and Sending

With this authorization in hand, Pomrenze could finally get to work. He and his staff estimated that there were more than one million books and other items in the depot, and Pomrenze set up sorting protocols to process them all. Early on he realized that many of the books in Offenbach were in a horrible state of disrepair. Some had broken bindings and were falling apart; others had gotten wet; many bore signs of mold. Fortunately Pomrenze learned that one of his employees was "a former Catholic Brother," who had worked with books and manuscripts back in his monastery days. The OAD had no equipment to repair and preserve the books, so Pomrenze instructed the ex-monk to jerry-rig a preservation system from the materials at hand.

Pomrenze directed his staff to separate the material into three categories: identifiable, "semi-identifiable," and unidentifiable.[10] The first category, the identifiable books, one might think would have been the simplest to process. If a book had a handwritten name on its inside-front cover, a library stamp on its title page, or some other marking indicating where it had been before the war, then the OAD should have been able to send it straightaway to its rightful owner. But of course in the chaos of postwar Europe, the situation was far more complicated. Many of the private book owners had been murdered; survivors could often not be found. It was not uncommon for entire Jewish communities to have been wiped out, leaving behind their prewar library books as material orphans of the war. To make matters even more complicated, many surviving communities had moved en masse to other countries—usually to the United States or the nascent State of Israel—and in other communities only a tiny remnant remained. Did it make sense to send large libraries back to places now depleted of all or most of their Jews?

Ultimately, however, none of these questions mattered. The Offenbach Archival Depot, like other Allied groups involved in postwar restitution, was operating under a legal principle known as escheat, which required that unidentified war loot be returned to the country from which it was taken. Returned to its home *country*, that is—its government, not individual citizens, local libraries, or nongovernmental agencies.[11] As a result, the OAD could deal only with national governments in its restitution efforts. Then, once another government received a book, that government could convey the book to its original owner . . . if it so desired.

It must have been frustrating for the OAD staff. When they came across a book that had clearly been taken from, say, the library of a small Jewish village in the Ukraine, their only option for restitution was to send it not to that village or any of its survivors, but rather to the Stalinist USSR government. Surely, Pomrenze and the others thought, there must be another option.

Many books, on the other hand, clearly did belong to foreign governments. As a result several countries assigned restitution officers to Offenbach, instructing them to identify their nation's books and facilitate their return. The Netherlands sent its chief archivist, Maj. Dirk Graswinkel, to help find the identifiably Dutch material. Graswinkel and Pomrenze hit it off immediately. "He was dedicated to his mission," Pomrenze later recalled, "and infected me with a strong desire to carry out mine." Pomrenze gave Graswinkel the full support of his staff and free run of the depot to help facilitate the identification of Dutch property.[12]

France sent three liaison officers—one from the Bibliothèque Nationale in Paris and two from the French army. Italy, Germany, and other countries later sent liaison teams as well. Additionally Offenbach received several agents who did not represent European governments, such as Koppel Pinson from the Joint Distribution Committee and David Clift from the Library of Congress.

When the workers in Offenbach first sorted through the books, they and the liaison officers identified several huge collections to which the principle of escheat could be sensibly applied. As early as March 8—a mere six days after the official establishment of the OAD—Pomrenze and his staff began loading a barge with 371 crates of books for shipment to Holland, and the barge departed down the Main River four days later. On March 22, workers loaded 730 cases of books onto five freight cars for shipment to France.[13] The numbers of outgoing books would continue to grow. Within the next four weeks, more than one million volumes were shipped—or would soon be shipped—to countries all over Europe. By October 1946, the numbers were downright staggering—700,000 books had been sent to Germany, 232,000 to Russia, and another 234,520 to Italy. The OAD also shipped smaller collections to Belgium, Czechoslovakia, Great Britain's Channel Islands, and twelve other countries. Simultaneously huge shipments of literature that were still being discovered throughout Europe continued to flow in. Millions of books would eventually pass into the Offenbach Archival Depot and out to the countries from which they were taken, restituted as part of the escheat-based nation-to-nation transfers.

The next category of books was the semi-identifiable ones. Ostensibly these bore hints but no definitive information as to where they had come from. Often there were faintly penned names on the inside of their front covers, some had semi-legible library stamps on their title pages, and in many cases the language or content of the books could

25. A barge loaded with books about to be transferred from the Offenbach Archival Depot to Holland. Courtesy American Jewish Historical Society, New York, and Newton Centre, Massachusetts.

help identify where the Nazis had gotten them. These books would need to be examined more closely. Pomrenze assigned dozens of staffers to the OAD sorting branch. Once the large governmental collections were removed, the sorters meticulously pored through the others, looking for stamps, notations, or anything else that might help identify them.

Leading the effort was the OAD's assistant director, Capt. Isaac Bencowitz. A forty-year-old Russian-born Jewish immigrant to the United States, Bencowitz had received a bachelor's degree in chemistry from University of Chicago and later a PhD from Columbia. He had been stationed at the Offenbach Collecting Point since the end of the war and became Pomrenze's assistant during the first few weeks of the OAD's official operations. Bencowitz was perfectly suited for the task. Not only was his scientific expertise of great help in preserving the damaged books and archives, but having come from eastern Europe, he also knew many of the languages in which they were written: Hebrew, Yiddish, Russian, Polish, and others.

Given the huge amount of material, the mere task of organizing the sorting process was a massive undertaking. There were, remember, *millions* of books. Some bore library markings; others didn't. Some were damaged; others were intact. Some were of great monetary value; others were not. They were written in a Babel of languages.

As soon as the identifiable material was removed, Bencowitz and his large sorting staff got to work, combing through the many crates of remaining material. Book, by book, by book. Many volumes lacked any identifying marks whatsoever—these the sorters set aside as unidentifiable. Others had incomplete markings—often faded, flaking away, or carelessly pressed library stamps, leaving vaguely legible smudges or half logos as the books' only sign of ownership. When the staffers could read the stamps, it still wasn't always clear where the books had come from. Many libraries had stamps that were similar to others. Some stamps included only a logo, and not the names of the libraries they represented. Many came from tiny little towns that nobody in the OAD had heard of. It had been clear from the outset that sorting so many *books* would be a huge undertaking, but now, Bencowitz realized, the mere task of sorting the *stamps* that identified them would be a big job as well.

What they needed, Bencowitz realized, was a stamp catalogue. Quickly he set up a photographic lab where his staff took pictures of every stamp represented in the Offenbach collection. He categorized the stamps into country groups and assembled the images into a two-volume catalogue, one for countries in western European and another for those from the east.

In June 2012 I had the opportunity see one of the only original copies of Bencowitz's library stamp catalogue at the Center for Jewish History, in New York. After navigating my way through security and a maze of hallways, I arrived at the reading room. It was large, quiet, temperature

26. Capt. Isaac Bencowitz. Courtesy Yad Vashem Photo Archives.

controlled, and serious. No pens or backpacks were allowed inside, just pencils, paper, and laptops. I requested the catalog and found a place to sit.

Soon a staff member arrived at my table and placed before me two large volumes bound in dark-green covers. Although the books reminded me of my grandparents' old photo albums, their content was utterly different from the bar mitzvah photos and vacation pictures I might have expected them to contain. To page through these albums, I discovered, was to see not the memories of a single family or individual, but to glimpse a lost world. The catalogue held more than four thousand images in all, categorized under tabs representing some three dozen countries. The photos, printed on glossy paper reminiscent of 1970s' Xerox machines, are each individually pasted onto the albums' heavy pages, with each leaf protected from the next by a flimsy, translucent sheet of what looked like rice paper. The pages are layered with glue and a patchwork of old photographs. They are as stiff as heavy parchment.

I looked through the first pages of the eastern Europe volume. There were forty-three different stamps from Jewish libraries in Czechoslovakia, sixty-six from Estonia, and forty-two from Greece. Each was different— one bore the name of its library inside a circular logo, another had it over a crude image of an eagle, and yet another provided the name without any adornments at all. Hungary, Latvia, Lithuania . . . Each page I saw was fascinating; I couldn't wait to see the next one, but I couldn't bear to leave the page I was on.

I continued flipping through the album—Poland, Russia, Ukraine . . . I tried to imagine what these libraries looked like. After all, somebody had designed each of those stamps; each one represented a different Jewish library—each from its own community, and each with its own caretakers and patrons, not to mention sounds, sights, and smells. And for the most part all of those libraries are gone. Who was behind these stamps? Who had read the libraries' books and couldn't wait to get their hands on the next one? Who had gone to those libraries just to see their friends and schmooze? What had the libraries looked like? The

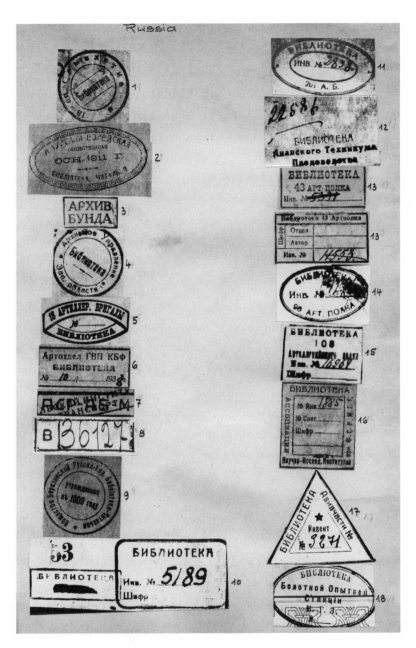

27. A page of stamps from Russian Jewish Libraries collected at Offenbach by Isaac Bencowitz. Courtesy American Jewish Historical Society, New York, and Newton Centre, Massachusetts.

very existence of each collection testified to the Jewish love of words. And each was a mini-memorial to the people who made that love real.

In the confines of that pristine, high-tech, New York reading room, it was almost as if every stamp in those albums was a hyperlink to a webpage. To click on any of them was not to surf through cyberspace, but to pay an imaginary visit to a real place in real time with real people. Yugoslavia, Vilna, White Russia . . . It was a lost world indeed. And if this was only a glimpse of it, I could barely imagine the magnificence of the riches it once contained.

I found it curious that many of the stamps in those albums were perfectly legible. One stamp in the Poland section, for example, shows just two words and no symbols: "Biblioteka Opolska." Even a non-Polish-speaker like me could tell that whatever book that stamp came from had been in the library of a town called Opolska (actually, I later learned that it was Opole—close enough). How is it that a book with such a clear stamp ended up in the OAD's "semi-identifiable" pile? In fact, most of the stamps in the Bencowitz catalogue were pretty clear. Shouldn't books with such stamps have been in the identifiable pile?

As it turns out, many of the books officially deemed "semi-identifiable" weren't semi-identifiable at all; they were *fully* identifiable. The handwritten names inside their covers were often quite clear, and many of their owners had survived the war and could be easily located. The OAD inspectors could have determined quite easily the Polish shtetl, Ukrainian seminary, or Lithuanian rabbi who had owned those books before the war. According to the rules, by all accounts those books should have joined the huge piles sent to foreign governments. Why, then, did the OAD classify them as semi-identifiable?

What was happening, perhaps, was tacit and subtle subterfuge—but in the climate of the time, the subterfuge was understandable. Pomrenze, as we have noted, was an observant Jew. Isaac Bencowitz was also Jewish, and Koppel Pinson, historian of the Joint Distribution Committee who helped in the OAD's identification process, was Jewish as well. We can imagine any of these men coming across one of the "semi-identifiable" volumes, *identifying* it, and having to decide in which pile to place the book. To deem the book "identifiable" would effectively mean casting it over to the other side of the Iron Curtain and consigning it to the waiting hands of the Ukraine, Poland, Lithuania, or another Eastern Bloc government. Many of these countries were ruled by regimes decidedly unfriendly to Jews and Judaism, and the prospect of shipping them these precious Jewish treasures was often one that the OAD's Jewish book-keepers couldn't stomach.

All of this unfolded, of course, during the early days of the Cold War. It was on March 5, 1946, in fact—just three days after the OAD was officially established—that Winston Churchill's famous "Iron Curtain Speech" at Missouri's Westminster College articulated the profound changes in the political and ideological landscape of the postwar world. The "Soviet menace," many Americans feared, was growing; all of eastern Europe had come under its influence. Even worse, many of the countries now part of the USSR were complicit in the Holocaust! In such an atmosphere, it is easy to imagine that the thought of sending looted Jewish books to the Communists of the east was utterly repugnant to many Americans— Jews and non-Jews alike.

This is not to say that Pomrenze and his staff were deceitful. Indeed, during the entire span of the OAD's existence, there is no evidence of any systematic duplicity at all on the part of its leaders. What we can conjecture, however, is that for books that might have gone to the Soviet Union or to other Eastern Bloc countries there was a built-in bias on the part of Bencowitz, Pomrenze, and the others to keep them as unidentifiable as possible. Better have them in limbo, the thinking probably went, than to put them in the hands of Communist antisemites. When they came across books marked as having come from the shtetls, yeshivot, and metropolitan libraries of the once-thriving Jewish world of eastern Europe—and when they couldn't bear the thought of sending them off in a huge shipment to a government that despised both democracy and

Jews—Pomrenze and his staff now had another option. Calling them "semi-identifiable" would buy them some time. Even when a book's provenance was pretty clear, they may have reasoned, it wouldn't really be a lie to call them semi-identifiable. After all, the identities of those stamps and signatures did need to be confirmed. And if the American military occupation "happened" to end before the OAD could secure these confirmations . . . and if the army then "happened" to turn the books over to another group not bound by the technicalities of escheat . . . and if that group "happened" to be one that could use more humane and sensible criteria to decide the books' fate—well then, so be it.

The third and final category of books was the "unidentifiables." Many had arrived in large piles from Nazi collecting points, completely unorganized, with no identifying marks. Others had come in unmarked crates or in smaller batches with no way to tell who their rightful owners were. Frequently they had broken bindings, and their loose pages had become irretrievably mixed with those of other destroyed books. These books really were unidentifiable. Where were they to go?

Basically, the answer was simple: nowhere. Deluged with hundreds of thousands of books arriving each month, the unidentifiable ones would have to sit and wait until after the OAD could deal with the others. These unidentifiable books, however, did pique their caretakers' curiosity. If they could somehow be identified, might there be a way to return them to their rightful owners? Pomrenze scoured the bullet-riddled chaos of postwar Germany and drafted whatever Judaic experts he could find to help identify them. One of them was Capt. Isaiah Rackovsky, an Orthodox rabbi and army chaplain. His expertise was invaluable in identifying a great deal of the OAD archival material.

Another was Koppel Pinson, drafted to use his Judaic expertise for the OAD itself as well as for the Joint Distribution Committee he officially represented. As a historian, Pinson had an eye for the antique, a sense about which objects and relics were of true historical value. During his time in Germany, for example, Pinson frequently embarked on tours of the country, and along the way he took pictures—lots of them. He photographed the ruins of grand castles and government buildings, the DP camps, and eventually the daily operations of the OAD. Often he turned the camera around and asked friends, associates, or strangers to snap pictures of him at these sites as well (before selfies!). After his death Pinson's wife donated his photo albums to a museum in California, where they remain today—an invaluable photographic record of a ravaged country recovering from the devastations of war.

Pinson put his nose for history to use at the OAD, examining and identifying whatever books he could. Some of those he inspected in Offenbach, for example, were from the library of YIVO, the Yiddish Scientific Institute, which had moved its headquarters from Vilna to New York in 1940. In late November 1945 YIVO authorized Pinson to carefully identify "nonvaluable" books in the OAD's YIVO collection and send them to the DP camps through the offices of the JDC. The same month Pinson applied to Gen. Lucius D. Clay, head of the American Military Government in Germany, for permission to send an additional twenty-five thousand "nonvaluable" books to the camps. Clay approved Pinson's application the following January.[14]

As Pinson and his staff looked for nonvaluable books, they couldn't help but identify some valuable ones as well. As a result Koppel Pinson became one of Pomrenze's key point men in identifying important books in the Offenbach collection. Pinson returned to New York in December 1946. Under General Clay's authorization, he had transferred twenty thousand books to the camps, but he still had five thousand left in his allotment. To finish the work, the JDC sent a thirty-year-old historian named Lucy Schildkret to select more books for the camps from the OAD's stock.

### Lucy Schildkret Rediscovers the Treasures

Preparing for her trip, Schildkret realized the significance of what she was about to do. Though born in the United States, her parents were from

Poland, and many of her relatives had perished during the Holocaust. During the late 1930s, Schildkret herself had spent a transformative year at YIVO in Vilna, where she beheld the riches of eastern European Jewish culture. "I was keyed up by the prospect of holding in my hands the remnant, as it were, of the civilization of the East European Jews. I was even more agitated by the thought that I might see the remnants of the YIVO library."

Upon arriving in Germany, Schildkret learned that since she was an official representative of the JDC, army regulations required her to be uniformed like an American officer. Though chagrined to learn that she had to wear such a getup—she was a *historian*, after all—Schildkret dutifully donned her army greens like a real trooper. On the shoulders of her well-pressed, brass-buttoned outfit were badges featuring blue and white chevrons and the letters "AJDC"—American Joint Distribution Committee. Soon, Schildkret realized that the uniform had its benefits. It gave her the rank of army major, with all of the privileges and priorities thereof.[15]

When the young, uniformed historian arrived at the OAD warehouse on February 4, 1947, she learned that more than 2 million items had already been restituted to other countries, leaving 630,000 still in storage. Of these, only half had been identified. She was to dig into the remaining half and choose which 5,000 should go the DP camps. Schildkret, like most other visitors first seeing the collection, was astounded at its size. "The hundreds of thousands of books, brought from all over the American Zone, stretched wall to wall in a continuing vista of wooden boxes on two floors of the Depot," she later wrote. "The smell of death emanated from these hundreds of thousands of books and religious objects—orphaned and homeless mute survivors of their murdered owners."

Despite these feelings, Schildkret came to the depot the following morning, rolled up her sleeves, and got to work. During her first week, she set aside 2,000 books for the camps, only to learn that the American government now wanted a catalogue of the 20,000 volumes that Pinson had sent earlier. With the help of Joseph A. Horne, by then one of Pomrenze's successors as director of the OAD, she set up a system for staffers to compile the catalogue, then turned back to the books themselves. By March 8 she had identified all 5,000 volumes for the camps. Then she decided to stay on to help identify material for YIVO.

During her months in Offenbach, Schildkret continued to be haunted by the ghosts of the Holocaust. When Horne learned that she had inadequate lighting in her hotel room, he offered to lend her a menorah from the depot's stock of looted items. She returned it after just two weeks. "Every time I looked at the menorah, I invented another history for it," she wrote, "imagining to whom it might have belonged, where it had stood in that home, and what had become of its owners. I felt as if these imagined people had moved into my hotel room."[16]

And she continued to work. Schildkret stayed until June, identifying old manuscripts, Yiddish books, Hebrew literature, and much more. At one point she discovered office files from YIVO and, with her hands trembling, examined each sheet in search of the people she had known in Vilna. She found notes written by her friends, photographs of former coworkers, and at one point even her own name on a list of the institute's graduate students.

Schildkret would always remember her work in Offenbach as both emotionally exhausting and deeply significant. On the one hand, it was hard for her to be with those ghost-ridden books. "The human survivors," she later wrote, "had a will to live and even, at times, a will to forget, but the books had been dumb witnesses to mass murder. They were the relics of six million murdered Jews." On the other hand, she also realized how important it was that these relics be saved. Recalling her work with the YIVO material, Schildkret explained that by the time she left in June 1947, "I had come to see that Vilna had been reduced to fragments of paper and fragments of memory. I knew that whatever I rescued from oblivion was all that could ever be rescued from the ruins of Vilna."[17]

Lucy Schildkret would be forever haunted by those ghosts, particularly the ones that appeared in the books and papers of the OAD. The year after she returned from Europe, she married a man from Poland named Szymon Dawidowicz and took on his family name as her own. As Lucy S. Dawidowicz, she continued to write extensively about eastern European Jewry during the decades to come, earning particular acclaim for her 1975 book *The War against the Jews, 1933–1945*. By the time Lucy Dawidowicz died in late 1990, she was renowned as one of the world's most prolific and passionate historians of the Nazi Holocaust.

## Gershom Scholem and the Offenbach Book Heist

Gershom Scholem spent July 1946 in a storeroom at Offenbach sifting through old manuscripts. The German-born forty-nine-year-old professor of Jewish mysticism from the Hebrew University, in Jerusalem, had already made a name for himself in academic circles, especially for his 1941 collection of essays *Major Trends in Jewish Mysticism*. His many writings on Kabbalah and other areas of Jewish thought during the coming decades would eventually place him securely in the pantheon of twentieth-century Jewish scholarship.

His work in the storeroom, however, seemed far more librarian-staff than pantheon. He and his colleagues at the Hebrew University had heard of the massive literary hoard at Offenbach, and they had sent Scholem to examine its contents on their behalf. Another scholar, Avraham Yaari, accompanied him, but Yaari had to return after only a few weeks because of problems with his visa. That left Scholem all alone in that hot storeroom, paging through old Jewish manuscripts in search of something—*anything*—that might be of value.

What did he find? Not much, Scholem reported. In the pile of six hundred manuscripts that he inspected, there were a few old *pinkasim*, some interesting Chabad material, and not much more worth writing home about.[18] "One should not be surprised," he wrote, "by the fact that the Offenbach Depot is somewhat disappointing with respect to the search for cultural treasures, meaning rare books, important manuscripts or precious archival material, especially if one does not take into account the books which are going to be sent as a restitution to various countries."[19]

Anyone who saw Scholem in the storeroom would most likely have seen the balding, middle-aged scholar sitting droopy-eyed at his table paging through document after document after document. He sorted the material into five piles based on value. The junkiest, most humdrum manuscripts went into Pile V, the priceless material—if there was any—went into Pile I, and the rest of it went into one of the three roman-numeraled stacks in between. Ho hum. His bosses at the Hebrew University had told him to enter into negotiations for the most interesting and significant material, but it seemed like what he saw wasn't even worth the bother. As his time in Offenbach drew to a close, he packed the manuscripts into five large boxes and prepared to leave.

But professors who look bored on the outside, it turns out, aren't always truly bored on the inside. Scholem was actually astounded by what he saw. There were handwritten manuscripts, community records, rabbinic documents, and works of medieval Jewish literature. The stuff was priceless, and it sent Scholem's heart racing. He knew the American military employees at Offenbach were unlikely to let him take these things back to Jerusalem, especially if they knew how valuable they were. He also knew that if the material were to stay in Offenbach, there was no telling what could happen to it. Maybe the OAD would let it slip out into the black market somehow. Maybe the documents would get carelessly tossed into general collections, where they would be neglected and perhaps destroyed. Worst of all, perhaps the U.S. Army would negotiate one of their deals with the locals and let the documents go to some *German* institution. Regardless, Scholem knew that the proper place for this material was in Jerusalem, the ancient and now reborn center of the Jewish world. It had to go to the Hebrew University, and Gershom Scholem knew it was up to him to get it there.

Unsure how to proceed, Scholem approached Rabbi Herbert A.

28. Gershom Scholem. Courtesy Yad Vashem Photo Archives.

Friedman, a U.S. military chaplain he had met in Germany. "Scholem was beside himself with fear," Friedman recalled. "When he finished telling me the story, he actually broke down from fatigue, strain, and worry."[20] Friedman, an ardent Zionist, came up with an instant solution: "I would steal the books," he said, "and see that they reached safekeeping in Jerusalem."[21] Friedman insisted that he made the decision on his own, but it's hard to believe that his suggestion didn't make the "broken down" Scholem smile a little mischievously on the inside.

Friedman came up with a plan. He would set aside the most valuable manuscripts—the 366 that were in piles I and II—and ask Isaac Bencowitz to hold onto them until the Joint Distribution Committee could arrange for them to be shipped off for use in the DP camps. He would act as the JDC's driver and get them to Paris, where he could give them to representatives of the Jewish Agency in Palestine, who could then ship them to the Hebrew University in Jerusalem.

On December 30 the plan went into action. Friedman "borrowed" a JDC truck and asked Bencowitz for the books. Bencowitz ordered that the books be brought to the loading dock and prepared a receipt. Workers loaded the boxes onto the truck and handed Friedman the receipt for his signature. Friedman signed—"Koppel Pinson." In tiny letters, he added his own initials; this would protect him against possible forgery accusations he might face down the road.

Pinson drove the truck carrying the five boxes of priceless manuscripts to Paris, where he found the representatives of the Jewish Agency and excitedly told them what he had. The Jewish Agency representatives, it turns out, weren't so excited. They probably would have been delighted to see the material go to Jerusalem, but they weren't about to get into illegal trafficking of stolen U.S. goods. Friedman's contacts at the Jewish Agency did, however, share an important piece of information with him. The library of Chaim Weizmann—soon to become the first president of Israel—was being shipped from London to Palestine in a few days . . . dozens of boxes. The ship would leave from Antwerp. Surely no one would notice a few extra crates loaded onto the ship. Friedman drove to Antwerp; the boxes got loaded onto the ship with Weizmann's; a few days later, they arrived in Jerusalem.

And then, they got caught. Within a few days of the Friedman-Scholem manuscript heist, the OAD realized what had happened, and to say the least, they weren't happy. The OAD was embarrassed that such a thing could have occurred, and the JDC was mortified that its good name was implicated in the crime. Scholem, unrepentant, explained that it would have been "dangerous to leave these documents in the hands of a German staff for a longer period, and [so I] urged removal at the first possible moment.[22]

Bencowitz, Schildkret, and a military advisor on Jewish affairs named Rabbi Philip Bernstein were questioned. Schildkret acknowledged—probably incorrectly—that many people in her office were aware that the five boxes of books had been shipped to Jerusalem with the full knowledge of Isaac Bencowitz and Koppel Pinson. She added that another four to five thousand books from the OAD were known to be in Pinson's own library in New York. Someone suggested bringing in the FBI.

For his part Friedman was arrested and charged with grand larceny. He denied wrongdoing at first, but then to avoid court martial, he sheepishly approached Gen. Lucius Clay and explained what really happened. Clay took pity on Friedman, gave him a stern lecture, and then ordered the charges to be dismissed and the books retrieved from Jerusalem. To the best of anyone's knowledge, the latter order was never obeyed.

Writing about the events a half century later, Friedman recalled, "The last time I saw Professor Scholem, shortly before he died, he told me that occasionally he looked into the rare book vault of the Hebrew University National Library and smiled contentedly. So did I."[23]

By mid-1947, the unidentifiable books in Offenbach were becoming a source of conflict. Officials in Washington suggested that the Library of Congress should receive the remaining books. American military leaders in Europe looking to end their postwar occupation of Germany suggested that the United States should transfer the books to the Länderrat—an American-appointed council of German regional ministers—so that local German governments could figure out what to do with the material. And Jewish groups from the United States, Palestine, and other countries were chiming in too, each trying to lay its own claim to this massive hoard of Jewish treasures.

The military retreated. Amid such a storm of conflict, the occupational government realized that making a rash decision about the fate of these volumes was clearly inadvisable—doing so would only lead to further battles. Instead the Offenbach Archival Depot repeatedly set aside the books in question until the army brass could come up with a sensible policy that would determine their fate.

And so the work of the Offenbach Archival Depot progressed. Having organized its procedures, Seymour Pomrenze was reassigned to a stateside position in May 1946 and was succeeded by Isaac Bencowitz, who served until the following November. Three civilians—Theodore Heinrich, Joseph Horne, and James Kimball—each took a turn as director too. Finally, in preparation for the end of America's military occupation of Germany, the OAD closed its doors in April 1949. During the years it operated, the Offenbach Archival Depot returned more than three million books to the countries from which they were looted. It could not restore what the Nazis destroyed, of course, but it did help preserve one small piece of that lost world for the future. Many books it processed still sit on the shelves of libraries around the world today.

As it prepared to shut down, everyone—the OAD directors, General Clay, and others—became increasingly concerned about the hundreds of thousands of unidentifiable books still remaining in the old Offenbach warehouse. Since the U.S. Army would soon be going home, the restitution efforts would need to be taken over by somebody else. Determining just who that "somebody else" would be, it turns out, became a topic of—to say the very least—extensive and passionate debate.

# 9

# Looted Books in the New Jewish Landscape

[The Commission on European Jewish Cultural Reconstruction will] help redistribute the Jewish cultural treasures in accordance with the new needs created by the new situation of world Jewry.
—*Salo Baron, 1946*

On Sunday, December 1, 1946, Salo Baron arrived at the Waldorf Astoria Hotel in New York for a meeting that would determine the fate of millions of Europe's Jewish cultural treasures. It was a foggy day in the city and, with the temperature pushing fifty, unseasonably warm for that time of year.[1] The posh hotel was only about four miles from the book-lined office at Columbia University where Baron spent most of his days, but when Baron entered that grand skyscraper, it was as if he were entering a different world.

Baron was a fastidious man, meticulous in his daily routine and frugal in his spending habits. His home featured thousands of books, shelved three deep in every room, even the bathroom. He awoke early every morning to do his historical research and writing, with his wife Jeannette working beside him as his research assistant and editor, and was also sure to spend time with his two daughters in the evenings. He devoted himself not only to his scholarly pursuits, but also to various causes and to supporting his family. A serious, reserved man, Baron was never known to have told a joke. He was so extensively organized that he is said to have had a twenty-five-year supply of shoelaces stored at home.[2]

By the mid-1940s Baron felt as if he carried upon his shoulders the weight of a lost world. When he arrived from Poland in 1926, he'd had no idea that twenty years later the European Jewish world of his youth would be all but obliterated, and he certainly had no idea that the forces that destroyed it would have murdered members of his own family. As the Nazi menace grew in the early 1930s, Baron had worked frantically to save his parents and his two sisters back in Europe, writing to them and imploring American officials to intercede on their behalf. One of his sisters arrived safely in America, but despite Baron's desperate efforts to rescue his parents and other sister, their letters abruptly stopped arriving in mid-1942, leaving undeniable the tragic truth of their fate in the Nazi death machine.

Baron came to the United States with a bundle of degrees under his belt—three PhDs from the University of Vienna, as well as rabbinic ordination from the Jewish Theological Seminary in the same city. He first taught history to young rabbinic students at the Jewish Institute of Religion but soon received an appointment at Columbia University. From that lofty perch Baron was able to establish the study of Jewish history and texts as a valid academic pursuit. Jewish studies had entered the American academy, and Salo Baron was widely recognized and celebrated as its dean.

Still, it was to be an unusual meeting—the man he had come to meet rarely interacted with the likes of Jewish historians. Yet it was the precisely unusual nature of their discussion that made it so enormously productive. As he stepped in to the lobby, Baron noticed its richly colored carpeting, ornate woodwork, and crystal chandeliers, but he probably didn't stop to study the decor. He proceeded to the suite, knocked on the door, and was greeted by Gen. Lucius D. Clay, commander of the American military occupation of Germany. Clay's slender military bearing was only slightly softened by his affable smile and the Georgia accent warming his baritone voice. He greeted Baron politely, but in this conversation, as in most others, it soon became clear that he would be all business.[3] Baron and Clay were not the only ones at that meeting. Sitting with them were five other men. Clay had brought his legal advisor, Max Lowenthal, and Baron was accompanied by Dr. Wolf Blattberg of the World Jewish Congress, Prof. Alexander Marx of the Jewish Theological Seminary, Jerome Michael of the Commission on European Jewish Cultural Reconstruction, and Prof. Aron Freimann, former librarian of the Frankfurt Municipal Library. The seven men sat down and began discussing what to do with the remaining troves of Jewish cultural treasures in Europe.

## Who Gets the Orphaned Treasures?

A worldwide snapshot of the Jewish people at that moment would reveal a nation struggling to discern its path to the future. European Jews were still taking their first steps out of the murderous hell. Bewildered and dazed, they didn't yet even have a word to describe what had just happened to them; the word "Holocaust" would not come into widespread use to describe the event until the 1960s.[4] Survivors were struggling to find lost relatives, figure out where to live, and recover from the sheer physical brutality of what they had just endured. Almost ten million Jews lived in Europe when the war began; five and a half to six million of them had been murdered.[5] The bombs had stopped, the roaring had grown quiet, and for a time the surviving remnant of Europe's Jews stood blinking in the gray smoky light of the ruins that had once been their world. Indeed the war had transformed not only the Jews of Europe, but the Jewish people in its entirety, regardless of where they lived. Before the war, the two most visible Jewish population centers were in Europe and United States. Now most Jews of Europe were either dead, departed, or dispirited, and the Jews of the United States, though still visibly powerful, were orphaned and distraught. Refugees were everywhere. Hundreds of thousands came to America, many thousands more moved to Palestine, and others emigrated to Argentina, South Africa,

Australia, Canada, and other countries to rebuild their lives. Nothing was the same. The loss was overwhelming, the pain was searing, and the future unclear. The massive earthquake called Nazism had turned the Jewish world upside down, and until the debris settled, nobody had a clue as to what the new Jewish world would be.

Such times of transition are often rife for conflict, and indeed an important one broke out in the most unlikely of battlefields. For the staff of the Offenbach Archival Depot one final question hovered over the entire enterprise like a looming cloud: Who owned the ownerless books?

Many of the books, like many Jewish *people*, were orphaned. For now, the U.S. Army held a good share of them, but what were they to do with millions of Jewish books? To whom should the American military turn them over? Should they be transferred to European governments in the newly reconstructed postwar Europe? Should they be sent to the United States? Should they somehow be given to the Jewish people? And if so, which Jewish people should get them? Jews in the Land of Israel? American Jews? Organizations of survivors?

Who, in other words, would get to speak for the Jewish people? It was a new question for Jews and governments alike. Yes, there had been Jewish spokespeople before the war—wealthy, powerful Jews near the seats of power who could intercede, like the biblical Esther, on behalf of imperiled Jews and Jewish communities. But these spokespeople usually represented local or regional communities or sometimes the Jews of a single nation. Now many felt the need for an individual or a group to speak for the worldwide Jewish community. In the absence of a formal structure or hierarchy, who could possibly assume such a role with any authority whatsoever?

### The Battle of the Books

A "Battle of the Books" was brewing—a battle that was fundamentally more a struggle to determine the contours of the international Jewish landscape in the years after World War II. In some ways the battle had been brewing for more than a decade. Unlike the more well-known and more pressing issues (e.g., what to do with the refugees, how to prosecute war criminals), scholars had been thinking about the postwar fate of European Jewish culture for a long time. In 1933, the Nazis' rise to power had raised alarm bells in Jewish communities everywhere. Those in the United States felt a special obligation. Many American Jews were first- or second-generation immigrants from Europe themselves, now replanted in a new land not only of freedom and opportunity, but also of great international strength. By the time the war began, organizations such as the American Jewish Joint Distribution Committee and Hebrew Immigrant Aid Society were providing millions of dollars in aid and support to refugees. The American Jewish Congress and the American Jewish Committee were advocating the cause of European Jewry on the political front, and Jews throughout the country were frantically trying to help their friends and families back in Europe.

Scholars also did their part. As early as 1940 Salo Baron observed that American Jewish leaders were "equipped with the knowledge furnished them by the methods of modern social and historical sciences and imbued with the accumulated wisdom of the ages of rabbis and thinkers." As he observed the worsening situation in Europe, Baron called on those leaders to employ American Jewish know-how to "look courageously into the realities as they are and to adopt measures which they will consider best." Doing so, he argued, would "render an historic service lesser to none performed by their predecessors in other ages of great transformation."[6]

American leaders answered Baron's call with gusto. By 1943 there were fully thirty-two different Jewish institutions in the United States addressing questions about postwar Jewish Europe. The American Jewish Committee created a commission "charged with the function of ascertaining, integrating and publishing of the requisite facts that will promote a better understanding of the Jewish situation and by the scholarly and scientific integrity of its findings, provide a reliable basis for subsequent efforts in the field of reconstruction and rehabilitation."[7] The American Jewish Congress established its Institute of Jewish Affairs and called on its new organization "to present proposals of Jews for the guarantee of rights and the assurance of equality at a forthcoming Peace Conference; and to plan the reconstruction of Jewish life at the end of the war."[8] Even the Jewish Labor Committee had created an operation called the "Research Institute for Jewish Post-war Problems."[9] Curiously, all of these organizations assumed that the Allies were going to win the war. During the darkest and most difficult times of that conflict—even during the years when Allied victory against the Nazis was far from certain—the very existence of these groups looking ahead to postwar Jewish life in Europe attests to the optimism of American Jewry.

As all these groups looked ahead to peacetime, their efforts naturally grew specific. Some groups focused on resettlement, others on prosecuting war crimes, and still others set their sights on dealing with Europe's Jewish cultural treasures. Allied governments had been thinking about the issue for some time, of course; their efforts had yielded the Monuments Men (MFA&A) program. But as the war thundered on, scholars and librarians spurred more and more Jewish organizations to prepare for what they knew would be a postwar deluge of Jewish literary loot. By 1943 the campaigns began taking shape. They would rage strong until Baron's meeting at the Waldorf with Clay, and skirmishes would break out even afterward.

The first campaign was led by an unlikely combatant, a bookish-looking Oxford University historian named Cecil Roth. Roth, an Orthodox Jew and avid collector of Jewish books, was head of the Jewish Historical Society of England and would later gain renown as editor in chief of the first edition of *Encyclopaedia Judaica*. He was also an ardent Zionist; his brother Leon was rector of the Hebrew University, and when he retired from Oxford in 1964, Cecil himself would move to Jerusalem. By 1943 the forty-four-year-old had already emerged as one of England's leading

29. Salo W. Baron. Courtesy Jacob Rader Marcus Center of the American Jewish Archives, Cincinnati, Ohio, americanjewisharchives.org.

30. Judah Leon Magnes. Courtesy Library of Congress.

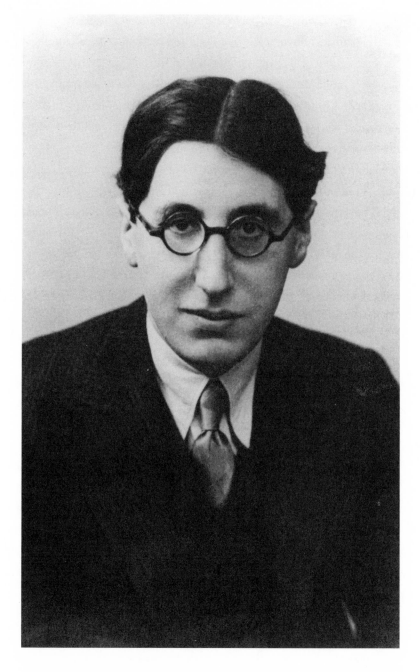

31. Cecil Roth. Courtesy Joseph F. Roth.

Jewish scholars, which may have been why an address he delivered at the Jewish Historical Society that April gained such widespread attention.

Mincing no words, Roth opened with a salvo against what he saw as the very foundation of Nazi antisemitism. The Nazis, he proclaimed, had attacked not only Jews, but also Jewish culture—its spiritual and intellectual values. "It is unthinkable," he continued, "that the German Government can be allowed to derive any profit from its campaign of murder and rapine, and it is obvious that it should be made to disgorge confiscated and stolen objects—to which must be added, too, those which have been disposed of by forced sale."[10] He called for all objects that the Nazis stole during the war to be returned to their rightful owners and for the material whose owners could not be identified to be sent to the Hebrew University in Jerusalem. Accordingly, the Jewish Historical Society of England set up a committee to deal with the postwar treasures, with Roth as one of its most prominent members. The committee was to work closely with Allied governments and cooperate with them in addressing all issues concerning stolen Jewish property and the reconstruction of European Jewish culture.

Roth's committee created a questionnaire to help assemble an inventory of looted property for use at the postwar peace conference, and it crafted some preliminary plans for working with Allied governments. To the best of anyone's knowledge, none of their work moved beyond the planning stage, but Roth remained proud of the fact that his group was the first to take on the work of postwar book restitution and cultural reconstruction in anything even resembling a systematic manner. As a result, he would later argue, his group should rightly be at the helm of later Jewish efforts in this area. When it came time to sort out the stolen books, he felt, the Brits should be in charge.

Of course Roth was far from the only Jewish scholar thinking about what to do with stolen Jewish literature after the war. One of the others—a man in some ways Roth's ally and in others his adversary—was Judah L. Magnes, founding president of the Hebrew University in Jerusalem. Born in San Francisco in 1877, Magnes was ordained a rabbi at the Reform movement's the Hebrew Union College in Cincinnati in 1900. He continued his studies in Berlin and Heidelberg, where he became not only a PhD, but also an ardent Zionist—both of which would define much of what he did for the remainder of his life. Magnes served as assistant rabbi of Temple Emanu-El in New York, the oldest and arguably the grandest of the city's Reform synagogues, and later as president of the New York Kehillah, an umbrella agency designed to coordinate and unite the city's many Jewish organizations. In 1922 Magnes moved to Palestine, where he took his position at the helm of the Hebrew University.

To Magnes, the nascent state that he and his fellow Zionists would soon create represented the spiritual and intellectual center of the Jewish people. Diaspora Jewish communities were important, of course, but Magnes argued that for the Jewish people to thrive, there needed to be a vibrant Jewish community in its ancestral land. As early as 1930 he had described the Land of Israel as "one of the chief means, if not the chief means, of revivifying and deepening the [Jewish] people and the Torah."[11]

With Palestine as the center of the Jewish world, could there be any question as to what should be done with the orphaned Jewish books? In Magnes's view, they had to come to Palestine. Period. The Hebrew University, located on a hilltop overlooking the ancient ramparts of Jerusalem, was the perfect new home for them. More fundamentally, given the role that the soon-to-be State of Israel would play in the postwar Jewish world, sending the books to the Hebrew University was the only logical choice. He said so explicitly in a 1946 letter to Koppel Pinson:

We are to be the chief country for the absorption of the living human beings who have escaped from Nazi persecution, and we are of course proud of this. That is one of the reasons why the Jewish National Home exists in Palestine. By the same token we should be the trustee of these spiritual goods which destroyed German Jewry has left behind. It will be nothing less than disgraceful if there were any competition between Jewish organizations for the receipt of books, manuscripts and other collections. As anxious as we are to build up our library, which is the greatest library among the Jews of all the world, we are much more anxious that the Jews of the world should recognize that it is our duty to establish our spiritual and moral claim to be in the direct line of succession to the Jewish culture and scholarship of European Jewry. I can well understand that putting forward different claims would confuse the military authorities. But we are not putting forward a claim to books or property, so much as we are putting forward a claim which no one else can put forward, i.e. the claim to be the chief spiritual heir of those Jewish institutions for whose books we want to be appointed trustees.[12]

With this in mind, Magnes sent his own representatives to Europe to catalogue the looted treasures. He also fostered ties with American Jewish military chaplains in Europe, ties that would serve him quite well as the battle for the books raged on. But Roth and Magnes would have to deal with yet a third general in their efforts to get their hands on the books.

On the other side of the Atlantic, Columbia's Salo Baron was also gearing up for his own campaign. Baron had been born in Galicia in 1895 and moved to New York as a young scholar in 1926. By the time of the war, he was just as much a leading light of Jewish studies in America as Roth was in England, if not more. Baron, however, found himself on the defensive during this period. Ever since the 1920s he had railed against what he called the "lachrymose conception of Jewish history." Many historians, he observed, had long propounded a view that the history of the Jewish people was one of suffering and travail only. But suffering in Jewish history, Baron insisted, was far from the whole story. A truer view of the Jewish past would show Jews as sometimes suffering, sometimes successful, and often somewhere in between.

Now, however, the horrors of the war seemed to provide more than ample proof for the lachrymose view. If nothing else, some historians argued, the Holocaust was screaming, howling, horrifying proof that being a Jew meant being part of a people doomed to undergo new agonies in each generation. To maintain his own position, Baron would need to be vigilant in his efforts to reclaim the fullness of Jewish history in all its complexity. Of *course* the Holocaust was terrible; like countless other Jews, Baron too had lost many family members and dear friends. But the Holocaust not only destroyed human lives, it also obliterated a magnificent Jewish culture. A student who studied *only* the Holocaust might come out feeling pretty lachrymose about the Jewish past, one that was dark and devastating. But a student who looked at European Jewry in the centuries *before* the war would certainly have a rosier view. And what better witness was there to the richness and complexity of Jewish history than its books?

Baron came to the battlefield by way of his involvement with the Conference on Jewish Relations, one of the American Jewish organizations looking ahead to life after the war in Europe. In June 1933 City University philosophy professor Morris Raphael Cohen convened a gathering of scholars to discuss Nazism and the implications of its rise to power in Germany. In 1937 the group officially became the Conference on Jewish Relations (CJR) and pledged to look not only at the oppression of European Jews, but also at alarming rates of antisemitism in the Unites States and elsewhere. The following year the CJR began publishing a quarterly journal, *Jewish Social Studies*, with Salo Baron as its editor. In 1941 Cohen stepped down, and Baron became president of the conference.

The specter of Nazism hung like a cloud over everything the CJR did. From early on, before the war, Baron and his cohorts realized that to respond effectively to the Nazi threat, they would need to have a full picture of the Jewish world that the Nazis were threatening, particularly that of Europe. With the outbreak of the war, the CJR, in an impressive demonstration of foresight, strove to take the American lead in preparing to aid in the postwar reconstruction of Jewish culture in Europe. As early as September 1940, it recommended "a program for a sustained and intensive study not only of the actual situation of Jews abroad and at home, and of the possible effects of various plans and proposals for post-war reconstruction, but also of the problems which are likely to confront the Jewish people after the war."[13]

The discussions continued, and by the end of the war the CJR had created the Commission on European Jewish Cultural Reconstruction. It consisted of sixty-nine scholars, librarians, and organizational leaders, representing many of the most prominent Jewish institutions in the world concerned with Jewish cultural reconstruction, including Theodor H. Gaster of the Library of Congress, Jacob Rader Marcus of the Hebrew Union College, Solomon Grayzel of the Jewish Publication Society, and Rabbi Edgar Magnin of Wilshire Boulevard Temple in Los Angeles. Significantly, most members of the commission were American, but there were people from other countries too, such as Rabbi Simon Langer of the Association Pour le Retablissement Israelite en France and Rabbi David A. Jessurun Cardozo of the Netherlands Jewish Committee. Tellingly, tragically, some members of the commission were listed only by their former positions: "Aron Freimann, Formerly Director, Frankfort Municipal Library," "Rachel Wischnitzer, Formerly Curator, Jewish Museum of Berlin."[14] The purpose of the new commission would be to serve as an advisory body to the United Nations and Allied authorities in rehabilitating the cultural institutions of European Jewry. The commission would, of course, need to be recognized as the official representative of the Jewish people in order to effectively perform its assigned tasks.

It wouldn't take long for Baron and his associates to realize that the CJR's Commission on European Jewish Cultural Reconstruction was tragically misnamed. In the wake of World War II, they learned, there wasn't much Jewish culture in Europe left to reconstruct.[15] Soon afterward the group dropped the word "European" from its title, calling it simply Jewish Cultural Reconstruction (JCR) instead. (The confusion wrought by an organization called the CJR creating a subgroup called JCR seems to have been lost on them.) Sadly, the work of reconstruction couldn't focus on Europe alone. Now Jewish cultural reconstruction would need to be a process by which the Jewish people worldwide adapted to the new realities of life after the cataclysm and destruction of World War II.

In late 1945, Baron headed a delegation that traveled to Germany to meet with Gen. Lucius Clay, the military governor of the American occupation. With great concern, the scholars told Clay that they had heard rumors of American soldiers and other passersby removing looted Jewish books, and consequently they asked the general to institute a systematic way to preserve the material. Clay, surely accustomed to similar such requests from the Monuments Men of MFA&A, responded cooperatively and ordered the establishment of the Offenbach Archival Depot (see chapter 8). After his initial meeting with Clay, Baron left behind a small staff of scholars to begin systematically collecting information about the looted treasures. The staff was led by a thirty-nine-year-old political theorist named Hannah Arendt.

## Assessing the Literary Loss

A strategy was coming together in Baron's mind, and in November 1945 he laid it out as the first substantive article in the inaugural issue of a new magazine called *Commentary*. His opening paragraph reveals not only the sense of confusion and fear perpetrating the Jewish world immediately after the war, but also Baron's deep commitment to reclaiming the culture of European Jewry, a culture that, whatever the details of its fate, he knew to have been horribly decimated under Nazi oppression.

> Although the blackout is slowly lifting from the areas where once flourished the largest centers of Jewish life in Europe, only fragmentary reports concerning the survivors have filtered through to the outside world. The simplest information, such as how many Jews remain alive—and where—is sparse and often contradictory; and we know practically nothing about the forms of their community

life, their religious observances, or the character of their hopes for survival as Jews. Under these circumstances, any discussion of the spiritual reconstruction of the Jewries of Europe must inevitably be little more than one man's personal estimate of long-term trends.[16]

Finally in 1946 Baron's staff was ready to issue its report. That year *Jewish Social Studies* issued a supplement to its regular quarterly publication cycle. Its title was rather pedestrian: "Tentative List of Jewish Cultural Treasures in Axis-Occupied Countries." But behind its lackluster cover lay the picture of a lost literary world.

Shortly after the war, the commission reported, it had assigned its researchers to compile a list of Jewish cultural treasures known to have existed in German-occupied lands before the hostilities had begun. The list contained only movable treasures—books, documents, and museum pieces. Other treasures such as synagogues and cemeteries were not included; their fate was more far more discernible than that of the smaller items. Compiling their data, the team was able to call on hundreds of informants for help. Some of their sources had fled to the United States during or after the war; others had remained in Europe. Some were librarians and scholars; others were chaplains and members of the press.

The list that they assembled was breathtaking in scope and magnitude: from the Lehranstalt fuer die Wissenschaft des Judentums in Berlin, 58,590 volumes, 40 manuscripts, "some incunables"; 10,000 volumes from the B'nai B'rith library in Vienna; 250,00 documents and deeds from the Archives of the Jewish Community of Prague, as well as 1,020 bound books, the oldest of which dated back to 1681; 20 kabbalistic manuscripts from the Jewish communal library in Mikulov (Nikolsburg); a "large library of rabbinic literature" from the Beth ha-Midrash ha-Gadol in Munkacevo; and a small collection from the Jewish Community Library of Alfred Rosenberg's hometown Talinn (Reval). In addition to the major collections from cities such as Frankfurt, Berlin, and Paris, the report also listed material from dozens of smaller towns, most of whose Jews had perished in the war. The library of Sanok in Poland was described only as "rich in Judaica"; the material of the Jewish community of Iasi, Romania, as "small collection." Genoa had yielded only "one Bible ms. [manuscript] in 7 vols." The list included material from twenty countries in all, and in addition to its millions of books and massive amounts of archival material, it also recorded priceless Torah scrolls, ritual items, and artwork.

The report was careful not to overstate its findings. The list was only tentative; surely it omitted important material, and soon *Jewish Social Studies* would issue a supplement to the supplement, listing even more treasures. More important, the list included only materials known to have existed prior to when the Nazis got access to them. It was a portrait of prewar European Jewish treasures, nothing else. "Information on the present state of these treasures," it noted, "is as yet insufficient to warrant publication." Nevertheless, the implication was clear: most of the material listed in the thick report was gone.

Looking ahead, the commission acknowledged that the project now at hand would be far more complicated than just collecting the books and sending them back to where they came from:

> In view of the wholesale destruction of Jewish life and property by the Nazis, reconstruction of Jewish cultural institutions cannot possibly mean mechanical restoration in their original form or, in all cases, to their previous location. The Commission intends . . . to devise if necessary some new forms better accommodated to the emergent patterns of postwar Europe. Ultimately it may also seek to help redistribute the Jewish cultural treasures in accordance with the new needs created by the new situation of world Jewry.[17]

The Jewish world, in other words, was now a different place than it had been just a few short years earlier. For Europe's Jews, healing wouldn't simply be a matter of cleaning up and moving on; it would demand new rules and new understandings regarding how best to live after the apocalypse.

Ordinarily it's pretty clear what victorious armies are supposed to do with war booty—they're supposed to return it. But this was no ordinary situation. In ordinary situations, winning armies can simply gather their plunder (or the plunder they reclaim from their enemies) and cart it off for return to their original owners. But in the cratered, devastated moonscape of postwar Europe, the "original owners" weren't usually easy to find—if one could identify them in the first place.

The staff at the Offenbach Archival Depot was doing what it could to return the books, and indeed they succeeded in shipping millions of volumes to the countries from which they were taken. But America's military occupation of Germany was going to end in the late 1940s, and soon it became clear that even with its secure facility, expert leaders, and large staff, the Offenbach Archival Depot wasn't going to finish the job.

## Salo Baron Takes the Helm

Given the size of the unidentifiable "what-are-we-supposed-to-do-with-*these*?" piles, and given the political heat that the whole matter was generating, everyone involved in the book restitution efforts soon realized that finishing the job was going to be a complicated assignment. That's why Baron issued his "Tentative List." His goal was understandably scholarly and philanthropic, but also political. Who, the report tacitly asked, should get to decide where the treasures should go? Why, the answer should be obvious, came Baron's not-so-tacit reply: the Commission on Jewish Cultural Reconstruction of course. From the outset, Baron made it clear that his body would be the one to coordinate all of the other groups working on the issue. He wrote, "It is planned to have the Commission serve as the central research and co-ordinating body for all American activities in the field of European Jewish cultural reconstruction and work in close co-operation with the Hebrew University in Jerusalem, the Committee on Restoration of Continental Jewish Museums, Libraries and Archives of the Jewish Historical Society in England and other national and international organizations."[18]

Baron, in other words, had taken his place at the helm of the struggle for control of Europe's Jewish books. As he continued to describe the work of his Commission on Jewish Cultural Reconstruction, he made it very clear: *The commission*, he said, would work with the UN and Allied governments. *The commission* would take charge of the books and assess claims of ownership. *The commission* would supervise the redistribution and reallocation of the books. Cecil Roth and his Jewish Historical Society of England could help if they wanted, as could Magnes and his associates at the Hebrew University. But the commission would be in charge.

By this time Cecil Roth, evidently willing to work with Baron, had effectively stepped into the background, and Magnes remained indignant at the very thought that anyone but the Hebrew University should get the books. To complicate matters even further, in late 1945 the Danish government came forward with an offer to bring the material to its country; doing so would not only keep the books in Europe, but also save on shipping costs.[19]

The planning and wrangling and squabbling continued. The Danish proposal was only short-lived, but the others weren't. Baron's commission staff worked tirelessly to assemble and update its "Tentative List"; Roth and his associates made plans and wrote memoranda; Magnes thundered that the unclaimed books must come to the Hebrew University, and he conducted reconnaissance of his own to begin gathering them.

Notably, at this juncture all of the contending parties agreed on one important point: that the Hebrew University should become the primary destination for the heirless European Jewish cultural treasures. They differed on several procedural matters—whose lists should be the official ones, which group should be in charge of the process, what the role of Allied governments and the UN would be—but with regard to the most important issue, they mostly agreed. Although they lived in the Diaspora, both Roth and Baron were ardent Zionists. Like Magnes, they too saw the nascent State of Israel as playing an essential and central role in the international Jewish community after the war, particularly with regard to the books.[20]

For the most part, in other words, they all agreed about what needed to happen. What they didn't agree about was who got to be the boss.

By the spring of 1946 it looked more and more likely that in this battle for the books of Jewish Europe, Baron and his Commission on Jewish Cultural Reconstruction were going to win. As it turned out, Baron's approach to the situation was far savvier than that of Roth or Magnes, and he had been hugely successful in forming a broad, worldwide coalition of many stakeholders concerned about the fate of these treasures. In fact Baron's commission included representatives of some of the very same groups that had originally opposed him.

Additionally, for all of its international character, Baron's Commission on Jewish Cultural Reconstruction was an *American*-based organization. This made it easier for him to work with the American army for the transfer of materials and also to get the support of key members of the American government and its military whom he would need to make the transfer happen smoothly. Theodor Gaster, chief of the Hebraica section of the Library of Congress, was actually a member of Baron's commission. In internal conversations at the Library of Congress, he took a position far more critical of the Hebrew University than did Baron himself:

The Hebrew University Library, however it may choose to describe itself, is not, in fact, the national library of the Jews, since there is no such thing as a Jewish state in Palestine. It is merely a Palestinian Jewish institution, no whit different from any corresponding institution here. To give it preferential treatment would therefore amount to discrimination against sister institutions in this country or elsewhere, and would be the more likely to be resented here seeing that the material was, in fact, liberated by American troops and that the non-Jewish portions of it will be going, apparently, to American institutions.[21]

Seymour Pomrenze was also supportive of Baron's group. Having returned to the United States from Offenbach in May 1946, Pomrenze encouraged the commission to get an official charter from the UN to become the sole trustee of the materials. He shared his views with officials from MFA&A, and like Gaster, he too weighed in with the Library of Congress. In a letter to Baron that month, he made his views clear: "When Prof. Pinsion [sic] gave me a copy of the list of treasures put out by your commission I said to him here is the Agency which can be the instrument of *geulah* (redemption) for these treasures."[22]

With the support of Gaster, Pomrenze, and other Jewish officials in place, the Commission on Jewish Cultural Reconstruction was finally in a position to make its case to the American government. During the spring of 1946 it prepared an official memo for submission to the Office of Military Government, United States (OMGUS) suggesting an advisory board be appointed to help with the restitution process. The board would consist of the commission, the Hebrew University, and the Synagogue Council of America (an interdenominational body representing Reform, Conservative, and Orthodox congregations throughout the United States). For items known to be stolen by the Nazis that were destroyed, damaged, or not found after the war, the memo called for "reparations in-kind." Accordingly the German government would be required to provide other items of similar value from its own collections to replace those taken during the war.

Overwhelmingly officials in the State and War Departments found the commission's reparations-in-kind proposal to be a nonstarter. The government was working to help Germany rebuild, and it feared that such a plan would create a bureaucratic behemoth of inventories, valuations, and political jockeying far more enormous than anyone would want. The rest of the commission's proposals might have sailed through more easily, but Magnes, still unwilling to concede defeat, complained to the War Department; the Jewish Agency of Palestine voiced concerns to the MFA&A; and the World Jewish Congress (WJC)—a federation of Jewish organizations that had long wanted in on the plans itself and felt slighted by being left out of Baron's commission—also complained and offered an alternative proposal that put the WJC at the helm.

Various government officials, particularly those in the State Department, were also concerned about the prospect of dealing with a body as amorphous as "the Jewish people." When dealing with established governments, diplomats rarely have much of a problem figuring out who they should work with. But here the State Department faced the prospect of returning property captured during the war to "the Jews"—a religious entity . . . or perhaps it was an ethnic group . . . or maybe, given the recent struggle for Jewish statehood in Palestine, the Jews constituted a national group after all. To anyone concerned with the legal and ethical protocols of international diplomacy, the situation seemed destined to become very messy. Very messy indeed.

For its part, different factions within the American government failed to see eye to eye on the issue as well. OMGUS had been charged with the task of denazifying Germany and reconstructing its government, a task that would demand the cooperation of local and regional government councils. For these German officials to work with the military of the army that had just vanquished them in war was hard enough, many felt, but to force them to work with an officially recognized *Jewish* restitution organization might seem downright vindictive. On the other hand, there was also an awareness throughout the American government—and indeed throughout the world—of the ghastliness of the Holocaust, and a genuine desire to empower the Jewish people in the postwar reconstruction efforts.

By the end of the summer, both the Commission on Jewish Cultural

Reconstruction and the WJC had incorporated the Hebrew University into its plans. Furthermore, although the WJC submitted its own formal plan, it had also joined Baron's team, and its proposal had become so similar to that of the commission as to render it effectively identical. Now the stage was set. For all practical purposes, Salo Baron and the Commission on Jewish Cultural Reconstruction could approach the American government as the fully—if unofficially—authorized representatives of the Jewish people. For its part, the American government was no longer caught in the middle of the internecine strife between these many groups of bickering Jews. Looking ahead to the end of its occupation of Germany, it finally had an identifiable, authoritative Jewish partner with whom it could work in determining the ultimate fate of the Jewish treasures it now held.

There remained, of course, myriad details to work out. How would the commission assure the officials of the State Department that it was okay to work with them as representatives of the Jewish people? How could they best set up a working relationship with Clay's Office of Military Government in Germany? What were they to do with books and other treasures taken from communities that were mostly, but not completely, decimated during the war?

## Government Approval

In June the Commission on Jewish Cultural Reconstruction, with Magnes's explicit approval, sent a memo to the State Department proposing a plan. Officially OMGUS, working on its own or through an appointed trustee, would be in charge of distributing the books. In reality, however, a Jewish advisory board would make the actual decisions, with the Library of Congress adding its expertise to help determine who had owned the books before the war. OMGUS would appoint tribunals to adjudicate the disagreements when there were conflicting claims regarding who should get the books. Private owners would get their property back, of course, while surviving Jewish communities and institutions would get theirs only to the extent that they could make full use of the material and to the extent to which the former Jewish population that owned them survived the war. All of the remaining material would be distributed to Jewish institutions and communities according to worldwide need.

The State Department agreed in principle to anything that would rid it of the responsibility for the books and get it out of the crossfire flying between the many warring Jewish groups. The State Department also specified that its decisions would certainly apply to material reclaimed in the American Zone and that it would seek "quadripartite approval" to have the material in the other three zones turned over to it or at least to receive the authority to determine the fate of this material on an ad hoc basis.[23]

Over the next several weeks there were informal discussions between Jewish leaders and officials at the State Department. Then, on August 26, Jerome Michael, vice president of the Commission on Jewish Cultural Reconstruction, wrote to Gen. John H. Hilldring, assistant secretary of state for occupied areas, with a revised proposal. He informed General Hilldring that the commission was setting up a "membership corporation" under the laws of New York, which would include representatives from all concerned parties: the American Jewish Joint Distribution Committee, the American Jewish Committee, the Synagogue Council of America, the Federation of Jews from Central Europe, the World Jewish Congress, and the Hebrew University. It would, in other words, be a widely representative entity, just as the State Department wanted.

The U.S. Army, the proposal continued, would appoint the corporation as the trustee for all Hebraica, Judaica, and other Jewish religious and cultural objects in the American Zone on behalf of the treasures' "former Jewish owners and the Jewish people." In cooperation with the American military, the corporation would examine and classify those objects that the American military had already found, endeavor to find additional material as yet undiscovered by Allied forces, search for material in the collections of German and Austrian libraries in the American Zone, and periodically report on its activities to the commanding generals of the American occupation. For their part, the commanding generals would provide housing, food, and clerical support to the corporation's staff as they conducted their work.

Objects that had been owned by private individuals would be restored to them or their heirs; those that had belonged to surviving institutions would likewise be returned to their prewar owners. Objects that had been owned by communities would be restored "in proportion to the prospective religious and cultural needs of the community and its capacity to retain, care for, and use such objects for their appropriate religious and cultural purposes." Un-returnable objects, on the other hand—those that could not be identified, or whose owners perished during the war, or belonged to communities that could no longer care for them—would "be distributed in such a manner as will in the judgment of the Corporation best serve the religious and cultural needs of the Jewish people and especially of the surviving victims of Nazi persecution, and satisfy the desire of the Jewish people to pay tribute to those victims who did not survive, as, for example, by establishing a library in the Hebrew University in Palestine as a memorial to those martyrs for their faith."[24]

Hitler and his henchmen coldly murdered the Jews of Europe while also gathering a library to preserve Judaism's destroyed culture. Now, shocked, grieving, and determined to reclaim what they could, the Jewish institutions of the free world lovingly strove to preserve the very same thing.

The memos and conversations continued. A host of legal and procedural issues needed to be worked out. How active would the American occupational forces be in the restitution of Jewish books? With Germany recovering, the world only beginning to heal, and the Iron Curtain slowly descending over a divided Europe, would Jewish books even merit a blip on the American military radar screen? Yes, Jewish leaders around the world were now mostly united under the leadership of Baron and the

Commission on Jewish Cultural Reconstruction, but with the support of the American military still in question, it remained to be seen whether such unity would matter.

The discussion at the Waldorf Astoria that day was cordial. Jerome Michael opened with a review of the proposal by the Commission on Jewish Cultural Reconstruction for a trustee corporation, touching on its complexities, the differences between various kinds of cultural property, and procedural matters regarding the transfer of such properties to a trustee. Baron chimed in with statistics from his "Tentative List" and some ideas as to how the corporation might distribute the material. Blattberg reminded the group of two important points: The proposed corporation was an international trusteeship—the World Jewish Congress stood behind it, as did the Hebrew University and other major Jewish organizations. Also the material under discussion wasn't just any old property. Rather it represented priceless cultural treasures of enormous sentimental value for Jews everywhere. The books would be crucial to any future study of and by the Jewish people. Marx and Freimann agreed and, bringing their scholarly knowledge to the table, added several technical details about the material under discussion.

Lucius Clay took it all in and then responded with the decisiveness that had brought him to his high position. Yes, some of the formalities of setting up a trusteeship of the type that the Commission on Jewish Cultural Reconstruction had suggested would need to go through the State Department. But once it was established (surely Baron and his cohort were thrilled at the first explicit, high-level sign of support for their proposal), the corporation would work directly with OMGUS, directly with Clay himself. Having said that, Clay reminded his Jewish visitors that the restitution of looted property would be conducted strictly in accordance with the law. Therefore, the commission's previous proposals for German in-kind reparations—taking valuable material from German libraries to replace items of similar value that were looted and subsequently lost during the war—was simply out of the question. The law provided no mechanism for this kind of restitution, and similar proposals from France and Holland had already been rejected as a result.

Most important, however, Clay agreed that all unidentifiable books and other cultural material should be turned over to the trusteeship as soon as possible. He rejected the notion that identifiable material from German communities with only a few survivors should receive only a small proportion of their material, but he suggested that many of these communities would probably be willing to cede portions of their collections to the trusteeship anyway.[25]

Clay touched on other questions in that two-hour conversation, but in their excitement the members of the Commission on Jewish Cultural Reconstruction likely missed the details. They had gotten what they came for; the highest-ranking American military official in Germany had given principled support to their plan. Now it was only a matter of writing up the paperwork.

On April 30, 1947, the articles of incorporation were filed in the State of New York. Jewish Cultural Reconstruction, Inc. had been created.

# 10
## Jewish Cultural Reconstruction

I perceive a desire on your part to undo, as far as was in your
power—a great wrong. . . . May it betoken an assurance that never
again will such misdeeds be allowed to be reenacted.
—*Bernard Heller to the workers at the*
*Offenbach Archival Depot, 1949*

As soon as Jewish Cultural Reconstruction began its work, there was
an enormous shifting of gears in the book restitution machine. The
Offenbach Archival Depot, after all, had operated as an agency of the
U.S. Army. Although most of the OAD's leaders were Jewish, it operated
within the framework of the larger postwar priorities of the American
government's occupation of Germany. Its job was to even the score
between *countries.* It could only deal with governments, not individuals or private agencies. It had to report up the chain—to General Clay,
to the War and State Departments, and eventually to the president of
the United States.

JCR, on the other hand, was a *Jewish* organization, so its priorities,
not to mention its authority structure, were different. JCR was a membership corporation, and its members were Jewish agencies; some were
among the most prominent Jewish agencies in the world. JCR focused
only on *Jewish* cultural objects, mostly books. Its role was to distribute

the material it found "in such a way as to best serve and promote the spiritual and cultural needs and interests of the Jewish people in particular and mankind in general, and especially the spiritual and cultural needs of the victims of Nazi or Fascist persecution."[1] Yes, the lion's share of the JCR work would take place in the old I. G. Farben warehouse that had been home to the OAD, at least at first; and yes, it too would designate some rooms for sorting the books, others for identification, and still others for shipping. But the infrastructure that operated it and the passions that drove it would be completely different.

## Jewish Cultural Reconstruction Sets Up Shop at Offenbach

After its incorporation in April 1947 the leaders of JCR knew that there was no time to waste. Despite the fact that the American occupation was still in place and the OAD was still in charge of the books, the directors of the OAD were kindly disposed to the Jewish scholars of this new organization, and General Clay was fully supportive of its work too. Perhaps there would be opportunities to get its operations in place ahead of time, so that when the American occupation ended, JCR could hit the ground running. There was certainly work to be done even before the Americans left. JCR leaders had received reports that there were many other troves of looted books that hadn't yet been reclaimed. Many of these collections had been discovered in Austria and France—areas where the American military government had no jurisdiction whatsoever—and contained vast amounts of priceless material. With the end of the occupation coming, JCR knew that it wouldn't have America's powerful military support in securing possession of the books for long. In addition, JCR leaders feared for the troves of material already sitting in the OAD. The American government was supporting the reconstruction efforts of local and regional German communities, and there was good reason for JCR to believe that its American military friends running the Offenbach depot might be inclined to turn over some of the recovered books to German libraries before they pulled up stakes and went home. Even though it wouldn't have full and unfettered access to the recovered material for some time, it was clear that JCR needed to act, and it needed to act quickly.

Its initial funding was modest: $10,000 from the Joint Distribution Committee and the Jewish Agency for Palestine.[2] That would be enough to cover the costs of only one scholar, a secretary, and incidental clerical help for a few months. Who would the team leader be? JCR leaders considered several American and European scholars for the job, but not surprisingly here too the Zionist issue surfaced again. David Werner Senator of the Hebrew University suggested that JCR send a team of five scholars to Europe, with at least two coming from his own institution. A few months later he and Gershom Scholem went even further and suggested that JCR move *all* of its activities to Palestine as soon as possible. After all, Palestine was soon to be fully enfranchised as the capital of the Jewish people, and as Senator asked, "Who would want to stay in Germany for so long a period?"[3]

Delaying matters even further was the fact that in 1947 yet another acronymed organization was added to the postwar restitution alphabet soup: the Jewish Restitution Successor Organization (JRSO). As the American occupational government under General Clay had worked with Baron and the other scholars to set up JCR, it was also keenly aware that the Nazis had confiscated many other types of material from Jewish families and institutions throughout Europe—ritual items, furniture, artwork, real estate, securities, and other properties. JCR was going to be fine for dealing with the cultural and literary material, but what about everything else? General Clay soon realized—and the Jewish organizations involved in the discussions soon agreed—that what would make the most sense would be to appoint one umbrella restitution organization to deal with all looted Jewish property and for JCR to act under its aegis to deal specifically with the books and cultural items.[4]

Like Jewish Cultural Reconstruction, the JRSO was also the creation of several leading Jewish organizations, and like JCR, its mission was also to facilitate the return of looted Jewish property to its rightful owners. However, the JRSO's mission was far broader than that of JCR. Whereas JCR was set up to deal with looted *cultural* property—mainly books and religious items—JRSO was established to deal with *all* heirless property of any kind: the artwork, home furnishings, land and houses, and so on. As soon as Allied governments established the JRSO as the primary vehicle for the restitution of Jewish property, it made sense to set JCR under its wing. Officially, then, JCR was a member organization of JRSO. In practice, however, JCR operated mostly on its own, free of much interference from its new adoptive parent.

What happened, then, was a weird reversal of organizational genealogy. Jewish Cultural Reconstruction was officially incorporated on April 25, 1947, and then three weeks later, on May 15, 1947, came the creation of its parent organization, the Jewish Restitution Successor Organization.[5]

## JCR's Starr Leader

But it took time to work these matters out. Finally in January 1948 JCR went ahead and chose its leader; it appointed a forty-one-year-old historian and communal worker, Joshua Starr, as its executive secretary. Starr, a quiet, dedicated man, had studied at the Jewish Theological Seminary, University of Chicago, New York University, Columbia University, and the American School of Oriental Research in Jerusalem. An expert in Byzantine and post-Byzantine Jewish history, he had also served on the staffs of the American Jewish Congress and the Joint Distribution Committee. He had also been an editor of *Jewish Social Studies* and had done important research for the Conference on Jewish Relations' population studies in 1943.[6] He was, to say the least, qualified for the job.

Starr was eager to get to work. His only problem was that he didn't yet have a visa to get into Germany. Undeterred, he traveled to England in February 1948; there, just across the Channel, Starr would at least be closer to the German warehouse storing the objects of his labors.

Upon arriving in Europe, Starr assessed the situation in France and Austria and was pleased that the JCR representatives on the scene from the Hebrew University were doing their jobs well. He also threw himself into a growing imbroglio over the Hungarian Gold Train: twenty-four freight cars of property looted from Jewish families and communities during the war and seized by Allied forces in May 1945. At the time, the Hungarian government and Jewish organizations estimated the value of its cargo (Jewish books and ceremonial objects) at $350 million—more than $4.5 billion today.[7] When Starr arrived in England, he learned that the train contained many valuables. Working through Abba P. Schwartz of the Intergovernmental Committee on Refugees, Starr was able to arrange for three tons of the material (450 cubic feet) to be transferred to Offenbach for later restitution.[8]

Finally in May, Starr was able to enter Germany, where he could get to work setting up JCR operations in earnest. Of immediate concern was a recently discovered collection of almost twenty-nine thousand books from Lithuania, Latvia, and Estonia, many of which had been owned by Jews. The American government didn't know what to do with the material. They certainly weren't going to send the books to back to Baltic lands, where they would be under Soviet control. And restoring the books to the German government or its decimated Jewish community would most definitely *not* "serve and promote the spiritual and cultural needs and interests of the Jewish people." After some prodding from Starr, the military government agreed to an interim step: the books would be turned over to JCR, which would hold them for two years until a solution could be worked out that would satisfy all stakeholders. JCR received the books, and by 1949 the departing American military apparently lost its appetite for Baltic Jewish books and agreed to let JCR take possession of them and fold the collection into its restitution program.

In November 1948 Starr left Germany to continue his work on behalf of JCR in the United States. Once home, Starr reported on the situation in Europe and began preparing staff to take over the work he had left behind. By this time the JCR budget had grown to $21,000. This meant a larger staff, better equipment, and increased morale for taking on the task at hand. The following February, the American military would turn over the keys of its Offenbach Archival Depot to JCR and give it custodianship of its 350,000 Jewish cultural items. Thanks in no small measure to Starr's dogged efforts in Europe, JCR leaders had every reason to believe they could complete their restitution work within six months.

In August 1949 Joshua Starr resigned his post at JCR. The reasons for his departure are unclear. The historical record suggests that he might have gotten into an argument with Salo Baron; Starr hinted that he had been offered a position with the government and also that he'd been asked to return to Europe. Some have suggested that he was seeking a position in academia and was dejected because he couldn't find one.

On December 6, 1949, Joshua Starr killed himself at his home in New York. He was forty-two years old.[9]

## New Leaders, New Challenges

Taking over the helm when Starr left Europe was a Moldovan-born, PhD-bearing Reform rabbi named Bernard Heller. Baron had originally hired him in December 1948, sending him to Germany to work under Starr's supervision, and he was a natural choice to become the JCR field director in Germany after Starr's departure. Assisting him were a librarian from the Jewish National and University Library in Jerusalem, Shlomo Shunami, who became the assistant field director, and Mordecai Narkiss, director of the Bezalel Museum in Jerusalem, whom Starr brought to Germany to select ceremonial objects for exhibit in Israel. When they arrived on the scene, Heller, Shunami, and Narkiss found that Starr had succeeded in getting JCR up and running quite well. Throughout the Offenbach depot, books were being sorted, identified, and distributed to libraries around the world, or, where possible, returned to their original owners.

From the get-go, however, Heller and his assistants feared that they might have a problem on their hands, and sure enough, their fears were soon confirmed: German libraries still had Jewish loot, and they weren't giving it up.

When JCR was first created, its obvious mission was to deal with the mountains of books awaiting its attention in Offenbach and other collecting points around Europe. But those who were in the know warned JCR that these collections represented only the proverbial tip of the iceberg. A lot of material, they suggested, hadn't even been discovered yet, and a great deal of it was probably sitting in libraries around Europe. If JCR was serious about getting Jewish books back into Jewish hands, they insisted, then JCR would do well to check out every German library and museum it could.    For its part, JCR was plenty busy dealing with the loot it already knew to exist. Now they should go out and find more? What could the overwhelmed and overworked JCR staffers do?

Enter "M. Bernstein"—Holocaust survivor, YIVO representative, and stealthy sleuth of purloined papers. Bernstein's identity has never been determined; all of the reports he wrote and all references to him in the JCR archives refer to him only as "M. Bernstein." Whoever he was, M. Bernstein embarked on a nationwide fact-finding tour on behalf of JCR beginning in the spring of 1949. He visited dozens of cities: Hamburg, Freiburg, and Wurms; Esslingen, Gottingen, and Floss. He even went to Sulzbach, where the large volume of Jewish law that first got me interested in this story was published. In each city M. Bernstein infiltrated his way into local libraries and checked out their Jewish collections. As his reports rolled into the JCR offices, the picture became clear. German libraries—in universities, large cities, and small hamlets—had Jewish books in their collections, and the librarians knew perfectly well that the material had been looted. Not only that, German institutions also held the archives of Jewish communities that had been destroyed during the war, and to make matters worse, there were even some Jewish libraries that had surreptitiously acquired looted archives from the war.

M. Bernstein's reconnaissance was stealthy and extensive—but lousy. His reports were so lacking in detail and documentation that they all but drove his JCR handlers mad, and evidently, in the fall of 1949 he was dismissed from his duties. Nevertheless when JCR sent out other investigators to see whether there was any validity to M. Bernstein's claims, they found that the overall message of his reports was correct. There were untold Jewish literary riches still being hidden in libraries and other institutions throughout the country. The material unearthed from castles and monasteries was only the beginning. To complete its work, JCR would somehow need to infiltrate German libraries and root out the portion of their holdings that had belonged to Jews before the war. Clearly it wasn't going to be easy.

Their problem was that the original law authorizing them to take possession of the books for restitution—Law 59, issued by General Clay on November 10, 1947—insisted that all claims for looted material be filed by December 31, 1948. Now that the deadline had passed, how was JCR going to get its hands on the additional material? Fortunately Benjamin Ferencz of the JRSO found a loophole. He pointed out that the same Law 59 that had once authorized JCR to get the material—the very same one that had instituted the deadline for the claims—also called on German institutions to report all of the confiscated material they held after the end of the war. Failure to comply could result in heavy fines. They were required to report only individual items or groups of items from single owners valued at DM 1,000 or more, but at least it was a start.

Without the Americans in Germany anymore, it was harder for JCR to get German individuals and institutions to comply with this law, but it did have the authority to approach libraries, universities, and private German citizens known to be holding stolen Jewish books and discuss the fate of their Jewish holdings.[10] Now, the agency did not just busy itself with sorting, identifying, shaping policy, and shipping; it had to negotiate as well.

But negotiations would need to wait. There was, after all, a warehouse full of books already on hand waiting for distribution, and under Heller's leadership, JCR leaders in Europe hired a staff of Jewish and non-Jewish

German workers to assist them in their efforts. Meanwhile, in the United States JCR set up a distribution protocol to govern the agency's efforts in Europe. When the board first articulated JCR's *raison d'etre* back in 1947, it was easy to say that its distribution would serve the spiritual and cultural needs and interests of the Jewish people, the survivors, and humankind in general. Now, however, they had to figure out what that really meant. By 1949 the JCR board had heard all the arguments—all of the conflicting claims to the material by the United States, Israel, survivor groups, and remaining Jewish communities in Europe—and surely the conflict had grown wearisome. Now they actually had the material. Now they were hiring a large staff. Now they actually needed to get to work. And now they needed a policy to guide them in their labor.

In the end, the solution they reached was simple: 40 percent of the unclaimed books and archives would go to libraries in Israel, another 40 percent would go to the United States, and the remaining 20 percent would go to Great Britain, South Africa, and other countries. Each receiving institution would agree to make all duplicates available to JCR for redistribution (or was it re-redistribution?); any library wishing to sell the material it received would need JCR approval to do so; libraries receiving book allocations had to supply JCR with a list of the books' titles and authors within six months of receipt; and, for a period of two years after receiving the material, libraries would agree to return any of their material in response to claims from owners or heirs.[11]

Once the JCR-JRSO framework was arranged, the member organizations of JCR could go ahead and work out the details of their own agreement with one another and their organizations' arrangement with the American occupational government. There was a good deal of fine print, of course, but the basic 40-40-20 formula indicating the percentage of JCR holdings that would go to the United States, Israel, and "other" was the primary guiding principle. Almost all of the stakeholders liked the formula. The Americans, glorying in their postwar prosperity and their power in almost everything, were pleased that it recognized the strength of their large Jewish community. The Israelis, now finally living in a sovereign country of their own, were gratified that the policy honored the centrality and significance of the newborn State of Israel. The British, South Africans, and other countries that made the JCR list were delighted to receive some of the material for their own communities.

In fact the only people who didn't seem to like this plan were the surviving Jewish communities in Europe. In all of the excitement about reconstructing Jewish communities after the war, the communities themselves seem to have gotten left out of the mix. Their frustration, of course, is understandable. European Jewry had been ravaged by war. Few of its residents had survived, and some had chosen to stay put rather than flee to faraway places. Others had fled to those faraway places or had already moved to those places before the war had begun. Now, to the great consternation of those who remained in Europe, the Jews who had left Europe behind wanted to come back and tell those who had decided to stay how to rebuild it. And for the most part they wanted to reconstruct European Jewish culture by removing Jewish books and ritual items from Europe. Jewish cultural reconstruction seemed to be occurring everywhere except where Jewish culture had been decimated in the first place.

By 1949 the smoke of World War II had largely cleared, and as it did, a new Jewish landscape came into view. Once, the Pale of Settlement teemed with millions of eastern European Jews. Once, the Jews of western Europe—those in Germany, France, Austria, and elsewhere—represented Jewish culture, sophistication, and prosperity at its finest. Once, American Jewry was struggling to get on its feet, and the Jewish community in Israel represented a tiny group of idealistic dreamers toiling to drain the swamps and make the deserts bloom. Now none of that was true. Now millions of eastern Europe's Jews were dead, and those who survived faced new terrors under Stalin's increasingly despotic rule. Now most Jews of western Europe were also gone—murdered or made refugees by the genocidal war that had just ended. And now the Jewish community of the United States had grown mighty, and the State of Israel had given the Jewish people the type of national, political power it hadn't enjoyed for almost two thousand years. The combined power of Israeli and American Jewry redounded well to Jews in other countries, too—to Jews in Bolivia, Brazil, Australia, Morocco, and Mexico. Not everything was perfect for Jews in those countries, far from it. But they were indisputably part of a new postwar Jewish world, still grieving a horrible loss, but far safer than only a few years earlier.

With the new distribution protocols approved and the European staff in place, JCR was able to quickly pack and ship the remaining books in the Offenbach warehouse. Twelve hundred cases were ready for shipment by the beginning of April 1949, three hundred more a few days later, and so on.

By the end of May—an astonishingly brief three months after the JCR distribution process had begun—the Offenbach Archival Depot was empty of its books. There was still more material at collecting points in Wiesbaden, Munich, and at who-knew-how-many libraries and museums throughout the country, but JCR had nevertheless reached an important milestone. Just four years earlier, the Offenbach depot had held the most colossal assemblage of Jewish literature anywhere—the literary remains of the murdered, decimated Jewish communities of Nazi Europe. Now, many of the books were back in the hands of the prewar owners, and those whose owners had been murdered or unidentifiable were at least back in the hands of the Jewish people or at institutions that could properly care for the books and make them available to Jews and others wishing to read them.

As Heller prepared to conclude his work in Offenbach, he and some of the other staffers surely noticed one of the great ironies of the entire project. Although Jewish scholars and administrators were in charge of what happened at Offenbach, much of the actual grunt work was performed by German employees. Germans had stolen Europe's Jewish books, and now Germans were helping put those very same books back in Jewish hands. Seymour Pomrenze had noticed this dynamic back in 1946, but by 1949 many Jews were involved too. The Nazis segregated Jews from Germans in order to destroy them; JCR, in its own small way, brought a small group of Jews and Germans together in order to rebuild Jewish culture.

On May 31, 1949, there was a small party for the workers at Offen-bach, celebrating the achievement they had all helped make possible. Speaking to the workers, Heller took note of the significance he saw in what had just happened:

In the work in which you have been engaged I see a deeper meaning. I do not merely wish to congratulate you on a task well performed. In your difficult and cooperative efforts to help the AMG [American mili-tary government] return the looted books and Torah scrolls I perceive a desire on your part to undo—as far as was in your power—a great wrong. You have collaborated in the work of making *some* restitution to the bereaved Jewish people. I see in the completion of this initial operation the first step towards a reconciliation between the greatest victims of Nazism, the Jews, and the de-nazified Germans. May this commingling of German and Jewish workers spell the beginning of peace and amity and good will between the peoples we represent. May it betoken an assurance that never again will such misdeeds be allowed to be reenacted.[12]

## *1949–1977: Hannah Arendt Empties the JCR Warehouses*

For all of the satisfaction that everyone involved with JCR must have felt, the lingering question of the books remaining at the other collec-tion points meant there was still a lot of work for the agency to do. Of particular concern were the tens of thousands of books that sat in the American military government's collecting point in Wiesbaden. In fact Wiesbaden held the largest remaining collection, and with the end of the occupation imminent, the American government was planning to shutter the facility on August 31, 1949.

One of the major Wiesbaden concerns had to do with the Baltic Collection—almost twenty-nine thousand books, some of which were rare and valuable—that the Nazis had looted from Jews in Latvia, Lithuania, and Estonia as they rounded up and murdered most of the people who owned them. Once the books had come into the hands of the American army, they posed a particularly difficult problem. It was clear that they had come from the Baltics, but the Baltics as independent countries no longer existed; the Soviet Union had annexed them after the war. To make matters worse, the United States didn't recognize the Soviet annexation of the Baltics. This meant that to U.S. diplomats, the countries that used to be Latvia, Lithuania, and Estonia were now a big, fat J-shaped hole on the map just to the right of the Baltic Sea. America could send the Baltic books only back to Baltic countries, but since the Baltic countries technically no longer existed, what were they to do? The Soviets, needless to say, didn't agree. They held that Latvia, Lithuania, and Estonia were bona fide countries just like Britain, France, and the Netherlands and that the Baltics states should therefore receive books just like other European countries did. Israel, however, was in a different position regarding the Soviet Union. It was now a democratic state, but many of its citizens had come from eastern Europe, and the ruling Labor Party was proudly socialist. In those early years of the Cold War, Israel had yet to cast its lot firmly with the United States and was still playing the field in the American-Soviet dating game. If Israel got the books, they might send them to the Baltics to curry favor with the Soviets. As a result many in the West were understandably concerned about the possibility that any Baltic books sent to Israel might eventually end up in Soviet hands.

Few American military officers wanted final say over what to do with this twenty-nine-thousand-volume literary hot potato, and the question of its disposition eventually reached the Joint Chiefs of Staff. Finally, on July 22, 1949, JCR got the Baltic Collection, but it had to keep the collection intact for two years to give individual claimants a chance to recover their books. JCR promptly sent about sixteen thousand volumes—most of which had identifiable owners—to its warehouse in Paris, and the rest went to the Hebrew University in Jerusalem. JCR then compiled a list of sixteen thousand people whom it could identify as original owners, published it, and invited the people on the list to come claim their books. Then in the summer of 1951, the remaining books were placed into JCR's larger 40-40-20 distribution process. Today the volumes of this priceless collection sit safely in libraries around the world.[13]

With Starr's resignation and Heller's departure for America in the summer of 1949, it became clear that JCR's new executive secretary would need to be "on the ground" in Germany and that the person who took the job would need to be the type of individual who knew Jewish books, was respected by scholars and government officials alike, and had the gravitas and diplomatic skills needed to negotiate the release of Jewish books from the German institutions where they were being hidden.

Hannah Arendt was perfect for the job. Arendt, a political philosopher and activist who grew up in a secular Jewish home in Königsberg, had completed her doctoral dissertation on the philosophy of Saint Augustine in 1929. Unable to secure a teaching position in the increasingly antisemitic atmosphere of prewar Germany, she worked as a researcher for the German Zionist Organization while also providing covert assistance to an "underground railroad," helping Jews flee Germany after Hitler's rise to power.

In 1940 Arendt married a Communist poet and activist named Heinrich Blücher. (Although she rarely went by her married name, the fact that Hannah Arendt *could* have been called "Frau Blücher" sadly seems to have been lost on Mel Brooks fans everywhere.) Arendt and Blücher were briefly interned in a French prison camp before fleeing to the United States in 1941.

In New York the couple quickly became active in the German Jewish refugee community, where some of Arendt's friends arranged for her

32. Hannah Arendt. Copyright estate of Fred Stein, fredstein.com.

to meet Salo Baron. Baron, who had been a professor at Columbia for twelve years by this time, took Arendt under his wing, encouraging her in her academic pursuits and helping the young scholar build a professional network. When it came time for Baron's Conference on Jewish Relations to hire a full-time research director in 1944, Hannah Arendt was the natural choice.[14]

In her new role—her first full-time job since immigrating to the United States—Arendt was in charge of compiling the CJR's "Tentative List of Jewish Cultural Treasures in Axis-Occupied Countries." She carried out her work from the United States, coordinating the CJR's research staff as it carried out its monumental task. With Arendt's knowledge of Jewish culture, her administrative skills, her many contacts in Germany, and perhaps most of all her passion for the commission's work, she was able carry out her tasks perhaps better than anyone else. Under her leadership, the CJR's research staff identified hundreds of rabbis, community leaders, and others who could give them the information they sought, slowly assembling their 103-page portrait of the prewar literary world of Jewish Europe. After this opus came to print, the CJR released three more such lists in quick succession: a list of Jewish educational institutions was published in 1946, one of periodicals in 1947, and one of Jewish publishers in 1948. The steady flow of information necessitated a list of addenda, also published in 1948. Arendt's work in assembling the material was invaluable. (After her death almost three decades later, Baron recalled her vital contribution to the postwar restitution effort, emphasizing that her work compiling the "Tentative Lists" "impressed the officials at the State Department" and helped pave the way for the Jewish Cultural Reconstruction, Inc.)[15]

At the end of 1949 JCR hired Arendt as its executive secretary and sent her to supervise the agency's book recovery and restitution efforts in Europe. By then most of the major collections discovered at the end of the war had already been dealt with, by either the American army, the French or British restitution organizations, or most recently the

JCR, when it took over for the army at the end of the occupation. Many people might have heralded these finds as a huge success, not to mention a good excuse to pack up and go home. As far as Arendt and her colleagues at JCR were concerned, however, their work was far from over. There was *a lot* of literary material that remained unaccounted for. For months JCR had been receiving reports indicating that Germany hadn't forked over all of the looted books and that many thousands of them—millions, perhaps—remained in libraries and museums around the country. Other collections were in the hands of their legal owners but still not receiving proper care, such as the 60 percent of the Bavarian State Library's collection that remained in depots or cellars. Many refugees had reclaimed their collections after the war but then moved to places such as the United States or Israel, leaving the books behind in the upheaval. News came out that the University of Marburg had up to one hundred volumes of rabbinic literature and eighteen Torah scrolls. Eighteen Torah scrolls? At the University of Marburg? Something was definitely amiss. And similar situations were coming to JCR's attention almost every day. To top it off, M. Bernstein's reconnaissance reports may have been clumsy, but for all of their vagueness and for all of the yawning gaps in the portrait they provided, it was nevertheless clear that the restitution work was far from over. Even after all of the restitution efforts that had taken place before she arrived, the task that greeted Hannah Arendt when she got to Germany was monumental.

Arendt threw herself into her work with gusto. She jumped into negotiations for the two-volume Worms *Machzor*, a beautifully illuminated, late thirteenth-century holiday prayer book looted on Kristallnacht and kept during the war in that city's Dom St. Peter Cathedral.[16] She entered into similar negotiations for the Jewish library of Mainz. She discovered with dismay that the Nazis had stored many of the looted books in Berlin and that these works were quietly disappearing behind the Iron Curtain.

Arendt also realized that in the discussions so far, JCR, the German librarians, and other concerned parties had all been a little fuzzy about

33. A page from the Worms *Machzor*. Photo by Leehe Bronstein. Courtesy National Library of Israel.

the term "Jewish books." Libraries in Frankfurt, for example, had received many books without explicit Jewish content from the American military after the war, not realizing—or perhaps closing their eyes to the fact— that these volumes had once belonged to Jewish families. Many would suggest that despite their subject matter, these books were "Jewish" because their owners were Jews. Arendt pointed this out to Hans Wilhelm Eppelsheimer, director of the Frankfurt Staats-und Universitätsbibliothek and a leading librarian in the region. In response, Eppelsheimer agreed to turn over to JCR those books that were undeniably owned by Jews before the war. Clearly there were many books once owned by Jews that he *hadn't* agreed to relinquish, but it was a start.[17]

There were, of course, still some Jews in Germany, desperately trying to reestablish their lives and reconstruct their ravaged culture. Understandably they wanted to get as many Jewish books as they could for their small communities. Arendt and her colleagues at JCR were sympathetic to their desires, but they also had to look at the bigger picture. The Jewish world was not what it was before the war. Although the remaining Jews in Germany needed and deserved support, Israel, the United States, and other countries had just seen their Jewish populations boom, often with Jews who had fled the small communities of survivors in Germany. The fact that this small group of German Jews wanted to stay in their homes may have been admirable, but it didn't necessarily mean that they should get a disproportionate number of books from the JCR book coffers.

So Arendt negotiated. Typically the agreements that came out of these talks involved local Jewish communities agreeing to retain a small percentage of these books, with the remainder going into JCR's worldwide distribution program. For example, in early 1950 Arendt worked out a deal with Rabbi Steven Schwarzschild, a young rabbi who had been ordained in 1948 at the Hebrew Union College in Cincinnati and returned to his native Germany to serve as rabbi of the Jewish community of Berlin. Arendt and Schwarzschild agreed that 15 percent of the Torah scrolls discovered in western Berlin would be retained by the local community for redistribution throughout the country. JCR would get the remainder of the scrolls and would pay for the needs of the local Jewish community library, allowing it to publish textbooks and other educational materials.

Arendt and her staff realized the historical significance of what they were doing. It wasn't only that the books represented a recently lost culture of the Jewish people, but perhaps even more fundamentally they represented a victory—albeit a small one—over the Nazi effort to murder all Jews and seize their books. The books that came through JCR had stories to tell—not only in the words they contained, but also as physical objects that were part of history. Future readers would be looking at these artifacts that had been involved in some of the greatest, most horrible, and perhaps in the end, also the most inspirational stories in history.

Arendt feared that future readers and owners of these books might be unaware of their historical significance. To make sure these future readers knew what had happened to the books, Arendt decided that each should somehow be marked, reminding readers forever of the epic path it had taken through history. To design this marking, Arendt turned to a concert violinist turned artist named Aaron Fastove. Fastove, a native of Chernobyl, Ukraine, had moved to the United States in 1922, where in the hurly-burly of 1920s' America he quickly realized that making a living as a musician would be difficult. So he taught himself to draw and paint and soon became a professional artist. He had a very precise, meticulous style, which is probably why the army hired him to illustrate their technical manuals during the war. For a long time Fastove lived in a cooperative housing colony in the Bronx, where he associated with a variety of Jewish intellectuals and progressive thinkers. His reputation grew, and eventually somebody mentioned his name to Hannah Arendt.[18]

Arendt commissioned Fastove to create a JCR emblem, a bookplate to be placed inside each of the volumes JCR distributed. The final product was a light-blue circle bearing the words *T'kumah L'tarbut Yisrael*, which both surrounded and was surrounded by Stars of David. For those who didn't understand the Hebrew, a translation appeared in gothic lettering underneath: "Jewish Cultural Reconstruction."

In a letter to the libraries that received JCR books, Arendt wrote:

In view of the extraordinary history of the books which are now being distributed by Jewish Cultural Reconstruction, Inc. to Jewish libraries and institutions of higher learning throughout the world, we feel that it will be of great importance to have each volume marked, so that present and future readers may be reminded of those who once cherished them before they became victims of the great Jewish catastrophe.

Without such a distinctive mark it will also be impossible for present and future scholars to retrace the history and the whereabouts of the great cultural treasures of European Jewry which once were the pride of scholars, institutions, and private collectors.

She requested that the libraries affix the bookplates she had sent with the letter inside the front covers of all the books they received.[19]

Arendt's work, conducted in the bombed-out remains of postwar Europe, was exhausting. In her letters home to Heinrich, she described her enormous workload and difficult living conditions. "Don't overexert yourself," he exhorted her, "they are only books."[20]

The haggling over the archival material was wearisome for Arendt and her colleagues, but it was also essential, for in the pre-Internet, pre-instant-printing days of the mid-twentieth century, the stakes of such discussions were far higher for librarians and curators than they are today. Now, books and archival material are often available to all—in the cloud, online, "Googleable" for the world to see. In the early 1950s, document owners had a far more exclusive hold on the information they contained than they do today. What was really at issue in discussions over who would get, say, the archives of a small Polish shtetl or the files of a Zionist religious school was the knowledge that the victor would get to hold onto the historical legacy left behind.

Back in 1936 the American Library Association had sanctioned the use of a new technology that eased some of the tension in these archival negotiations—microfilm. Joshua Starr had initiated the effort to commit JCR material to microfilm during his tenure, and Arendt continued it with added enthusiasm. Now if the archives of a German community were to remain in Germany, it could also be available to scholars around the world on microfilm. Eventually JCR delegated the large-scale microfilming of manuscripts to the Hebrew University and the State of Israel. By the time the work on the European material concluded, they had amassed more than fifteen thousand images.[21]

Slowly the collecting points emptied. Offenbach, Wiesbaden, Munich. And slowly Arendt and her colleagues rousted more books from their hiding places in Germany—450,000 altogether. And then, by late 1950, the flow of books into JCR's literary coffers had dwindled to a trickle. Baron and Arendt knew that there were more books out there—some libraries and museums had refused to part with their books, and others had certainly managed to keep their holdings secret—but it was becoming increasingly difficult to justify the cost and energy needed to maintain a fully operational JCR staff in Europe. Baron refused to close up shop completely, but in an August 1950 letter to Arendt, he did acknowledge that it was time to shift gears. "It would hardly pay to operate a full-fledged JCR office in Germany for the sake of the occasional driblets which might come through from time to time," Baron observed. "Probably five years from now, another attempt might be really worthwhile, if the international situation allows it. On the other hand, I am not sure about it in my own mind, and certainly cannot commit the organization to that policy."[22]

It was a good time for JCR to stop and take stock. By the beginning of 1952 it had redistributed more than 400,000 volumes. Books allotted to the United States were sent to a depot in Brooklyn and divided into smaller lots and shipped to libraries around the country. Brandeis University received 11,288, YIVO at its new headquarters in New York received 11,601, and Yeshiva University received 9,407. Several smaller libraries were on the list as well, as were the Library of Congress, the New York Public Library, and the libraries at ten non-Jewish universities, including Harvard, the University of Iowa, Johns Hopkins, and the University of Texas. There were four dozen U.S. allocations, ranging in size from the 13,275 that went to the Jewish Theological Seminary to the 22 volumes that went to the New York Board of Rabbis. Fortunately JCR was also able to return almost 9,000 of the volumes from the Brooklyn depot to their original owners. The books sent to the United States traveled from Germany to New York, and from there they scattered around the country to their new homes—libraries where they would be kept safe and available to scholars and students who wanted to read them.

In Israel—the country receiving the most books—the lion's share of the shipments went to the Hebrew University. The university chose to take most of the major collections of rare books so as to preserve the collections' integrity and helped itself to many of the other volumes as well. The Ministry of Religious Affairs and the Ministry of Education divvied up the remaining 53,500 volumes, sending shipments to schools, libraries, and yeshivot around the country. The other countries receiving smaller numbers of books worked out similar distribution processes for themselves.

### Number of books redistributed by the JCR, by country

| | |
|---|---|
| Israel | 191,423 |
| United States | 160,886 |
| Canada | 2,031 |
| Belgium | 842 |
| France | 8,193 |

Germany        11,814
Great Britain  19,082
Holland        1,813
Sweden         696
Switzerland    7,843
South Africa   7,269
Morocco        378
Australia      3,307
Argentina      5,053
Bolivia        1,281
Brazil         2,463
Chile          1,219
Costa Rica     442
Ecuador        225
Mexico         804
Peru           529
Uruguay        1,670
Venezuela      456
Others         2,044
Total          431,745

(JCR, Inc., World Distribution of Books 1 July 1949–31 January 1952, July 1952, Geneva IV/32/1B, JDC Archives, Jerusalem). This tally is incomplete due to the archival record being compromised, the disorganized character of the original list, and the nature of the materials being listed. Some of the numbers were compiled based on unopened cases. The total reached here does not correspond exactly to the total reached by Hannah Arendt. There is a surplus of 4,824 books on this list that cannot be accounted for. Courtesy Dana Herman, "*Hashevat Avedah*: A History of Jewish Cultural Reconstruction, Inc." (PhD diss., McGill University, 2008), 225–26.

Hannah Arendt, now back in the United States, was able to free herself from the heavy burdens of Europe, and her life became a whirlwind of writing, teaching, and planning. She published many essays during this time, and her book *The Origins of Totalitarianism*, published in 1951, was a systematic analysis based in no small measure on her experiences before and immediately after the war. She was also able to reconnect with old friends, getting to know them in ways that had been impossible while performing her duties in Europe. Salo Baron's daughter Shoshana was one of the many people in Arendt's world to reap the benefits of these new opportunities. In the early 1950s Shoshana was able to turn to Arendt for help as she wrote her college philosophy papers.[23]

Small caches of material continued to appear even after JCR completed these large allocations, and Baron and Arendt continued setting the staff to work on cataloging and microfilming what they could. The book piles on JCR's warehouse floors shrank in size and then disappeared altogether. The flow of material into the JCR book coffers dwindled from a deluge to a trickle, and then to almost nothing. Still, Baron was reluctant to close shop. The books that remained in Germany needed to be microfilmed, and there needed to be a German law guaranteeing the safeguarding and return of books for the future. And, most important, there still might be books out there, awaiting the discovery and restitution that JCR was uniquely qualified to provide.[24]

By the early 1950s, however, there was a palpable shifting of gears in the way that Jewish leaders and institutions were dealing with the Holocaust and its aftermath. Most of the funding that had supported the international institutional work of JCR and other similar organizations was now flowing toward efforts aimed at directly supporting the survivors and their families. JRSO, for one, was engaged in an effort to secure financial compensation for the survivors and had lost its enthusiasm for the large-scale book restitution that JCR had championed during its heyday.

Nominally JCR continued to exist for another two and a half decades, dealing with an occasional claims issue here, another newly discovered group of books there, but not much more. Arendt and Baron aged, growing grayer and less suited for the trench work they had done so well in the years right after the war. Then on December 4, 1975, while dining with Salo and Jeannette Baron at their home in New York, Hannah Arendt died at the age of sixty-nine.

Two years later, on November 9, 1977, Salo Baron gathered some of JCR's directors in a New York law office and officially dissolved the organization. Even then Baron remained aware that there was still restitution work to be done. In 1988, the year before his death, he told an interviewer that he thought he'd closed JCR's doors prematurely. For all of its important work, Jewish Cultural Reconstruction's name was often misleading. Yes, during the thirty years of its existence, it did strive to reconstruct Jewish culture, but only in the broadest sense. It did not try to rebuild damaged shtetl libraries, nor reopen destroyed yeshivot, nor in any way restore European Jewish culture to what it once was. Early on its leaders saw clearly that in Europe there wasn't anything left to rebuild. Instead, as Jews stepped shakily away from the ruins the Holocaust, JCR strove to get Jewish books and other cultural items back into Jewish hands, wherever Jews might live. The few who chose to remain in Europe would get a few of the books, of course, but in the new landscape of postwar Jewish life, Europe—at least for now—was a large, mostly empty hole. The "reconstruction" that this new situation called for was not of *European* Jewish culture, but of worldwide Jewish culture. JCR, as we have seen, played an important role not only in helping this reconstruction take place, but also in helping Jews around the world maintain their ties with the culture and literature of the world that the Nazis destroyed.

The books that went to Canada, we should note, don't carry the JCR bookplate inside their covers. Instead the Canadian Jewish Congress designed its own plate for the books it received. To Arendt's dismay, it didn't acknowledge the work of JCR, but she could hardly quibble with the sentiment its words expressed:

> *eleh ezkarah . . . [These I will remember]*
> *This book was once the property*
> *of a Jew, victim of the Great Massacre*
> *in Europe. The Nazis who seized*

*this book eventually destroyed the owner.*
*It has been recovered by the Jewish*
*People, and reverently placed in*
*This institution by the Canadian Jewish*
*Congress, as a memorial to those who gave*
*Their lives for the sanctification of the Holy Name*
*gvulin nisrafin ve'otiot porkhot [scrolls aflame and letters flying up*
*through the air].*[25]

The Nazis set the scrolls aflame. But it was the efforts of people like Salo Baron and Hannah Arendt and their work with JCR that helped the letters to fly through the air—perhaps to heaven, but certainly to shelves in safe, well-lit libraries all around the world.

# 11

# *Where Are They Now?*

All that remains of her now
are those grey pearls
smoldering in the ash.
—Abraham Sutzkever

## *Salonika . . .*

In 2003 a nineteen-year-old American college student named Devin
Naar traveled to Salonika, Greece, for a project that many might have
considered tedious at best: he was going to help catalogue the disorganized
records of that city's Jewish community.[1] Naar, however, couldn't wait
to begin. He had a passionate interest in Salonika's Jews—and for good
reason. Back when there were eighty thousand Jews in the "Jerusalem of
the Balkans," the Naars were one of its many prominent Jewish families.

Today the Jewish community of Salonika is quite small. Most of the
Naars—and for that matter, most of the other Jewish families who lived
in Salonika before the war—are gone too, more than 90 percent of them
having been murdered during the Holocaust. On the site of what was
once the city's great Jewish cemetery now sits the University of Salonika.
Many headstones that once marked the graves of Salonika's Jews can now
be found mortared into the foundations of the city's postwar buildings,
their Hebrew letters and Jewish symbols giving fragmentary testimony
to the lives and the culture of the city's Jewish past. Sadly this Jerusalem
is one that shines mostly in memory.

After World War I, Devin Naar's great-grandfather, Rabbi Benyamin Haim Naar, migrated to the United States with nine of his ten children; one son, Salomon, decided to remain in Salonika. The Naars landed in New Jersey, and even as Benyamin's children had children and grandchildren of their own, the family continued to cherish its Salonikan roots. Pictures of the old country hung on the walls of Naar homes, and Naar family elders told stories about life in Salonika—its rich Jewish culture, its synagogues and sages, its businesses and leaders, and the lives they once lived that were now distant memories yet still almost close enough to touch. Even when Devin and his generation had become part of the picture, older relatives still spoke Ladino—Judeo-Spanish—just as their ancestors had done back in the old country.

Devin Naar had been interested in his family's history ever since he had first heard the stories. What was it like to live in Salonika back then? What was this strange language that he heard at family gatherings? What had happened to his great-uncle Salomon, who had somehow disappeared from the family? Devin came to believe that the answers to some of these questions may have been at YIVO (the Yiddish Scientific Institute), in New York City. As an undergraduate history major at Washington University in St. Louis, he learned that YIVO had gotten piles of archival material after the war, most likely in a shipment from the Offenbach Archival Depot. In 2003 he spent time in New York helping YIVO catalogue and organize the heaps of Salonikan Jewish papers: birth certificates, marriage records, correspondence of the Jewish Community Council, and much more. In the collection he found three volumes of a twenty-four-volume, seventy-five-thousand-name census that had been taken by the Jewish community during World War I, and as luck would have it, one of the volumes he found was the "N," which listed Naar, after Naar, after Naar.

In 2005, after Devin graduated from college and before beginning his doctoral studies in history at Stanford, he went to Greece on a year-long Fulbright scholarship to conduct an in-depth study of Salonikan Jewry. It was exciting work for a twenty-one-year-old student. He planned to investigate the archives of Jewish Salonika, interview its old-timers, and examine the physical evidence attesting to the greatness of the bustling Jewish community that was once home to his own family as well as thousands of others.

When Naar arrived, he went to the Jewish community's recently established museum to check out its archives. What he found shocked him. The entire written record of Salonikan Jewry—the births, the deaths, the weddings, the scandals, the gossip, the trials, the tribulations, the deeds, the literature, the love letters, and all the rest—amounted to a stack of papers just a few inches thick. Jews had lived there since the second century BCE—hundreds of thousands of them, perhaps millions over the generations—and the written records they left behind amounted to little more than a phone-book's worth of material.

Was this all? Surely there must have been more. Naar started asking around, and everyone seemed to give him a different answer. "The Nazis destroyed it," one resident claimed. Perhaps, but Naar knew that the Nazis saved far more of their looted books and archives than they destroyed. "The Nazis took it away," said someone else, "and after the war it ended up in the former Soviet Union." Hmm. . . perhaps, but still, it didn't seem to add up.

When Naar consulted the OAD's records about its Salonikan material, the mystery deepened. It turns out that the Nazis *had* looted a lot of books and archives from Salonika. Evidently some of the material did end up in the former Soviet Union (a few years later, in Moscow, Naar would have the opportunity to see it), and there was some additional material at the Central Archives of the Jewish People, in Jerusalem. But Naar also found a document indicating that the OAD had shipped eight tons of books and archives back to Salonika through Hamburg after the war.

Eight *tons*? This was a lot more than the small sheaf of papers Naar had found at the museum. Where was the rest of it? Naar continued to ask around, receiving little more than mumbled guesses and resigned shrugs in response. Finally, one day when he was schmoozing with a clerical worker employed by the Jewish community, he said, "By the way, do you know what happened to the archives that were sent back to Salonika after the war?"

"Sure," said the clerk, pointing toward one of the buildings in the Jewish community complex. "They're in the basement."

Naar immediately strode to the building, went down into its basement, turned on the light, and was thrilled at what he saw. The large room was overflowing with box after box of old books and archives. Not all eight tons of the material was there, but a lot of it was! He opened a couple of the boxes to see what was inside. Most of what he found was from the twenties and thirties. Some of the documents were in Greek, Hebrew, and French, but most were in Ladino. And stapled to some of them were translations of the Greek into German.

Later, as he perused the archives, Devin discovered that, contrary to local memory, it was not the Nazis who destroyed the local Jewish cemetery; it was the Greeks. They had been trying to get their hands on the property since the 1920s, and once the Nazis arrived, they felt freer to confiscate it—and did so over the objections of Nazi leaders.

One letter in the collection was of particular interest to Devin Naar. It was a letter, written in Greek, inviting a member of Salonika's Jewish community to join the committee of the soup kitchen that the community ran for its needy citizens during the German occupation. The letter was addressed to Salomon Naar, Devin's great-uncle—the one who never got out. Salomon Naar's name is not engraved into the brickwork of local buildings, for Salomon Naar never had a proper grave to begin with. His name is, however, preserved in the papers of Salonika's Jewish community—papers that were stolen by the Nazis, recovered by the Americans, and re-discovered by his great-nephew in the early twenty-first century.

So this is one story of saved Jewish books and documents from one European Jewish community—a story that concludes the way it does thanks to the efforts of a dedicated young scholar with a passion to understand and preserve his Jewish roots. But many millions of Jewish books were looted and many millions recovered—where are they now?

In a word, everywhere. After the war, as we have seen, the Offenbach Archival Depot returned vast quantities of books to other countries in government-to-government transfers. Later, Jewish Cultural Reconstruction took possession of the remaining books, restored many of them to their original owners, and distributed more than a million volumes to libraries around the world. Many millions of books found by the Soviet army in their zone of Germany after the war made their way back into Eastern Bloc libraries and were never seen again. Complicating matters further, many of the libraries that received the books after the war "de-acquisitioned" parts of their collections, selling off sets or individual volumes to dealers and other customers. One looted copy of *Hilkhot Alfasi* even made its way to Woodinville, Washington.

For the most part, the fact that the books are now "everywhere" is a good thing. Many are in the hands of the original owners or their heirs, and most of the unidentifiable books have made their way into libraries where they receive good care and are widely available to readers. Some of the books, however, haven't been so fortunate.

Although many of the books looted by the Nazis during World War II now sit quietly and relatively unnoticed upon the shelves of libraries around the world, others are the subjects of bitter dispute—sometimes between governments, sometimes between Jews themselves, and sometimes both.

### *Moscow . . .*

One collection that has proved to be particularly contentious is the library that was once owned by Rabbi Yosef Yitzchak Schneersohn, the sixth rebbe of Lubavitcher Hasidism and the father-in-law of Menachem Mendel Schneerson, the movement's last leader, who died in 1994. Yosef Yitzchak Schneersohn's library was a grand collection of twelve thousand books and more than twenty-five thousand manuscripts. Many of them were books that he had obtained on his own; others he had inherited from his five predecessors—the Lubavitcher rebbes who had led the group ever since it began in the late 1700s. It was a priceless collection, containing Jewish legal literature, manuscripts of great historical value, and a large number of priceless Hasidic books and manuscripts as well.

In 1918, as the oppressive restrictions of the new Soviet government fell into place, the Bolsheviks confiscated half of Schneersohn's library, nationalized it, and installed the collection in Moscow's Lenin Library. Then in 1927 Schneersohn was arrested for "counterrevolutionary activities" and sentenced to death. Fortunately there was a howl of protests from the West, and as a result Schneersohn's sentence was reduced to exile from the Soviet Union. On his way out of the country, Schneersohn was able to retrieve the remaining half of his collection, most of which was manuscript and responsa material.

The good news is that Schneersohn and his library—or at least half of it—were able to depart the Soviet Union for safe haven elsewhere. The bad news is that Schneersohn decided to move to Warsaw as his next home—a choice of safe haven that proved inauspicious, to say the least. With the beginning of World War II, Schneersohn found himself fleeing again, this time to the far safer destination of Brooklyn, New York. Sadly this time he was not able to bring his books with him and instead needed to leave them behind in a Warsaw warehouse. When the Nazis conquered Poland, they discovered this invaluable trove and transported the books to Berlin for safekeeping. Having moved from Russia to Poland to Germany, it was becoming a very well-traveled collection.

But the journey wasn't over. At war's end, Berlin was in the Soviet Zone of Germany, and when Soviet soldiers discovered the books, they promptly shipped the collection back to Russia, where it was placed in the USSR's military archives, near Moscow, and forgotten for decades. The first half had been looted by the Soviets, the second by the Nazis, and now those that had fallen into Nazi hands had been taken yet again by the Soviets. The books were all back in their country of origin, but it was hardly a happy homecoming.

The books sat in storage for decades. Chabad Lubavitch, now operating out of its new Brooklyn headquarters, began teaching children and adults in the freedom of their new American home. Yosef Yitzchak Schneersohn died in 1950, and under the leadership of his son-in-law Menachem Mendel Schneerson, the movement grew exponentially throughout the second half of the twentieth century. And for all those years, the books and archives sat unused—half in the Lenin Library and the other half in the military archives. Chabad knew that they were there. Few others outside of the movement paid the books any attention whatsoever. Maybe they could have complained, but in the days of Khrushchev and Brezhnev, what would have been the point?

But then, of course, came a change—a change with a big red birthmark on top. Mikhail Gorbachev rose to power. The Berlin Wall fell to the ground. Perestroika flourished. Chabad, whose Russian operations had dwindled after the war, gained new strength. In the late 1980s Gorbachev signaled that he might be willing to revisit the question of the library's ownership and maybe even negotiate its terms of release. With the collapse of the Iron Curtain and the downfall of totalitarian regimes, this was a heady time for everyone. And now, with the possible release of the Rebbe's library at hand, Chabad responded with almost messianic fervor. They brought the case to the Russian courts, who ordered that the collection be sent to New York. Menachem Mendel Schneerson sent a delegation to Moscow to inspect the library. The librarians dissembled, hemming and hawing, and throwing up massive blockades of Soviet red tape, effectively responding to the court-ordered release of the Schneersohn library with a heartfelt *"Nyet!"*

Having gotten so close to reclaiming their books, Chabad was not about to give up now. The Moscow delegation worked on the librarians at the Lenin Library to show them the books, "The Rebbe [Menachem Mendel Schneerson] did not permit us to come home without the books," said Rabbi Berel Levin, Chabad's chief librarian and a member of the delegation. "So, we stayed there for a year and a half." In the meantime, other Chabadniks went to Washington DC and lobbied congress for further American intercession. They succeeded in getting letters of support from seventy U.S. senators.

In the spring of 1992 Menachem Mendel Schneerson suffered a stroke, leaving him unable to speak. Chabad's Moscow negotiators sat on their hands for a couple of months, not knowing what to do. Finally the delegation got its answer. "I asked the secretaries of the Rebbe what to do," recalled Levin. "They asked the Rebbe and he shook his head, and I came back. We lost."[2] But maybe not. In May 1992 the U.S. Senate sent a letter to Boris Yeltsin calling on him to return the books. The following year Al Gore was able to arrange for the return of a century-old edition of the *Tanya*, a collection of the first Lubavitcher rebbe's mystical writings. Soon afterward, Bill Clinton secured the release of seven more books. But then the Russians dug in their heels again and, to Chabad's dismay, closed off the looted-book spigot. Chabad brought the case to the U.S. courts. The Russians participated at first but eventually pulled out, arguing that the American court had no jurisdiction over what it decided to do with its books. The case dragged on, and by 2011 Russia was refusing to lend any artwork to American museums, lest it be used as ransom for the Schneersohn collection.

In June 2013 Vladimir Putin announced that the Schneersohn material would be moved to Moscow's Jewish Museum and Tolerance Center, a magnificent edifice that Putin himself had supported by kicking in a month of his own salary.[3] In his announcement he said, "I hope transferring the Schneersohn collection. . . to the Jewish Museum and the Moscow Tolerance Center for storage purposes, will put an end to this problem." Local Chabad leaders stood together with Putin as he made the announcement and heralded it as a great victory. "Today you have made an important step that I would even call a heroic deed," said Rabbi Berel Lazar to Putin at the event. "We would call it as 'Solomon's decision.'" Afterward, Lubavitchers who were in attendance broke out into a celebratory dance.[4]

In New York, however, Chabad leaders didn't feel like dancing. They had long insisted that the books rightly belonged to *Chabad*. Not to a Russian library, nor even to its beautiful Jewish museum. The Jewish museum, after all, was a state institution. Though built with private funds, it belonged to the Russian government. The Russians, therefore, weren't giving up the books but only moving them into a nicer home. Although there's no record of the private telephone conversations between Brooklyn's Berel Levin and Moscow's Berel Lazar, we can almost still hear the echo of the incredulous Brooklyn Berel to his colleague in Russia: "What! You're taking that deal? What a sucker you are! Putin's pretending to be generous, but in reality he's not giving us anything! Didn't you notice that he said he was moving the books to the museum 'for storage'?"

The difference in responses between Chabad's Brooklyn leadership and its on-the-ground people in Moscow reflects two radically different perspectives regarding the looted books. To the international leaders of the movement in Brooklyn, the books were stolen property, and the Russian government needed to give them back. Period. Until Chabad received the books stolen from the Rebbe during the two World Wars, they would not put the issue to rest. To the leaders in Russia, however, the issue wasn't one of stolen property nearly as much as it was one of realpolitik. In Russia the government can make things very difficult for any of its religious organizations if it decides to do so, and the local community needs to stay on its good side. As journalist Avital Chizik noted, "While Chabad's U.S. legal representatives refuse to surrender, [the Russian Chabad leaders] are not so worried about the principle of the matter—they're bending to the will of Russian policy, for the sake of the future of the Russian Jewish community. Furthermore, Russia gives financial support to its religious groups, and Chabad—to the great dismay of many other Jewish groups—has succeeded in getting the lion's share of the funds allocated to the Jewish community. If Chabad doesn't behave, that situation could change in an instant."[5]

Chabad in Russia, in other words, isn't looking for Russia to come clean. It's looking to put the problem behind them as quickly as possible. Yes, the books were stolen. Now Putin is putting them in a place where we can all see them. Let's call it good and go on to other things before anyone gets angry, okay?

Brooklyn grumbles and Moscow dances, and still, in determining the fate of these looted treasures, the modern Jewish world tries to find its footing.

### *Lithuania . . .*

When Abraham Sutzkever and Shmerke Kaczerginski returned to Jewish Vilna after the war, they were devastated. The *shulhoyf*, with its synagogues and Jewish community center—gone. The famous Romm Publishing House—gone. With the Strashun Library and most of the hiding places where they and their fellow Paper Brigade members had so carefully hidden the books also mostly gone, Sutzkever and Kaczerginski salvaged what they could, smuggling several hundred books out of Lithuania to YIVO in New York. Tens of thousands more remained, most of which went to New York in the late 1940s and became "the Vilna Collection" at YIVO. Finally what remained of the great Jewish literary legacy of Vilna was reunited, albeit very far away from home.

Or so everyone thought. In the 1990s YIVO learned that some of the archival materials and eight thousand of the books that Dr. Antanas Ulpis saved had actually remained in Vilna and were stored in the country's national archives and library. When YIVO's head librarian, Lyudmila Sholokhova, found this out, she approached the National Library of Lithuania to discuss what might be done with them. After all, they had belonged to YIVO before the war, so, by all rights YIVO should get them now.

The National Library of Lithuania acknowledged that the books had come from YIVO, but it was not eager to part with them. The books, it felt, were part of the Lithuanian National Heritage, and the Nazis had stolen them from Lithuanians. Moreover, there are about three thousand Jews who live in Lithuania today. That's only a small fraction of what the country's Jewish population was before the war, but still, the National Library argued, the local Jews could use the books. In fact some people wanted to create the conditions for a renaissance of Jewish life in Lithuania, and what better way would there be to do so than by preserving what they could of the literary heritage of the community? Yes, the books might once have belonged to YIVO, but YIVO had moved to America, thus forfeiting its claim on the literature. Now the books were in Lithuania once again, and as far as the Lithuanian National Library was concerned, that was where they belonged.

If the early discussions between YIVO and the Lithuanian National Library had occurred on a middle-school playground, they would have engendered an anticipatory pre-fight hush. But YIVO wasn't looking for a fight; it just wanted access to its books. For their part, the Lithuanian librarians, while unwilling to hand over the material to YIVO for keeps, did seem reasonable and cooperative. They even loaned some of the books and archives to YIVO in the late 1990s, which YIVO was then able to photocopy and catalogue.

What YIVO wanted most was *access* to its books. Having the actual volumes in hand would have been great of course, but obtaining ownership of them would have meant making an international issue of the matter. Fortunately, YIVO realized, modern technology now made it possible for patrons of its New York headquarters to have full access to the books that remained in Lithuania. The Rothschild Foundation agreed to fund the project, and in October 2013 a team from YIVO went to Lithuania to make arrangements to digitize the archival material and several hundred books from the Strashun Library. The team—library director Lyudmila Sholokhova, YIVO director Jonathan Brent, and director of digital initiatives Roberta Newman—succeeded in its mission, and the digitization is currently under way. The Lithuanian Jewish community is also participating, fully supportive of the now worldwide effort to preserve and share the literary heritage of its community. The Nazis tried to confiscate and seal off this material in one of its research institutes. Soon, however, some of it will be available to the world—to Jews and non-Jews alike—a public testimony to the uncontainability of the Jewish written word.[6]

Reflecting on the collection, Brent observed that the Jewish community left us little in the way of a physical legacy of its presence—no castles, cathedrals, or Towers of London. Instead, he observed, "what for a thousand years they made and possessed was for the most part invisible: a life of activity, structures of thought rather than things . . . . The invisible structures created by the Jewish people of Eastern Europe over a thousand years were given shape and transmitted through the books and the documents collected by YIVO. These structures still move us. If we do not know what they are, we do not know ourselves."[7]

### . . . and Everywhere Else

Some books, then, remain in Europe—hidden in back rooms, moldering in basements, resolutely shelved in the stacks of national libraries in the Eastern Bloc countries that were first able to lay claim to them after the war. Some of the books will surely remain in government collections, others will be transferred to Jewish libraries and perhaps even to individual survivors or their families, and still others will remain hidden indefinitely.

But then there are the other books—the ones that were discovered by the Allies and shipped to libraries large and small in countries all over the world. Many of these books have made their way into the larger library collections. They're well protected and properly catalogued, of course, although more often than not their catalogue entries say nothing about the books' eventful histories. Some are kept in rare-book rooms, others are in the general stacks. Sometimes students seek out particular volumes to study, and sometimes curious library patrons idly pull out other volumes because they find the old bindings interesting and enticing. Many of the once-looted books, in other words, just kind of sit there; few people think to tell their stories. They are like old, wheelchair-bound warriors sitting mutely in the halls of nursing homes. All you need to do is take a little interest in them and their jaw-dropping stories could come alive.

Why do they attract so little attention? How could they sit so quietly? How could it be that the hushed silence of the libraries housing these collections isn't disturbed every time a reader finds one of these treasures? "Whoa, Janey, c'mere! You've gotta see what I just found!" When I show people my volume of *Alfasi* with the JCR sticker inside its cover, they usually ooh and aah, then sheepishly ask if they can touch its pages. There are hundreds of thousands of such looted books at libraries all over the place these days. Why doesn't such oohing and aahing happen all the time?

Part of the reason is simply an accident of history. Remember that these books arrived in Western libraries in the late 1940s and early 1950s, a time when the Jewish world was still coming to grips with the enormity of the Holocaust and focused on the absorption and resettlement of the refugees it left behind. The books were important to the scholars and librarians of the OAD, JCR, and other organizations, but to a world still recovering from one of the greatest military cataclysms in human history, the books amounted to little more than background noise.

More fundamentally they represented something people really didn't want to focus on back then. The war was over, the victims dead, their villages in ruins. Now it was the early 1950s. To many Israelis, the recent calamity was proof of what they'd been saying all along—that Judaism in the Diaspora was doomed. Newly arrived immigrants seeking to rebuild their lives in the young country knew that continued focus on relics from their lives in Europe wasn't going to get them very far at all.

In the United States, of course, it was also the 1950s. It was the decade when the GI Bill shone forth in all its glory, a time of unbridled optimism and amazing opportunity. Jews, along with many other Americans, were moving to the suburbs, building homes, and watching *Father Knows Best*. In such an atmosphere, Jews calling attention to tattered literary remnants of their old lives would have been a real drag. Worse, it might have imperiled Jewish attempts to be accepted into the new social and religious landscape of postwar America. Yes, in the 1940s the Germans were the bad guys, but now it was the 1950s, and the Germans—at least the West Germans—were our friends. Now it was the Russians who were the bad guys. To focus on the Holocaust would be to make our German friends look bad, and at a time when they're accusing some of us Jews of being Communists, why invite trouble?[8]

To put it most simply, when the looted books of the Holocaust arrived in America, people weren't talking very much about the Holocaust. Remember, this was before there were blockbuster Holocaust movies, before there were Holocaust museums, before top universities had Holocaust studies programs. Jews in America and other Western countries were aware of the recent calamity, but at the time many tended to view it as one horrible element in the horrible war that they had just put behind them. "The Holocaust" as a distinct historical event simply didn't exist yet. And since the Holocaust didn't exist, there was no reason to get all excited about its books.

Finally, the books didn't garner much attention because, well, I can hardly bring myself to say it, but. . . they were just books. There were huge piles of them everywhere, and while a few were rare and quite valuable, most, at least monetarily speaking, were all but worthless. In the years after the war, a load of recovered Jewish books would have seemed like the typical shelf of used books at a thrift shop today. Yes, there might be some gems in the collection, but most of the stuff was just junk.

In short, the books arrived at a time when nobody cared about them very much. The artwork garnered far more attention and became the subject of books and movies. The books, however, drew far less attention.

The few times when rare and valuable volumes could be identified were exciting, of course, but most of those books had been removed back in Europe. As a result the librarians who received shipments from the OAD or JCR duly cataloged each volume, placed it in the appropriate spot on their shelves, and promptly turned their attentions elsewhere.

Nowadays, of course, these books do excite many of us. Their provenances reveal stories of adventure and survival, and they seem to reflect something of the eternality of written words. Additionally, they're *books*— printed pages between two covers. And books like those are becoming rarer and rarer these days. It's an irony of modern technology: the more digitized our books become, the more drawn we feel to the printed word. Nowadays printed books are on their way to becoming antiques and rarities. Yesterday's trash is today's rare book treasure. As the Holocaust moves deeper into the recesses of history, maybe this is just as it should be. Yesterday the books sat in homes and libraries throughout Europe. Today their owners are gone, and we remain speechless in the shadow of the evil that killed them.

But we do have some of their books. And because we do, the departed still speak.

# Afterword

One July morning in 2012 I took a gray, briefcase-sized archival box from
a bookshelf near my writing desk and carried it to my bedroom. Setting
the box on my bed, I untied the heavy string holding it shut. Inside,
nestled within a frame of crumpled paper, was my eighteenth-century
*Hilkhot Alfasi*—the one that Nazis had looted from some long-forgotten
Jewish community during the war.

Carefully I retied the box and placed it safely in a large trunk, cush-
ioned by clothes all around. I stowed the trunk in my car along with
some other luggage and promptly began an hour-long drive that took
me along winding two-lane roads through the evergreen-covered foothills of the Cascade Mountains. Halting before a closed metal gate at
the end of a narrow wooded lane, I pressed a button on an electronic
console and identified myself. As soon as I did, the gate opened, and a
voice crackled through a small speaker: "Welcome to Camp Kalsman!"

Camp Kalsman is the Reform movement's religious and educational
summer camp in the Pacific Northwest, and I had come for my annual
two-week stint as a faculty member. I'm not sure why I brought my
*Alfasi* with me, though maybe it was simply that, having spent so many
months immersed in the story of Nazi book looting, I was eager to tell
the story to whomever I could, and a camp full of eager young Jews
seemed like it might be the perfect place.

A week later I got my chance. One sunny afternoon in the shade of an old broad-leaf maple tree, I met with a group of twenty campers between the ages of ten and twelve. It was their hour with the rabbi. My instructions were to "teach them something—something Jewish." It was almost as if Isaac Alfasi himself was pulling strings across the vast span of history to get himself an introduction to the kids.

The campers were still a little groggy from their rest hour, and they were also eager to get to the pool after they were done with me. Still, I wasn't going to let this opportunity go to waste. To begin, I briefly described what happened to Jewish books during World War II—how the Nazis stole so many of them with an eye toward opening a library to study Jews and Judaism after they'd wiped out the Jewish people. To help them understand the story, I asked the kids to imagine a certain Jewish book: an old book of laws written by a man named Isaac Alfasi. I told them about the wise rabbi, a Moroccan sage who was devoted to helping Jews see the richness in their Jewish heritage. I explained how, other than Torah, the only book Jews could use back then was the Talmud and how complicated this made it to be a Jew. I described Alfasi's magnificent collection of Jewish law and the impact it had on Judaism everywhere. Then I asked them to imagine an eighteenth-century edition of this work, printed by Jews in Germany, and shipped by horse cart to some distant community in eastern Europe—perhaps a small town in Poland. I encouraged the kids to imagine generations of young Jews intently studying the book. Then I had them imagine Nazi soldiers stealing the book along with millions of others and storing it in a castle or monastery, where it remained until American soldiers discovered it after the war. The soldiers, I said, sent the book to a depot in Germany, where it was eventually processed by Jewish book experts as part of a massive book recovery operation called the Jewish Cultural Reconstruction. I told the campers about the light blue book stamp. I told them that this copy of *Hilkhot Alfasi* was later shipped to a library in Israel, then sold to an antiquarian book dealer, and finally made its way to a book-loving Jewish customer in nearby Seattle, a man who'd ordered the book online.

Then I said, "I'm that customer. Do you want to see the book?"

They did.

I removed the much-traveled *Alfasi* from its gray archival box. "*Whoa!*" said the kids. And "*Wow!*" and "*I've never seen a book that old!*"

I asked if they wanted to see it up close.

"*Yeah!*" came the reply.

Borrowing a sweatshirt from the most well-showered camper in the group, I spread the garment on a picnic table and placed the book on top of it. I showed the kids the Alfasi text in the middle of the pages and explained the later commentaries arrayed in concentric frames around it.

"Can we touch it?" asked a girl named Hannah.

"Sure," I said. "If you're careful."

Six hands from the half dozen kids in the front row drifted slowly and tentatively toward the old book; a second later more than a dozen other hands snaked their way in from behind. Soon twenty index fingers gently caressed the book's timeworn rag-paper pages.

Most of these kids—kids with surnames like Shevitz and Birnbaum and Silverberg—were descendants of European Jews. Most had family trees with branches that came to abrupt ends in the early to mid-1940s. Many had grandparents or great-grandparents who had just barely gotten out and who could have told stories about their frantic, futile efforts to rescue those who had stayed behind. To these young campers, however, that world was the stuff of history books, not real life. With their twenty-first-century lives of Facebook and Select Soccer and summers at Camp Kalsman, their European Jewish heritage was so distant from their own daily reality as to render it almost unreal.

Gathered with me under the maple tree, however, the kids connected with that past, more directly perhaps than ever before. It was just a book, an old edition of Jewish laws and commentaries, but as they ran their fingers over the letters on its pages, their wide-eyed expressions and awed silence made it clear that at that moment they felt themselves to be part of something far greater than they had ever fully realized. Here

34. Camp Kalsman, near Arlington, Washington, July 2012. Photo by Leehe Bronstein.

was a Jewish object that had survived the destruction of the Holocaust, one whose soft pages had been touched by members of a generation of their families nearly wiped out.

With entire villages and urban districts obliterated during the war, opportunities for young Jews to connect with the world of their European forebears are tragically rare. But we do have some of its books. They sit quietly on shelves around the world. As memory grows fainter, we can still honor the dead in many ways. One way is to do what the kids and I did on that sunny summer day—open a book and let the words shine forth once again.

*Notes*

INTRODUCTION

1. Babylonian Talmud, *Ketubot* 17a; *Pesachim* 9b ff., *Sukkah* 23a–b.
2. *Encyclopaedia Judaica* (Jerusalem: Keter, 1971), 2:602. Translation slightly edited for clarity.
3. Raphael Posner and Israel Ta-Shema, eds., *The Hebrew Book: An Historical Survey* (Jerusalem: Keter, 1975), 98.
4. Ch. B. Friedberg, *Bet Eked Sepharim* (Israel, 1928), 1:291.
5. Fraenkel Family Tree, "Aaron ben Uri Lipmann Fraenkel's Tree," http://www.geni.com/family-tree/index/6000000006911140325.
6. Evidently Meshulam's father and his son were both named Aaron.

1. LOADING THE JEWISH BOOKSHELF

1. The general information in this chapter about Vilna and its book world is accurate. Khaykl Lunski's tour of the Strashun Library is imagined.
2. Yad Vashem, "The Jerusalem of Lithuania: The Story of the Jewish Community of Vilna," http://www1.yadvashem.org/yv/en/exhibitions/vilna/overview.asp.
3. Mordechai Zalkin, "Strashun, Shemu'el, and Matityahu," trans. I. Michael Aronson, in *The YIVO Encyclopedia of Jews in Eastern Europe*, http://www.yivoencyclopedia.org/article.aspx/Strashun_Shemuel_and_Matityahu; Yad Vashem, "The Jerusalem of Lithuania: The Story of the Jewish Community of Vilna, The Interwar Period, Cultural Life," http://www1.yadvashem.org/yv/en/exhibitions/vilna/before/libraries.asp#!prettyPhoto.
4. On Khaykl Lunski, see Dina Abramowicz and Jeffery Shandler, eds., *Profiles of a Lost World: Memoirs of East European Jewish Life before World War II* (Detroit: Wayne State University Press, 1999), 260–64; and Itzik Nakhmen Gottesman, *Defining the Yiddish Nation: The Jewish Folklorists of Poland* (Detroit: Wayne State University Press, 2003), 78–81.

5. Exodus 31:18, 32:19, 34:28.

6. Ezra, 3:10–12.

7. Raphael Posner and Israel Ta-Shema, eds., *The Hebrew Book: An Historical Survey* (Jerusalem: Keter, 1975), 6.

8. Posner and Ta-Shema, *The Hebrew Book*, 4.

9. Babylonian Talmud, *Yoma* 68b.

10. See Walter J. Ong, *Orality and Literacy: The Technologizing of the Word* (London: Routledge, 2002), 30–57.

11. Babylonian Talmud, *Temurah* 14b. Jerusalem Talmud, *Gittin* 60b; *Peah* 2:6, 17a and parallels. From Martin S. Jaffee, "A Rabbinic Ontology of the Written and Spoken Word: On Discipleship, Transformative Knowledge, and the Living Texts of Oral Torah," *Journal of the American Academy of Religion* 65, no. 3 (Autumn 1997): 525–49.

12. Tovia Preschel, "Amram ben Sheshna," in *Encylopaedia Judaica* (Jerusalem: Keter, 1973), 2:891–93.

13. Henry Malter, *Saadia Gaon: His Life and Works* (Philadelphia: Jewish Publication Society, 1921), 137.

14. *Book of Beliefs and Opinions*, quoted in Talya Fishman, *Becoming the People of the Talmud: Oral Torah as Written Tradition in Medieval Jewish Cultures* (Philadelphia: University of Pennsylvania Press, 2011), 38.

15. Bernard Cerquiglini, *Éloge de la variante: histoire critique de la philologie* (Paris: Seuil, 1989), 111, quoted in Fishman, *Becoming the People of the Talmud*, 5.

16. Based on Shraga Abramson, *Perush Rabbenu Hananel la-Talmud* (Ramat Gan: Bar Ilan, 1995), cited in Fishman, *Becoming the People of the Talmud*, 69.

17. Quoted in Fishman, *Becoming the People of the Talmud*, 76.

18. Fishman, *Becoming the People of the Talmud*, 134.

19. Talya Fishman, "The Rhineland Pietists' Sacralization of Oral Torah," *Jewish Quarterly Review* 96, no. 1 (Winter 2006): 9–16.

20. Posner and Ta-Shema, *The Hebrew Book*, 85.

21. Joseph Jacob, "Typography," in *The Jewish Encyclopedia* (New York: Funk and Wagnalls, 1906), xii, 295ff. Also Zeev Gries, *The Book in the Jewish World: 1700–1900* (Oxford: Littman Library of Jewish Civilization, 2010), 4.

22. Gries, *Book in the Jewish World*, 4. Also Posner and Ta-Shema (*The Hebrew Book*, 86) suggest that there were 50,000 editions of Jewish incunabula, but this number is certainly way off. Jacob ("Typography," 295) states that there were "about 100" Jewish works produced before 1500, and Posner and Ta-shema's more updated list puts the number at 175. I put the upper limit at approximately 200 to account for the possibility of lost titles.

23. David B. Ruderman, *Early Modern Jewry: A New Cultural History* (Princeton NJ: Princeton University Press, 2011), 102–3.

24. Posner and Ta-Shema, *The Hebrew Book*, 97.

25. Posner and Ta-Shema (*The Hebrew Book*, 91) list the date as 1493; Gries (*Book in the Jewish World*, 4–5) puts the date of publication as 1504.
26. Ruderman, *Early Modern Jewry*, 105.
27. Gershom Scholem, *The Messianic Idea in Judaism and Other Essays in Jewish Spirituality* (New York: Schocken Books, 1971), 91.
28. Gries, *Book in the Jewish World*, 25–26.
29. "Tsene rene," in *The YIVO Encyclopedia of Jews in Eastern Europe*, http://www.yivoencyclopedia.org/article.aspx/Tsene-rene.
30. Ora Schwarzwald and Aldina Quintana Rodriquez, eds., *Seder Nashim: Sidur Tefilot be-Ladino, Saloniki, ha-me'ah ha-shesh 'esreh* (Jerusalem: Ben Zvi Institute, 2012).

2. ANTISEMITES AND THE JEWISH WRITTEN WORD
Epigraph: Heinrich Heine, "Almansor," in *The Complete Poems of Heinrich Heine: A Modern English Version*, trans. Hal Draper (Boston: Suhrkamp Verlag, 1982), 187.
1. Quoted in Jacob Rader Marcus, *The Jew in the Medieval World: A Sourcebook, 315–1791* (Cincinnati: Union of American Hebrew Congregations, 1938), 149.
2. The details of this book burning remain unclear. William Popper (*The Censorship of Hebrew Books* [New York: Knickerbocker Press, 1899]), for example, records the date as June 17, 1244; Yvonne Glikson ("Talmud, Burning Of," in *Encyclopaedia Judaica*, 2nd ed., ed. Michael Berenbaum and Fred Skolnik [Detoit: Macmillan Reference USA, 2007], 19:482) puts it in June of 1242. Marcus (*Jew in the Medieval World*, 145) argues that burnings probably took place at both times. Similarly, the various sources differ in the number of books destroyed, estimates running from 14,000 to 20,000.
3. Popper, *Censorship of Hebrew Books*, 6–11.
4. Marcus, *Jew in the Medieval World*, 146
5. 1 Maccabees, 1:56–57, *The Oxford Annotated Bible with Apocrypha*, expanded ed., rev. standard version (Oxford: Oxford University Press, 1973).
6. Alfredo Mordechai Rubello, "Justinian Code: *Corpus Iuris Civilis*," in *Antisemitism: A Historical Encyclopedia of Prejudice and Persecution* (Santa Barbara: ABC-CLIO, 2005), 393–94.
7. "Medieval Sourcebook: Justinian: Novella 146: On Jews," Fordham University website, http://www.fordham.edu/halsall/source/novell46.asp.
8. William Popper, "Confiscation of Jewish Books," in *The Jewish Encyclopedia* (New York: Funk and Wagnalls, 1906), 4:221–24.
9. Quoted in Fr. William G. Most, "Private Revelations and Discernment of Spirits," http://www.ewtn.com/faith/teachings/maryd8.htm.
10. Popper, "Confiscation of Jewish Books."
11. Yoel Kahn, *The Three Blessings: Boundaries, Censorship, and Identity in Jewish Liturgy* (Oxford: Oxford University Press, 2011), 46.

12. Popper, "Censorship of Jewish Books."

13. Arlen Viktorovitch Blium, "The Jewish Question and Censorship in the USSR," in *The Holocaust and the Book: Destruction and Preservation*," ed. Jonathan A. Rose (Amherst: University of Massachusetts Press, 2001), 79–103.

### 3. FROM BONFIRES TO BOOKSHELVES

Epigraph: Quoted in Richard L. Rubenstein and John K. Roth, *Approaches to Auschwitz: The Holocaust and Its Legacy*, rev. ed. (Louisville KY: Westminster John Knox, 2003), 116.

1. Leonidas E. Hill, "The Nazi Attack on 'Un-German' Literature," in *The Holocaust and the Book: Destruction and Preservation*," ed. Jonathan A. Rose (Amherst: University of Massachusetts Press, 2001), 14.

2. Peter Weidhass, *A History of the Frankfurt Book Fair*, trans. C. M. Gossage and W. A. Wright (Toronto: Dundurn Press, 2007). Eliezer ben Natan mentions simply Frankfurt's "fair of the non-Jews." Its specific association with books emerged in the late fifteenth century.

3. *Mein Kampf*, http://gutenberg.net.au/ebooks02/0200601.txt.

4. Matthew Fishburne, *Burning Books* (New York: Palgrave Macmillan, 2008), 36.

5. Fishburne, *Burning Books*, 34.

6. Fishburne, *Burning Books*, 39.

7. Fishburne, *Burning Books*, 37.

8. Hill, "Nazi Attack on 'Un-German' Literature," 16

9. Fishburne, *Burning Books*, 40–41.

10. "Adolf Hitler: First Anti-Semitic Writing," Jewish Virtual Library, http://www.jewishvirtuallibrary.org/jsource/Holocaust/Adolf_Hitler's_First_Antisemitic_Writing.html.

11. Alan E. Steinweis, *Studying the Jew: Scholarly Antisemitism in Nazi Germany* (Cambridge MA: Harvard University Press, 2008), 11.

12. On Seraphim, see Steinweiss, *Studying the Jew*, 142–47.

13. Max Weinreich, *Hitler's Professors: The Part of Scholarship in Germany's Crimes against the Jewish People* (New York: YIVO, 1946), 77.

14. Steinweis, *Studying the Jew*, 142–47.

15. On Kittel, see Robert P. Ericksen, "Theologian in the Third Reich: The Case of Gerhard Kittel," *Journal of Contemporary History* 12, no. 3 (July 1977): 595–22.

16. Steinweis, *Studying the Jew*, 75–76.

17. Steinweis, *Studying the Jew*, 153–54.

18. David E. Fishman, "Like Embers Plucked from the Fire: The Rescue of Jewish Cultural Treasures in Vilna," in Rose, *Holocaust and the Book*, 67. Steinweis (*Studying the Jew*, 116) puts Pohl in Jerusalem from 1932 to 1934.

19. Deborah Lipstadt, *The Eichmann Trial* (New York: Schocken Books, 2011), 48–50.

20. Werner Willikens, February 21, 1934, quoted in "Working Towards the Führer:

Reflections on the Nature of the Hitler Dictatorship," *Contemporary European History* 2, no. 2 (July 1993): 116.

4. TALMUD SCHOLARS, HEBRAISTS, AND OTHER LOOTERS

1. Robert Cecil, The Myth of the Master Race: Alfred Rosenberg and Nazi Ideology (London: Bastford, 1972), 3.
2. Cecil, Myth of the Master Race, 14–15.
3. Cecil, Myth of the Master Race, 12–13.
4. Cecil, Myth of the Master Race, 13.
5. Alfred Rosenberg's Memoirs, http://issuu.com/creact/docs/www.jurgenmarechal.nl, 9.
6. Cecil, *Myth of the Master Race*, 25.
7. Cecil, Myth of the Master Race, 29.
8. Ian Kershaw, Hitler: A Biography (New York: Norton, 2008), 110.
9. Cecil, *Myth of the Master Race*, 34.
10. Cecil, Myth of the Master Race, 82–83.
11. Cecil, Myth of the Master Race, 100–101.
12. Fritz Nova, *Alfred Rosenberg: Nazi Theorist of the Holocaust* (New York: Hippocrene Books, 1986), 8.
13. Quoted in Cecil, *Myth of the Master Race*, 102.
14. Max Weinreich, *Hitler's Professors: The Part of Scholarship in Germany's Crimes against the Jewish People* (New York: YIVO, 1946), 22–25.
15. Weinreich, *Hitler's Professors*, 47. Punctuation edited for clarity.
16. Weinreich, *Hitler's Professors*, 49.
17. "Nuremberg Trial Proceedings Vol. 7, fifty-second day, Wednesday, 6 February 1946, Morning Session," Yale Law School, Lillian Goldman Law Library, http://avalon.law.yale.edu/imt/02-06-46.asp.
18. Cecil, *Myth of the Master Race*, 98.
19. Weinreich, *Hitler's Professors*, 99.
20. Weinreich, *Hitler's Professors*, 91.
21. Patricia Kennedy Grimsted, "Roads to Ratibor: Library and Archival Plunder by the Einsatzstab Reichsleiter Rosenberg," Holocaust and Genocide Studies 19, no. 3 (Winter 2005): 395.
22. Nazi Conspiracy and Aggression, Supplement B (Washington DC: Office of United States Chief of Counsel for Prosecution of Axis Criminality, 1948), 1335.
23. Mark Neocleous, "Theoretical Foundations of the 'New Political Science,'" in The New Police Science: The Police Power in Domestic and International Governance, ed. Markus D. Dubber and Mariana Valverde (Stanford CA: Stanford University Press, 2006), 35.
24. Michael Wildt, *An Uncompromising Generation: The Nazi Leadership of the Reich Security Main Office* (Madison: University of Wisconsin Press, 2009), 161–62.

25. Wildt, *An Uncompromising Generation*, 9.

26. Carl Tighe, "Six, Franz Alfred: A Life in the Shadows," Journal of European Studies 37 (2007): 5.

27. Wildt, An Uncompromising Generation, 489n101; ci Preliminary Interrogation Report (ci-fir) No 102, Records Prepared for War Crimes Proceedings at Nuremberg, 1945–1947, http://www.fold3.com/image/232064362/#232064362/.

28. On Six's work with the rsha library, see Dov Schidorsky, "The Library of the Reich Security Main Office and Its Looted Jewish Book Collections," Libraries *&* the Cultural Record 42, no. 1 (2007): 21–47.

29. Schidorsky, "Library of the Reich Security Main Office," 31.

30. Schidorsky, "Library of the Reich Security Main Office," 29. Also see Dov Schidorsky, "Confiscation of Libraries and Assignments to Forced Labor: Two Documents of the Holocaust," Libraries & Culture 33, no. 4 (Fall 1998): 347–88.

31. "Statement of Col. Robert G. Storey, 18 December 1945," *Trial of the Major War Criminals before the International Military Tribunal* (Nuremberg: International Military Tribunal, 1947–49), 4:81, quoted in Donald E. Collins and Herbert P. Rothfeder, "The Einsatzstab Reichsleiter Rosenberg and the Looting of Jewish and Masonic Libraries During World War II," Journal of Library History 18, no. 1 (Winter 1983): 21.

5. PILLAGE

1. On the Cairo Genizah, see Mark Glickman, *Sacred Treasure—The Cairo Genizah* (Woodstock VT: Jewish Lights, 2011).

2. Cambridge University, Taylor-Schechter Genizah Research Unit, "Fragment of the Month: January, 2011," http://www.lib.cam.ac.uk/Taylor-Schechter/fotm/january -2011/index.html; Sem C. Sutter, "Looting of the Jewish Collections in France by the Eisatzstab Reichsleiter Rosenberg," in *Jüdischer Buchbesitz als Raubgut: Zweites Hannoversches Symposium*, ed. Regine Dehnel (Frankfurt am Main: Klostermann, 2006), 123.

3. Michael Marrus, "France," in *Encyclopedia of the Holocaust*, ed. Israel Gutman (New York: Macmillan, 1990), 505–19.

4. Donald E. Collins and Herbert P. Rothfeder, "The Einsatzstab Reichsleiter Rosenberg and the Looting of Jewish and Masonic Libraries During World War II," Journal of Library History 18, no. 1 (Winter 1983): 27.

5. Sutter, "Looting of the Jewish Collections," 126–31.

6. Patricia Grimsted, *Descriptive Catalogue on Looted Judaica*, 2nd ed. (New York: Conference on Material Claims against Germany, 2012), 332–34; Leonidas E. Hill, "The Nazi Attack on 'Un-German' Literature," in *The Holocaust and the Book: Destruction and Preservation*," ed. Jonathan A. Rose (Amherst: University of Massachusetts Press, 2001), 30.

7. "Report of Oberbereichsleiter Schimmer to Nuremberg War Tribunal, Document

176-PS, Part 01" [translation], in *Nazi Conspiracy and Aggression*, vol. 3, *Documents 001-PS-1406-PS* (Washington DC: GPO, 1947), 203–7.

8. Commission on European Jewish Cultural Reconstruction, "Tentative List of Jewish Cultural Treasures," supplement, *Jewish Social Studies* 8, no. 1 (1946): 12–27; "Addenda and Corrigenda to Tentative List of Jewish Cultural Treasures in Axis-Occupied Countries," supplement, *Jewish Social Studies* 8, no. 1 (1946): 6–7.

9. Commission on European Jewish Cultural Reconstruction, "Tentative List," 22.

10. U.S. Holocaust Memorial Museum, "Interview with Walter Lachman, July 31, 1992," http://collections.ushmm.org/search/catalog/irn509147.

11. I am grateful to Walter Lachman for providing me a copy of this inventory and to Ursula Behre for translating it.

12. Michael Sontheimer, "Retracing the Nazi Book Theft: German Libraries Hold Thousands of Looted Volumes," *Der Spiegel*, October 24, 2008.

13. Sontheimer, "Retracing the Nazi Book Theft"; Tom Berg, "A Child's Book, Looted By Nazis, Finds Its Owner," *Orange County Register*, January 19, 2009; Melonie Magruder, "A Holocaust Survivor's Childhood Book Comes Home," *Malibu Times*, July 22, 2009.

14. Meir Michaelis, "Rome," in Gutman, *Encyclopedia of the Holocaust*, 1300–1302.

15. Diacrone: Studi di Storai Contemporanea, "Olocausto: Seciale Diacronie—2012," http://www.studistorici.com/2012/01/26/27-gennaio-giorno-della-memoria/.

16. Diacrone: Studi di Storai Contemporanea, "Olocausto: Seciale Diacronie—2012."

17. Stanislao G. Pugliese, "Bloodless Torture: The Books of the Roman Ghetto under the Nazi Occupation," in Rose, *Holocaust and the Book*, 51.

18. Isaia Sonne, "Scelta di Manoscritti e Stampe Della Biblioteca Della Universita Israelitica di Roma," http://www.mosaico-cem.it/archivio/intervento/la-biblioteca-razziata-nel-1943-a-roma.

19. Diacrone: Studi di Storai Contemporanea, "Olocausto: Seciale Diacronie–2012."

20. Diary of Rosina Sorani, http://www.studistorici.com/2012/01/26/27-gennaio-giorno-della-memoria.

21. Pugliese, "Bloodless Torture," 51.

22. Giacomo Debenedetti, *October 16, 1943; Eight Jews*, trans. Estelle Gilson (Notre Dame, IN: University of Notre Dame Press, 2001), 33.

23. Michaelis, "Rome."

24. Dario Tedeschi, "Research of the Roman Jewish Community's Library Looted in 1943," in Dehnel, *Judische Buchbesitz*, 248–49.

25. Yitchak Kerem, "The Confiscation of Jewish Books in Salonika during the Holocaust," in Rose, *Holocaust and the Book*, 60.

26. "Emmanuel, Rabbi Isaac," in *Zikhron Saloniki: G'edulata v'Chorbana shel Yerushalayim d'Balkan*, ed. David A. Recanati (Tel Aviv: Hava'ad L'hotza'at Sefer K'hillat Saloniki, 1972).

27. Joshua Eli Plaut, *Greek Jewry in the Twentieth Century: 1913–1983: Patterns of Survival in the Greek Provinces before and after the Holocaust* (Cranbury NJ: Associated University Presses / Farleigh Dickinson University Press, 2000), 64.

28. Patricia Kennedy Grimsted, "The ERR versus the RSHA: Patterns of Plunder and Migration of Books and Archives as Factors in Restitution." I thank Professor Grimsted for providing me with this unpublished manuscript.

29. Solly Ganor, *Light One Candle: A Survivor's Tale from Lithuania to Jerusalem*, 2nd ed. (New York: Kodansha America: 2003), 208.

30. Josef Rosin, "Kaunas," http://www.jewishgen.org/yizkor/pinkas_lita/lit_00542 .html.

31. Ganor, *Light One Candle*, 21.

32. Ganor, *Light One Candle*, 21.

33. Grimsted, "Patterns of Plunder," 4.

34. Patricia Kennedy Grimsted, "Roads to Ratibor: Library and Archival Plunder by the Einsatzstab Reichsleiter Rosenberg," Holocaust and Genocide Studies 19, no. 3 (Winter 2005): 414–415.

35. Grimsted, "Roads to Ratibor," 395.

36. Otto Dov Kulka, "Theresienstadt," in Gutman, *Encyclopedia of the Holocaust*, 1463.

37. On the Theresienstadt library, see Miriam Intrator, "'People Were Literally Starving for Any Kind of Reading': The Theresienstadt Ghetto Central Library, 1942–1945," *Library Trends* 55, no. 3 (Winter 2007): 511–22.

38. Patricia Kennedy Grimsted, email message to author, July 8, 2013.

6. RESISTANCE

1. Abraham A. Foxman, Israel O. Lehman, et al., "Vilna," in *Encyclopaedia Judaica*, ed. Cecil Roth (Jerusalem: Keter, 1972), 16:138–51.

2. David E. Fishman, *Embers Plucked from the Fire: The Rescue of Jewish Cultural Treasures in Vilna (New York: YIVO, 2009)*, 1–2.

3. Fishman, *Embers Plucked from the Fire*, 2.

4. Herman Kruk, *The Last Days of the Jerusalem of Lithuania: Chronicles from the Vilna Ghetto and the Camps, 1939–1944*, ed. Benjamin Harshav and Barbara Harshav (New Haven CT: Yale University Press, 2002), diary entry for February 28, 1942, 220.

5. See Fishman, *Embers Plucked from the Fire*.

6. Quoted in Fishman, *Embers Plucked from the Fire*, 3–4.

7. Fishman, *Embers Plucked from the Fire*, 4–5.

8. Fishman, *Embers Plucked from the Fire*.

9. Quoted in Lawrence Langer, *Art from the Ashes* (Oxford: Oxford University Press, 1995), 570–71.

10. Rachel Pupko-Krinsky, "Laurel Trees of Wiwulskiego," in *The Root and the Bough:*

*The Epic of an Enduring People*, ed. Leo W. Schwarz (New York: Rinehart, 1949), 158.

11. I am grateful to Professor Barbara Henry of the University of Washington for her translation of this poem.

12. Pupko-Krinsky, "Laurel Trees," 162.

13. I am grateful to Ann Brener of the U.S. Library of Congress for making me aware of the medieval imagery that this poem evokes.

14. David H. Hirsch, "Abraham Sutzkever's Vilna Poems," *Modern Language Studies* 16, no. 1 (Winter 1986): 38.

15. David E. Fishman, "Like Embers Plucked from the Fire: The Rescue of Jewish Cultural Treasures in Vilna," in *The Holocaust and the Book: Destruction and Preservation*, ed. Jonathan A. Rose (Amherst: University of Massachusetts Press, 2001), 72.

16. Yehiel Szeintuch, "Kaczerginski, Shmaryahu," in *Encyclopedia of the Holocaust*, ed. Israel Gutman (New York: Macmillan, 1990), 775–76.

17. "Avrom Sutzkever" (obituary), *The Telegraph*, February 16, 2010, http://www .telegraph.co.uk/news/obituaries/culture-obituaries/books-obituaries/7252012 /Avrom-Sutzkever.html.

18. Rita Reiff, "AUCTIONS; 1400's Bible from Prague," *New York Times*, April 13, 1984, http://www.nytimes.com/1984/04/13/arts/auctions-1400-s-bible-from-prague.html.

19. Herbert C. Zafren, "From Hochshule to Judaica Conservancy Foundation: The Guttmann Affair," *Jewish Book Annual* 47 (1989/1990): 10–11.

20. Douglas C. McGill, "Hebrew Books Sale Protested," *New York Times*, June 19, 1984, http://www.nytimes.com/1984/06/19/books/hebrew-books-sale-protested .html.

21. *CCAR Yearbook* 94 (1984): 152.

22. Douglas C. McGill, "Hebrew Books and Manuscripts Sold," New York Times, June 27, 1984.

23. Douglas C. McGill, "State Accuses Sotheby's of Fraud in Selling of Hebrew Manuscript," *New York Times*, August 14, 1984, http://www.nytimes.com/1984/08/14/ arts/state-accuses-sotheby-s-of-fraud-in-selling-of-hebrew-manuscripts.html.

24. Michael A. Meyer, *Hebrew Union College–Jewish Institute of Religion at One Hundred Years* (Cincinnati: Hebrew Union College Press, 1976), 125–27.

25. Douglas C. McGill, "Ohio Professor Says He Was Smuggler of Hebrew Books," *New York Times*, August 16, 1984, http://www.nytimes.com/1984/08/16/books/ ohio-professor-says-he-was-smuggler-of-hebrew-books.html.

26. Zafren, "From Hochshule to Judaica Conservancy Foundation," 20.

27. Unless otherwise specified, information about the Sarajevo Haggadah is from Geraldine Brooks, "The Book of Exodus: A Double Rescue in Wartime Sarajevo," *New Yorker*, December 3, 2007.

28. For information on this story, see http://www.lib.usm.edu/legacy/degrum/public
_html/html/research/findaids/dg0812f.html. See also Louise Borden, *The Journey
That Saved Curious George: The True Wartime Escape of Margret and H. A. Rey*,
illus. Allan Drummond (New York: Houghton Mifflin, 2005).

29. Dinitia Smith, "How Curious George Escaped the Nazis," *New York Times*,
September 13, 2005.

## 7. RESCUE

1. Almanach de Saxe Gotha, "House of Solms," http://almanachdegotha.org/id102
.html.

2. Joseph Driscoll, "Stolen Jewish Religious Data Is Recovered," *New York Herald
Tribune*, April 16, 1945, 13.

3. Jeremy Howard, "'*Schottenschift*: A Quiet Mix': Artists of the Scottish Diaspora,
Their Integration with and Contribution to European Visual Culture," in *A
Shared Legacy: Essays on Irish and Scottish Art and Visual Culture*, ed. Fintan
Cullen and John Morrision (Burlington VT: Ashgate, 2005), 20. Driscoll lists
Princess Solms-Braunfels's husband as "Pitcairn Knowles"—no first name—and
describes him as "an English national and a concert pianist," but every other
reference I have found describes him as a painter.

4. Robert Richards, "Nazi Art Loot Seized in Lair of Jew-Baiter: Treasure Uncovered
by Brooklyn Boy Who Fled Hitler Race War," *New York World Telegram*, April
9, 1945.

5. Violet Brown and Walter Crosby, "Jew Finds Hebrew Collection Nazis Stole in
Lie Drive: Boro Lieutenant's Discovery of Manuscripts, Paintings Avenges His
Flight from Vienna," *Brooklyn Eagle*, April 9, 1945.

6. National Archives and Records Administration, Records Concerning the Central
Collecting Points ("Ardelia Hall Collection"): Wiesbaden Central Collecting
Point, 1945–1952, "Monthly Report: Supreme Headquarters Allied Expeditionary
Force, April 1945," http://www.fold3.com/image/231965766/, 16.

7. National Archives and Records Administration, "Report of the American Commission for the Protection and Salvage of Artistic and Historic Monuments in
War Areas, Washington, 1946," National Archives Catalog ID: 1518823, http://
www.fold3.com/image/270463369/.

8. Driscoll, "Stolen Jewish Religious Data."

9. "Geschichte, Sanierung, Räume: Entwicklung des Hungener Schlosses," Schloss
Hungen website, http://www.freundeskreis-schloss-hungen.de/geschichte.

10. U.S. Supreme Court Chief Justice Harlan Stone to FDR, December 8, 1942.

11. Lynn Nicholas, *The Rape of Europa: The Fate of Europe's Treasures in the Third
Reich and the Second World War* (New York: Vintage Books, 1994); Robert M.
Edsel, *The Monuments Men: Allied Heroes, Nazi Thieves, and the Greatest Treasure
Hung in History* (New York: Center Street, 2009).

## 8. RESTITUTION

Epigraph: Adele Tauber, "Seymour Pomrenze and the Spoils of War," *Heritage* (Winter 2013), http://www.mydigitalpublication.com/display_article. php?id=1257685.

1. Chaya Pomrenze, personal interview with author, May 1, 2012.
2. Col. S. J. Pomrenze, "Offenbach Reminiscences: The Netherlands Experience," William J. Clinton Presidential Library and Museum, "The Presidential Advisory Commission on Holocaust Assets in the United States," JCR/JRSO[3] Pomrenze, 2.
3. Col. S. J. Pomrenze, "The Restitution of Jewish Cultural Treasures after the Holocaust: The Offenbach Archival Depot's Role in the Fulfillment of U.S. International and Moral Obligations (A First Hand Account)," Association of Jewish Libraries, Rosaline and Myer Feinstein Lecture Series, 2002, 2.
4. Jonathan Mark, "The Monuments Men," *Jewish Week*, October 23, 2012.
5. Pomrenze, "Offenbach Reminiscences," 3.
6. Pomrenze, "Offenbach Reminiscences," 14.
7. Mark, "The Monuments Men."
8. Chaya Pomrenze interview.
9. "Offenbach Archival Depot Monthly Report, March 31, 1946," 8.
10. Tauber, "Seymour Pomrenze and the Spoils of War."
11. Dana Herman, "*Hashevat Avedah*: A History of Jewish Cultural Reconstruction, Inc." (PhD diss., McGill University, 2008), 5.
12. Pomrenze, "Offenbach Reminiscences," 10.
13. "Offenbach Archival Depot Monthly Report, March 31, 1946," 54.
14. Lucy S. Dawidowicz, *From That Place and Time: A Memoir, 1938–1947* (New Brunswick NJ: Rutgers University Press, 2008), 312–13.
15. Dawidowicz, *From That Place and Time*, 279.
16. Dawidowicz, *From That Place and Time*, 323.
17. Dawidowicz, *From That Place and Time*, 322, 324.
18. Herman, "*Hashevat Avedah*," 173.
19. Quoted in Herman, "*Hashevat Avedah*," 172.
20. Herbert A. Friedman, *Roots of the Future* (Jerusalem: Gefen, 1999), 107–8.
21. Friedman, *Roots of the Future*, 108.
22. Quoted in Herman, "*Hashevat Avedah*," 179.
23. Friedman, *Roots of the Future*, 112.

## 9. LOOTED BOOKS IN THE NEW JEWISH LANDSCAPE

Epigraph: Commission on European Jewish Cultural Reconstruction, supplement to "Tentative List of Jewish Cultural Treasures," *Jewish Social Studies* 8, no. 1 (1946): 6.

1. Weather Source, "Official Weather: New York NY, http://weathersource.com /account/official-weather?location=New+York%2c+ny&start-date=12%2f01

%2f1946&end-date=12%2f01%2f1946&subscription-demo=1&sid=n687s
8alab4rdcqabboduvf6i5&search=1&station-id=27638&latitude=40.7484
&longitude=-73.9861.

2. Shoshana Baron Tancer, personal interview with author, March 9, 2014.

3. On Clay's personality, see "Booknotes" interview with Jean Edward Smith, November 18, 1990, http://www.booknotes.org/Watch/15031-1/Jean+Edward+Smith .aspx.

4. Peter Novick, *The Holocaust in American Life* (New York: Houghton Mifflin, 1999), 133–34.

5. Israel Gutman and Robert Rozett, "Appendix 6, Estimated Losses during the Holocaust," in *Encyclopedia of the Holocaust*, ed. Israel Gutman (New York: Macmillan, 1990), 4:1799. Gutman and Rozett list the prewar Jewish population of Europe as 9,796,840 and the Jewish losses as at least 5,596,029 and no more than 5,800,129.

6. Salo Baron, "Reflections on the Future of the Jews of Europe," *Contemporary Jewish Record* 3, no. 4 (July–August 1940): 369, quoted in Dana Herman, "*Hashevat Avedah*: A History of Jewish Cultural Reconstruction, Inc." (PhD diss., McGill University, 2008), 36–37.

7. Herman, "*Hashevat Avedah*," 39.

8. Herman, "*Hashevat Avedah*," 39–40.

9. Henry L. Feingold, *The Jewish People in America*, vol. 4, *A Time for Searching: Entering the Mainstream, 1920–1945* (Baltimore: Johns Hopkins University Press, 1992), 261.

10. Cecil Roth, "The Restoration of Jewish Libraries, Archives and Museums," *Contemporary Jewish Record* 7, no. 3 (June 1944): 253, quoted in Herman, "Hashevat Avedah," 45.

11. Judah Leon Magnes, "'Like All the Nations?' (1930)," in *The Zionist Idea: A Historical Analysis and Reader*, ed. Arthur Herzberg (New York: Atheneum, 1982), 444.

12. Magnes to Pinson, May 3, 1946, quoted in Herman, "*Hashevat Avedah*," 60–61.

13. Robert Liberles, *Salo Wittmayer Baron: Architect of Jewish History* (New York: New York University Press, 1995), 237.

14. Commission on European Jewish Cultural Reconstruction, "Tentative List," 1–103.

15. Liberles, *Salo Wittmayer Baron*, 238.

16. Salo W. Baron, "The Spiritual Reconstruction of European Jewry," *Commentary* 1, no. 1 (November 1945): 4.

17. Commission on European Jewish Cultural Reconstruction, "Tentative List," 7.

18. Commission on European Jewish Cultural Reconstruction, "Tentative List," 5.

19. On the Danish proposal, see Herman, "*Hashevat Avedah*," 66–80.

20. Herman, "*Hashevat Avedah*," 57.

21. Theodor Gaster to Dr. Luther Evans, December 30, 1945, quoted in Herman, "*Hashevat Avedah*," 75.

22. Seymour Pomrenze to Salo Baron, 15 May 1946, quoted in Herman, "*Hashevat Avedah*," 75n147.

23. OMGUS (Signed by Clay) to Adjutant General, War Department, Ref # WX-94368, National Archives and Records Administration, pub. # DN1924, National Archives ID # 4857882, HMS Entry Number A1 589, July 15, 1946.

24. To General J. H. Hilldring, Assistant Secretary of State, from Jerome Michael; Commission of European Jewish Cultural Reconstruction, letter, August 26, 1946, Library of Congress, Library of Congress European Mission Papers, Restitution of Unrestituted Materials File, Box 34.

25. Dr. Blattberg's report on the conference with General Clay on 1 December 1946 at the Waldorf Astoria (lasted two hours), 3 December 1946, 361/C232/7, American Jewish Archives, Cincinnati OH.

10. JEWISH CULTURAL RECONSTRUCTION

1. JCR certificate of incorporation, quoted in Herman, "*Hashevat Avedah*," 129.

2. Herman, "*Hashevat Avedah*," 181.

3. Senator to Baron, August 31, 1947, quoted in Herman, "*Hashevat Avedah*," 182.

4. Michael J. Kurtz, *America and the Return of Nazi Contraband: The Recovery of Europe's Cultural Treasures* (Cambridge: Cambridge University Press, 2009), 160–62.

5. *Plunder and Restitution: Findings and Recommendations of the Presidential Advisory Commission on Holocaust Assets in the United States and Staff Report, December 2000*, chap. 5, "Restitution of Victims' Assets," http://govinfo.library.unt .edu/pcha/PlunderRestitution.html/html/StaffChapter5.html#anchor2702685.

6. David Jacoby, "Starr, Joshua," in Berenbaum and Skolnik, *Encyclopaedia Judaica*, 2nd ed., 15:342–43.

7. Adam Dunn, "Nazis and the Mysterious 'Gold Train,'" CNN, October 30, 2002, http://edition.cnn.com/2002/SHOWBIZ/books/10/30/gold.train/index.html; http://www.futureboy.us/fsp/dollar.fsp?quantity=350&currency=dollars&from Year=1945.

8. Herman, "*Hashevat Avedah*," 183–84.

9. Samuel C. Heilman, *Portrait of American Jews: Last Half of the 20th Century* (Seattle: University of Washington Press, 1998), 37–38.

10. Herman, "*Hashevat Avedah*," 190–91.

11. Kurtz, *America and the Return of Nazi Contraband*, 163–64.

12. Kurtz, *America and the Return of Nazi Contraband*, 164; Herman, "*Hashevat Avedah*," 194–95.

13. On the Baltic Collection, see Kurtz, *America and the Return of Nazi Contraband*, 166–68; Herman, "*Hashevat Avedah*," 267–68; *Plunder and Restitution*, chap. 6,

"Heirless Assets and the Role of Jewish Cultural Reconstruction, Inc.," http:// pcha.ushmm.org/PlunderRestitution.html/html/StaffChapter6.html.

14. Cf. Elisabeth Young-Breul, *Hannah Arendt: For the Love of the World* (New Haven: Yale University Press, 1982). Curiously, even though Arendt's spent six months in Europe working on behalf of JCR and continued leading the organization until her death in 1975, Young-Breul's 563-page biography devotes only two pages and a few additional passing references to Arendt's work with the organization.

15. Salo Baron, "Personal Notes: Hannah Arendt (1906–1975)," *Jewish Social Studies* 38, no. 2 (Spring 1976): 187–89.

16. Malachi Bet-Arié, "The Worms Mahzor: Its History and Its Paleographic and Codicological Characteristics," in *Worms Mahzor*, ed. Malachi Bet-Arié (Vaduz: Cyelar, 1985), accessed from http://www.jnul.huji.ac.il/dl/mss/worms/pdf/1eng .pdf.

17. Herman, "*Hashevat Avedah*," 204–5.

18. Bob Fastovsky, personal email correspondence with the author, April 7–8, 2014.

19. Arendt to libraries receiving JCR books, September 1949, William J. Clinton Presidential Library and Museum, "The Presidential Advisory Commission on Holocaust Assets in the United States, Yeshiva University."

20. Heinrich Blucher to Hannah Arendt, December 8, 1949, quoted in *Within Four Walls: The Correspondence between Hannah Arendt and Heinrich Blucher, 1936– 1968* (New York: Harcourt, 2000), 103.

21. Herman, "*Hashevat Avedah*," 211–14.

22. Salo Baron to Hannah Arendt, August 10, 1950, quoted in Herman, "*Hashevat Avedah*," 222.

23. Shoshana Baron Tancer, personal interview.

24. Herman, "*Hashevat Avedah*," 326.

25. Quoted in Herman, "*Hashevat Avedah*," 280.

11. WHERE ARE THEY NOW?

1. Devin Naar, interview with the author, February 29, 2012.

2. Avital Chizik, "Putin Refuses to Let the Lubavitcher Rebbe's Library Leave Moscow," *Tablet Magazine*, September 30, 2013.

3. Ellen Barry, "In Big New Museum, Russia Has a Message for Jews: We Like You," *New York Times,* November 8, 2012.

4. Meir Alfesi, "Putin Announces Books Return," *COLlive*, June 13, 2013, http:// collive.com/show_news.rtx?id=25714&alias=putin-announces-books-return.

5. Chizik, "Putin Refuses."

6. Roberta Newman, "Reuniting YIVO's Prewar Collections: Digitally," *Yedies fun YIVO: News from YIVO*, November 8, 2013, http://www.yivo.org/blog

/index.php/2013/11/08/reuniting-yivos-prewar-collections-digitally/; Lyudmila Sholokhova, personal email correspondence with the author, February 2014.

7. Jonathan Brent, "The Last Books," *Jewish Ideas Daily*, May 1, 2013.

8. Peter Novick, *The Holocaust in American Life* (New York: Houghton Mifflin, 1999), 103–23.

# Index

HUC-JIR. *See* Hebrew Union College–Jewish Institute of Religion (HUC-JIR)
Hungarian Gold Train, 255
Hungen, 144, *145*, 185–90
Hushiel, Hananel ben, 38

ibn Daud, Abraham, 38
ibn Tibbon, Judah, 15
identifiable books of restitution process, 202–4
IEJ. *See* Institut der NSDAP zur Erforschung der Judenfrage (Institute for the Study of Jewish Influence on German Church Life) (IEJ)
"Immorality in the Talmud" (Rosenberg), 99
incunabula, 35, 300n22
*Index Librorum Prohibitorium*, 60–61, 103
India, 95–97
in-kind reparations from Germany, 243–44, 248–49
Innocent III, Pope, 59
Institut der NSDAP zur Erforschung der Judenfrage (Institute for the Study of Jewish Influence on German Church Life) (IEJ), 91, 108, 110, 111, 143–44
Institute de Bibliographic (Paris), 188
Institute of Jewish Affairs, 228
Institute for the Study of the Jewish Question, 91, 143
Intergovernmental Committee on Refugees, 255
Iron Curtain Speech (Churchill), 211
Islam, 2–3, 4, 44–45
Israel, land of, 3, 22–23, 29–33, 233
Israel, state of, 203, 219, 242, 259–61, 263, 273, 291

Israel Museum, 32
Isserles, Moshe, 43–44
Italian Rabbinical College, 131–36
Italy, 6, 40, 44, 59–60, 131–36, 190–91, 204

James I of Aragon, King, 62
JCR. *See* Jewish Cultural Reconstruction (JCR)
JDC. *See* Joint Distribution Committee (JDC)
Jerusalem, 22–24, 57, 217
*Jesus and the Rabbis* (Kittel), 86
Jewish Agency, 218–19, 244, 253
Jewish Antiquities Museum, 188
Jewish Community Library in Rome, 131–36
Jewish conspiracy theory, 38, 88, 97, 98–99, 105, 116–17, 123
Jewish Cultural Reconstruction (JCR), 11–12, 236–37, 251–52, 276, 283; Baltic Collection and, 262–64; book distribution by, 259–62, 272–74; dissolution of, 275–76; emblem and bookplate of, 11–12, *12*, 270–71; Hannah Arendt's work for, 266–72; under Joshua Starr, 254–56; JRSO and, 253–54; loot in German libraries and, 257–58; Offenbach setting up of, 252–53; planning and trusteeship of, 245–49. *See also* Commission on Jewish Cultural Reconstruction
Jewish Cultural Reconstruction, Inc. (JCR), 246–49
*The Jewish Encyclopedia*, 65–66, 67–68
Jewish Enlightenment, 50–51
Jewish Historical Society of England, 228, 232, 241
Jewish Labor Committee, 228

Lenin Library in Minsk, 146
Lenin Library in Moscow, 284–86
Levin, Berel, 286, 287
Lewis, Agnes, 119–20
libraries: in Germany, 76–77, 257–58, 267; and Jewish society, 51. *See also specific libraries*
library at Theresienstadt Ghetto, 147–50
Library of Congress, 150, 220, 242–43, 245, 273
library stamps, 202, 206–10, *209*
Lipschuetz Bookstore, 124
*Literary Digest,* 82
Lithuania, 140–43, 263, 288–90. *See also* Vilna
Lithuanian National Heritage, 289
Louis IX, King, 55–57
Lowenthal, Max, 225
Lubavitcher Hasidism, 283–84
Lubavitcher rebbes, 283–84, 286–87
Ludwig, Emil, 82
Lunski, Khaykl, *19,* 52; as conscripted worker, 154–55; imaginary tour of Strashun Library and, 19–20, 24–25, 33–35, 39–44, 46–48, 51–52, 299n1

Maccabean revolt, 57
Magnes, Judah Leon, *230,* 232–34, 241–42, 244, 245
Magnin, Edgar, 236
Maimonides, 5, 59, 60
*Major Trends in Jewish Mysticism* (Scholem), 216
*Manchester Guardian* newspaper, 82
Mann, Erika, 77
Mann, Thomas, 77
Marcus, Jacob Rader, 236, 301n2
Markeles, Naomi, 161
Martini, Raymond, 62

Marx, Alexander, 225, 248
Masonic materials, 144
Mayence, looted collection from, 127
*Mein Kampf* (Hitler), 78, 103
Mendelssohn, Moses, 169
MFA&A program (Monuments, Fine Arts, and Archives), 190, 191–94, 228, 243, 244
Michael, Jerome, 246, 248
microfilm, 272, 275
Middle Ages, 32–39, 61–64, 131
Mishnah, 30–31, 38, 41, 58, 59
Monuments, Fine Arts and Archives (MFA&A) program, 190, 191–94, 228, 243, 244
Monuments Men program, 190, 191–94, 228, 243, 244
Moses, 21–22, 25, 31, 38
Municipal Library of Frankfurt, 76, 106, 108
Museum Jüdischer Altertümer, 188
Muslims, 2–3, 4, 33, 177. *See also* Islam
Mussolini, Benito, 132–34
mysticism, 46–47, 48, 216
*Der Mythus des zwanzigsten Jahrhunderts* (Rosenberg), 102–4

Naar, Benyamin Haim, 280
Naar, Devin, 279–83
Naar, Salomon, 280, 282
Nachman, Moshe ben, 62
Nachmanides, 62
Narkiss, Mordecai, 256
Nash Papyrus, 32
Natan, Eliezer ben, 76, 302n2
National German Socialist Student Federation (NDS), 79
National Library of Lithuania, 288–90
Nationalsozialistische Deutsche Arbeiterpartei (NSDAP). *See* Nazi Party

Romans, 29, 32

Rome: Jews in, 131–36; printing in, 40, 131

Romm family, 152

Romm publishing, 288

Roosevelt, Franklin D., 110, 191

Rosenberg, Alfred, 95–100, *96*, 101–3; ER book looting and, 110–12, 118, 122–24, 137–38, 143–45, 147; Hohe Schule and IEJ formation and, 107–10; rising in Nazi Party of, 104–7

Roth, Cecil, 228–32, *231*, 241–42

Rothschild, Edmond James de, 121–22, 124

Rothschild Foundation, 289

Rothschild Libraries, 76–77, 108, 124, 144, 146, 188, 196

RSHA. *See* Reichssicherheitshauptamt (RSHA)

Russia, 7, 64–66, *68*, 285–88. *See also* Soviet Union

SA (Sturmabteilung), 101, 112–13

Saadia Gaon, 36–37, 120

Sabbatean literature, 47

sacred books, care and handling of, 38

Salonika, 44, 137–38, 279–82

Sarajevo, 176, 180

Sarajevo Haggadah, 177–80, *179*

saving books: *The Adventures of Fifi*, 181–83; Guttmann Collection, 169–76; overview of, 151; Sarajevo Haggadah, 177–80; in Vilna, 157, 158–68

Schechter, Solomon, 119–22

Schidorsky, Dov, 117

Schildkret, Lucy, 213–16, 219–20. *See also* Dawidowicz, Lucy S.

Schimmer, Oberbereischsleiter, 125–26

Schloss Hungen, 144, *145*

Schloss Solms-Braunfels, 185–90

Schneersohn, Yosef Yitzchak, 283–85

Schneersohn's library, 283–88

Schneerson, Menachem Mendel, 285–86

Schoenfeld, Robert, 186–88

Scholem, Gershom, 216–20, *218*, 253

Schutzstaffel (SS), 78, 89, 113–14, 115, 117, 142–43

Schwartz, Abba P., 255

Schwarzschild, Steven, 269–70

scientific library for the Jewish question, 106–11

scribes, 28

SD (Sicherheitsdienst), 114, 115–16

Second Temple, 28, 29–30

secular literature, 49–51

*Seder Rav Amram* (Amram), 36

Seeligmann, Sigmund, 125

*Sefer Hasidim* (Yehudah He-chasid), 38

Seideman, Lawrence, 129–30

semi-identifiable books of restitution process, 204–6, 210–12

Senate, U.S., 286

Sephardic Jews, 43–44, 50

Seraphim, Peter-Heinz, 85–86

Shabbetai Tzvi, 47–48

Shlomo Zalman Kremer, Elijah ben, 152

Sholokhova, Lyudmila, 288, 289–90

Shulchan Arukh, 43–44

Shunami, Shlomo, 256

Sicherheitsdienst (SD), 114, 115–16

Six, Franz Alfred, 115–18, 126

Snyder, George, 169

Sonne, Isaia, 132

Sonsino Press, 132

sorting of books by Nazis, *75*, 117–18, 146, *152*, 155–60

Sotheby's auction house, 169–75

universities of Germany, 75, 85, 107. *See also specific universities*

University of Heidelberg, 75

University of Marburg, 267

University of Salonika, 279

U.S. Army: book and artwork recovery by, 186–88, 190–94; restitution and, 195–97, 201–2, 214, 220–21, 226, 242, 246–47

U.S. Senate, 286

U.S. State Department, 243–44, 245–46, 248

U.S. War Department, 243–44

Utitz, Emil, 150

Veit-Simon, Heinrich, 172, 173–75

Vilna, 8, 15–18, 34, 52, 151–57, 160–68, 215, 288–89, 299n1. *See also* Strashun Library

Vilna Collection, 288–90

Vilna Gaon, 152

Vilna University Library, 155–58

Vincennes, Talmud burning in, 55–57

Virbilis, 163–64

Vistorini, Giovanni Domenico, 179

*Völkischer Beobachter,* 77, 79, 101

von Müller, Karl Alexander, 106

Von Pless castle, 146

von Solms-Braunfels, Luise Anna, 185

Wagner, Richard, 97

Wahl, Albert, 146

Waldstein, Margarete Elisabeth, 181–83

*The War against the Jews* (Dawidowicz), 216

Warsaw, 7, 284

Weizmann, Chaim, 219

Werner, David, 253

western European Jews, 50, 260

Wiesbaden collection point, 261, 262–63

Wilhelm Leibniz Library, 136

Willikens, Werner, 90–91

Wischnitzer, Rachel, 236

*Wissenschaft des Judentums,* 50–51

women, reading by Jewish, 7, 50

World Jewish Congress (WJC), 244, 246, 248

"World Jewry" seminar by Adolphe Eichmann, 89

Worms *Machzor,* 267, *268*

written words of Judaism, history of: early books, 34–39; Hasidic, 48–49; manuscripts, 29–34, 39, 45; printed kabbalistic texts, 46–47; printed sacred texts, 39–45, 300n22, 301n25; scrolls, 24–29; tablets, 21–24

Yaari, Avraham, 216

Yad Vashem Holocaust Memorial, 181

Yavneh, 29–30

Yehudah Hanasi, 30–31

Yehudah He-chasid, 38

Yeltsin, Boris, 286

Yeshiva University, 175, 273

Yiddish, 50, 88, 152

Yitzchaki, Shlomo, 40

Yiddish Scientific Institute (YIVO), *152*, 153–54, *167*; book sorting center at library of, 158–65, 213–14; fate of materials from, 166–68, 213–15; Peter-Heinz Seraphim and, 85; postwar, 273, 280, 288–90; visitor's book from, 164

YIVO. *See* Yiddish Scientific Institute (YIVO)

Yugoslavia, 176, 180

Zionism, 51, 87, 89, 233

Zunz, Leopold, 169

Zyklon B, 195